C0-AVR-070

MAY 21 2003

DEMCO, INC. 38-2931

SISTERS FOR THE
21st CENTURY

By the Same Author

The Education of Sisters (1940)

Then and Now (1946)

Devotedly Yours (1950)

A Woman Named Louise (1956)

SISTERS FOR THE
21ST CENTURY

Sister Bertrande Meyers, D.C.

with a Preface by Cardinal Ritter

66603

ST. JOSEPH'S UNIVERSITY STX
BTQ 2345 .M61R
Sisters for the 21st century.

3 9353 00011 4643

SHEED AND WARD : NEW YORK

© Sheed & Ward, Inc., 1965

Library of Congress Catalog Card Number 65–12196

Imprimi Potest:
George E. Dolan, C.M., Ph.D.
Director, Saint Louis Province

Nihil Obstat:
Nicholas E. Persich, C.M., S.T.D.
Censor Librorum

Imprimatur:
† Joseph Cardinal Ritter, D.D.
Archiepiscopus Sancti Ludovici

Manufactured in the United States of America

To
Sister Mary Rose McPhee and Sister Catherine Sullivan
My Present and Past Provincial Superiors
Whose Encouragement Made This Book Possible

To The
Major Superiors of Women's Institutes
Who so Generously Collaborate
with the Church
In Its Efforts at Renewal and Adaptation

To The
Pioneer Leaders of the Sister Formation Movement
With whom I shared the Honor and Effort of
Updating the Pre-Service Preparation of Sisters

and to all
My Sister Colleagues—My Comrades-in-Arms
Who share with me great Love and Admiration
For the New Generation of Religious who will be

The Sisters of the 21st Century

This Book is Dedicated with grateful Love

"The future is hidden from us as in an impenetrable mist. But you can control it because in your hands are fashioned those who shall dominate and mould future generations."

—POPE PIUS XII

Contents

Contents

Preface

Aggiornamento! The word has become a part of almost every living language. The idea has found its way into the mind, the ideal into the heart, of every thoughtful and zealous Catholic. From the word, the idea, and the ideal have come speeches, articles, and books too numerous to count. Unfortunately, much of this activity has been anything but encouraging: it has been so little in keeping with the spirit and meaning of the *aggiornamento* called for by Pope John XXIII and his Council.

Above all, the updating, the renewal of the Church calls for a clear, accurate understanding of what the Church should be according to the mind of her divine Founder, for a profound, objective criticism of what she is as a matter of fact, and for a determined, prolonged effort to plan and execute reforms. The Church must become the recognizable, irresistible, and effective sacrament of God's love present and active in the contemporary world. The task is one that belongs to each and every group, each and every individual, within the Church. The understanding, the criticism, and the reforms must be concerned primarily with one's own self, with one's own group.

The interested and zealous response to Pope John's proclamation and summons is a source of joy and gratification to all. Laymen, priests, bishops—almost every group within the Church has seen or heard its own point of view expressed by suitable representatives. One group, however, that of women religious, has been particularly conspicuous because of the apparent silence with which it met the call for renewal and because of the easy frequency with which it has come under criticism, especially during the past year. It is rather ironic—and indicative of the wayward character of some renewal efforts—that this group, perhaps above all others, has been working for years, quietly and effectively, toward a genuine *aggiornamento* in the fullest conformity with the Johannine and Conciliar spirit.

It is time that the story be told! For this reason, it is a joy and a privilege to welcome and to introduce to others this informative and edifying work of love. Sister Bertrande Meyers, a Daughter of Charity in St. Louis, has long been an esteemed figure in educational circles, in the Sister Formation Movement, and in allied groups. She is the guiding spirit behind Marillac College, an outstanding institution of learning, dedicated to the preparation of young women religious for the many and varied works of the apostolate. In the present book, she has made a valuable and multi-faceted contribution to the spirit and advancement of Church renewal.

First of all, she recounts a bit of history that may well serve all of us as an example of selfless and humble dedication. It is the history of the Sister Formation Movement, of its accomplishments and of its hopes for the future, a story which has found but little understanding and recognition in the Catholic journals and periodicals. The story gives credit to that group of women to whom so many Catholics owe so much, without whom the Church in the United States would be but a shadow of itself, and because of whom we can look forward to an energetic and effective program of renewal in this country.

True to the spirit of genuine *aggiornamento,* Sister Bertrande clearly understands and readily discusses the deficiencies of her own group. But she is far more interested in suggesting remedies and in encouraging progressive and constructive reforms. Many religious Communities have already inaugurated and developed renewal programs. Many others will find the courage and the incentive from this book to follow their example. Rest assured, no one will find reason for complacency.

Finally, the book fills a tremendous need of the present moment! The criticisms which have been lodged against women religious over the past months have largely been grounded upon fact. And yet, in the context of the vast renewal programs undertaken by religious Communities, they have scarcely been just. Whatever their purpose, many Nuns and Sisters, precisely because of their own sense of fairness and humility, have come to doubt their usefulness in and to the Church. Young girls, possibly the religious of tomorrow, influenced by these criticisms, have mistrusted their own sense of vocation; many others have been advised that a more effective apostolate is open to them in the lay state.

Sister Bertrande's book will leave no doubt about the need for women religious in the Church. While it does not pretend that Christian perfection can be found only in the religious life, it does succeed in showing that the religious life is the most effective means of achieving perfection in charity and loving service toward God and the neighbor. In this respect, it is an eminent commentary on the words of Pope Pius XII: "The apostolate of the Church is almost inconceivable without the help of religious women."

✠ Joseph Cardinal Ritter
Archbishop of St. Louis

August 15, 1964

Foreword

Major Superiors of women's Communities are gravely aware of the need for keeping very close to the Church today; of being well informed on the Church's thinking in regard to religious Communities; of being guided by its directives. These directives, under the general term of *aggiornamento,* deal with the updating of constitutions, rules, customs and traditions, so that religious women may best serve the interests of the Church and society today. The thinking of the Church is the unifying element of Sister Bertrande's book: *Sisters for the 21st Century.*

Aggiornamento was first presented to religious Communities by Pius XII at the First International Congress of Mothers General in Rome in 1950. *Sisters for the 21st Century* is a compact, comprehensive account of the implementation of those recommendations by Communities during the intervening fifteen years.

That the Sister Formation Conference and later the Conference of Major Superiors developed directly from the recommendations of the Church is historically established. The steady progress of religious Communities in the programs of renewal and adaptation is clearly traced in *Sisters for the 21st Century*. It is a convincing exposition of the obedience of the Sisters of the United States to the Church. A careful distinction is made between essentials, which cannot be changed, and non-essentials, which may be thoughtfully studied. Sister Bertrande rightly points out that the ultimate responsibility for change lies with Major Superiors. Her long-term friendship with this group in all parts of the United States and her wide experience in the field of education are decided assets in writing a book of this kind. She was one of the pioneer workers in the Sister Formation Conference, a consultant at the Everett Curriculum Workshop, and a member of the Leadership Group of Sister Formation for a number of years.

Sisters for the 21st Century is extraordinarily well timed, and timely. The value and relevancy of religious life in today's world is being challenged by word and writing. The question has frequently been asked: "Why do not the Sisters speak out?" *Sisters for the 21st Century,* by one with long and varied experience, does speak out authoritatively and effectively.

Throughout the book, documentation is drawn largely from Holy Scripture, Papal pronouncements from Pius XI to Paul VI, and spokesmen for the Sacred Congregation of Religious. This book is not just to be read but, as Francis Bacon says "to be chewed and digested."

Sister Bertrande's chief qualification for writing this book is her own love and appreciation for the religious life, her strong convictions as to the dignity, grandeur and permanence of the religious vocation. The writing has been truly a labor of love. Every paragraph and page bespeaks her affection for Sisters, her faith in their divine call to follow Christ, and her firm hope for a glorious and fruitful future for Sisters in the remainder of this century, the 21st century—and beyond.

Sister Mary Rose McPhee
Provincial, St. Louis Province
Daughters of Charity of St. Vincent de Paul

Introduction

When, just about three years ago, Mr. Philip Scharper of Sheed and Ward asked me if I would write a book "about Sisters," I was delighted. Sisters are the people I like best. I have been associated with Sisters on the professional and apostolic levels in all parts of the United States. The better I know them, the more I love them.

This is a book about Sisters. Specifically, it is about the response of Sisters to the Church's call to *aggiornamento*. This call, first sounded by Pius XII, accentuated and dramatized by John XXIII, and now being put into effect by Pope Paul VI and Vatican Council II, closely affects religious Communities because of their ecclesial position. The various schemata now under consideration in Vatican Council II have as their purpose the restoration of the Church to its primitive beauty and to its universal appeal. The program of renewal and adaptation recommended by the Church to religious Communities has, within its smaller scope, the same goals as has the Ecumenical Council now in progress.

Aggiornamento touches every phase of a Sister's life, interior and exterior: her life of prayer and her life of work, her particular apostolate, relationships with her Superiors, her companions and members of the laity. It affects her parish and professional activities, her intellectual, cultural and civic interests.

The changes now taking place within religious Communities are proof of their strong vitality. The process of growth, development and adaptation by religious women to contemporary times is the subject of *Sisters for the 21st Century*. There is only one valid source of information as to what Sisters are doing about *aggiornamento,* how they feel about it, and how it has affected the structure of Community living. This source is the Sisters themselves, their Mothers General and Provincials in whose hands rest largely the destinies of their respective Communities. Most happily, their collaboration was made available to me in a most generous and far-reaching manner.

Through the kindness of Reverend Mother M. Consolatrice, B.V.M., then National Chairman of the Conference of Major Superiors of Women's Institutes, I was given an opportunity to speak with the Executive Committee. To them I presented the nature and the scope of the book I had been asked to write and sought their cooperation and their prayers. The response to my request was magnificent. The Reverend Mothers assured me of a hundred per cent cooperation and "beyond." Results proved that the "beyond" was no mere figure of speech.

From that meeting came the impetus to proceed with the writing of the book as rapidly as would be consistent with the reading, research and comprehensive analysis required by the matter to be covered. The Reverend Mothers communicated to me a sense of urgency which I can best express by paraphrasing St. Paul: *Now* is the acceptable time; *now* is the day for publication. It was, they felt, the precise historical moment when Sisters themselves, as well as the society they serve, should be renewed in the conviction of the relevancy of Sisters to the Church of today, in the world of today. This conviction will enable Sisters to set their sights calmly and confidently on the world of tomorrow. This would be a presumptuous task for any one person to assume. Therefore, I sought co-authors of *Sisters for the 21st Century* among the Major Superiors and other Sisters in the following manner:

After meeting with the Executive Committee of CMSW, I mailed questionnaires to 407 Major Superiors, asking these questions:

1. What topics would you like to see covered in this book?
2. What new avenues of service or unusual apostolate has your Community engaged in recently?

3. What personal recommendations or observations would you wish to offer that would make this book more helpful at this time?

The result was phenomenal. Within 61 days after mailing 407 questionnaires I had received exactly 762 replies. I can best explain the "over-returns" by citing extracts from two letters, typical of scores:

(1) Dear Sister, I am so interested that I decided to mimeograph your questionnaire and send it to 125 houses. . . . Thus you will hear directly from both local Superiors and rank-and-file Sisters, which will broaden our base of opinion and interest.

(2) I have sent your questionnaire to five different Sisters who have broadly varied interests and viewpoints. This will add to the variety and objectivity of the opinions you will receive.

To safeguard anonymity I destroyed the return-address envelopes in which the questionnaires were mailed. Hence I must depend upon these pages to thank personally the 762 Sisters who have so concretely and so whole-heartedly demonstrated the *ecce quam bonum* of the religious life.

More than 100 of the questionnaires were supplemented with from 2- to 8-page letters of further information. These letters and the questionnaires are the framework of *Sisters for the 21 Century*. Every topic in the book was selected on the basis of the frequency with which it was mentioned in the returned questionnaires and letters. As a matter of fact, each chapter could have been developed into a full-length book, so rich and relevant was the material supplied.

The preparation of young religious for the apostolate has been stressed throughout this book because the directives of the Church and the experiences of Major Superiors make such preparation of primary importance. One of Christ's most striking parables deals with two houses: one built upon sand the other upon rock. The one built upon sand could not resist the fury of tempests and torrents, and great was its fall. The other, built upon rock, amid all assaults remained firm. The parable has a timeless and universal application. Every enterprise, material or spiritual, stands or falls in proportion to the soundness of its foundation. The multiplication of Juniorates shows that Major Superiors are building on the bedrock of obedience to the Church, a strong and sturdy edifice—the spiritual and intellectual formation of their young Sisters.

A word about the title of this book. It is the all but unanimous choice of the Reverend Mothers who were circularized for an expression of opinion as to: (1) *Sisters in Contemporary Society,* (2) *The Modern Sister in the Modern World,* (3) *Sisters for the 21st Century.* The first was my original choice; the second was Sheed and Ward's; the third was that of a heavy majority of Major Superiors. The last named, as you see, "have it."

There may be those who find in this book an overt tone of triumphalism. This the author disavows. Sisters are cognizant of what the present historical reality means for them and for others. Under the guidance of the Church they have assessed and taken advantage of opportunities to serve society in greater depth. But Sisters themselves know that there is yet a long way to go.

Sisters are for the most part yielding to neither complacency nor discouragement. From their wealth of contact with all classes of persons they know that the greatest unhappiness derives from failing to find a purpose in life. This purpose has been abundantly vouchsafed them through the medium of their religious vocation. Christ is indeed their Way, their Truth and their Life.

This brings me to the easiest, and by far the most pleasant, part of my writing. That is, the heart-warming duty of expressing gratitude to all those who contributed, in so many and such varied ways, to the beginning, the continuation and the completion of this book. My mind and heart again go back to those Major Superiors, "co-authors" of the book, who made so vivid the ecumene of love.

My filial thanks go to my own Provincial, Sister Mary Rose McPhee who, despite a crowded schedule, gave time to the thoughtful reading of each chapter as I completed it. Her unfailing interest, suggestions and encouragement were sources of strength and inspiration. I am indebted deeply to the Very Reverend Nicholas Persich, C.M., for his reading of the typescript from the viewpoint of a theologian. The Very Reverend George E. Dolan,

C.M., the spiritual director of the Daughters of Charity, gave cordial approval to my writing the book.

My former Provincial, Sister Catherine Sullivan, rendered yeoman service in the matter of documentation, of acting as a "sounding board" as I wrote, and in giving generously and with love her moral support. So conscious was I of this that on one occasion I asked her if both of our names might not be attached to the book. Her reply was silently to pass over to me a clipping which referred to "another of those horrendous two-author books." She declined to be partner to anything "horrendous." To those Reverend Mothers who read various chapters and made valuable suggestions, I extend my appreciative gratitude. Sister Noreen Slattery, S.S.N.D., was another reader of the painstaking kind with which an author is seldom blessed.

After my experience with the librarians and typists who helped far, far over and above the call and line of duty with the preparation of the manuscript, the word "amanuensis" will forever have a new and shining meaning. They have been "hands" to me in every warm, endearing sense of the term. They did not lend their hands, they gave them joyously, generously, untiringly, efficiently. So, after the quaint fashion of my Irish Mother, I turn to the Giver of all gifts and ask that He "may bless them with *both* hands."

Perhaps my last word should be addressed to those Sisters of the 21st Century who even now are being prepared to catch up and carry the torch when we will pass it on to them. On what strange scenes shall its glow fall? How limitless will be the boundaries to which they will carry it? We do not know, possibly we can see "but through a glass darkly." But they have our confidence. Speaking to them we say, "I am convinced of this, that He who has begun a good work in you will bring it to perfection, until the day of Christ Jesus."

S.B.M.

August 15, 1964

1

Relevance of Religious Life to the Church

A few years ago, the publication of Hans Küng's *The Council, Reform and Reunion* was greeted with shocked surprise.[1] But when its full implications were realized, shock and surprise gave place to relief and approval. So the Church, after all, was not static. Vatican Council II, with its opening to debate and discussion of many points long thought of as closed issues, with its heavy emphasis on the pastoral, taking into account the demanding needs of contemporary society and moving swiftly towards adjusting the Church's service thereto, gave to all men in general a sense of renewed hope and a basis for understanding and security. Catholics, who know by faith that the Church is essential to society, were now seeing its relevancy to contemporary problems—problems that are national and international, social and economic, political and psychological in scope, the uncertain and tentative answers to which beget an anxiety that fills the very atmosphere that man breathes.

Aperatura of Vatican II

Vatican II, in seeking to establish beyond doubt the Church's relevancy to modern-day problems, began by a thorough inquiry into the nature of the Church itself. By examining what the Church had been in apostolic times, and by questioning long-standing prac-

1 New York: Sheed and Ward, 1961.

tices and centuries-old customs growing out of unexamined traditions, it sought to eliminate whatever could draw a detrimental line between clergy and people, between the Church of God and the People of God. Far from demonstrating either weakness or failure, this self-examination of the Church shows her divine vitality and her enduring ability to adapt as time and changing circumstances require, in order to achieve the purpose of Christ's incarnation and death—the redemption of the world.

This *aperatura* of Vatican II has, on a grand scale, set an example to religious Communities. Like the Church, religious Communities have, through the years, gathered many accretions in the way of spiritual exercises, practices, and customs—accretions which were, in their way and day, the result of adaptations to the times. But in our modern, swift-moving era, they are seen as nonessentials which may indeed, in spirit and in truth, mitigate the service religious Congregations seek to render the Church in her progress towards aiding society in the solution of its pressing problems. In the thinking of many churchmen, these accretions, these non-essentials, cannot be phased out or discarded as slowly as they were acquired as part of the daily Community life. In the words of Cardinal Suenens,[2] they must be "mercilessly" pruned and replaced by practices more in accord with contemporary living. In doing this there would seem to be grave danger that society in general, and some Sisters in particular, might not distinguish clearly between the true non-essentials of the religious life and the very essence of the religious life itself. A questioning attitude has been aroused. The problem should be recognized for what it is. It should be realistically and intelligently analyzed and fearlessly answered.

Is Religious Life Relevant Today?

Is religious life for women relevant, then, to the Church today? Many Sisters, as a reflex from what they hear and read, both from sacerdotal and lay sources, are asking themselves this question. They ponder whether religious life is not an anachronism, swept into the 20th century by tradition and reverence, but actually hav-

[2] Address to Major Superiors and leaders of religious Communities, Mundelein College, Chicago, Illinois, May, 1964.

ing no longer a solid, substantial base of its own. It is reasoned that today's well-educated laity are better fitted and providentially equipped to carry on those works once thought of as exclusively the domain of religious women. It is well to set out all of these questions plainly. They need realistic answers that are neither superficial nor sentimental.

Most of the opinions questioning the relevancy of the religious life in today's world are based on the premise that the works for which religious were hitherto thought indispensable can now be better performed by lay persons. Let us look at the premise—is it valid? What relation do the works of religious bear to the religious life itself?

Religious Life Defined

The religious life is defined by Archbishop Philippe, Secretary of the Sacred Congregation of Religious, as "a state which, as a whole, constitutes a system of life organized to form and to train religious to Christian perfection. The religious life is this privileged way of perfection because it is essentially constituted by the three vows of religion."[3] His Excellency further adds: "The vows free the religious from the obstacles which might hold back the impulse of his love towards God, and insofar as they consecrate him to God, they make his life a divine service."[4]

The last two words, "divine service," need underscoring. The special or multiple ends of each religious Community—teaching, nursing, missionary works—are only secondarily services to their fellow men; primarily, by reason of the religious vows, they are a divine service bearing witness to Christ. The relationship between the striving of a religious for perfection and her apostolic works is the relationship between love of God and love of the neighbor. There is no substitute for a person wholly, publicly dedicated to God. All works flowing therefrom are part of that dedication, they are acts of religion. Therefore religious, by the very nature of their life consecrated to God by vows, cannot be replaced by the laity any more than religious can substitute for the laity, who have their

[3] Paul Philippe, *The Ends of the Religious Life* (Athens, Ohio: Graphic Arts, 1962), p. 36.
[4] *Ibid.*

own special vocation in the Church of God. This special vocation, as will be seen in later chapters of this book, places upon them obligations and responsibilities incompatible with apostolic demands which are an integral part of the vocation to a religious life.

Secular Institutes

Neither can secular institutes substitute for organized religious Communities. Secular institutes are a modern form of religious life, recognized as such by the Apostolic Constitution of Pius XII, *Provido Mater,* February 2, 1947. This approval demonstrates the fecundity of the Church, which draws from its treasures "new things and old." To see in them a possible substitute for active Orders of religious women is an unfounded assumption. The outstanding differences between secular institutes and established active Orders of women are: the absence of habit, communal life and visible organizational structure.

These three features, far from lessening the services of religious Communities, increase them. The religious habit is a continuous, potent reminder of the Church's existence and influence. The wearing of it is a witnessing to Christ. In proof of this, have we not noted through the years that one of the first steps taken by anticlerical governments has been the prohibition of a religious habit? To this day, in those countries where the Church is under persecution, the religious habit is banned.

Religious Communities

Communal living and the organizational structure of religious Communities bring them into close harmony with the Church—so close as to impart to them a hierarchical character. They are recognized by the Church as one of the three basic canonical states: clerical, religious and lay. They are, in fact, not private societies but public bodies approved by the Church.

Religious Communities furnish the Church with an always available force; they are to the Church what an elite corps is to a government. Through their dependence upon the hierarchy and the prescriptions of Canon Law, their lines of communication and authority reach through the proper channels, from the individual religious to the Supreme Pontiff, the commander-in-chief. By their diverse ends, religious Communities constitute different service divisions, prepared and mobilized, ready without delay to be used as the Church sees fit in answer to any and all of the needs of society. The secular institute renders its own notable service to the Church and to society, and this implies its own special vocation, but—as with the laity—it is not a substitute for the older established communal forms of religious life.

Christ and Communal Living

Spiritual writers tell us that in essence Christ founded the first religious Community. He laid down the first principle: "If thou wilt be perfect, leave what thou hast and come follow Me." This is what He demanded of His apostles; and they, with Him, formed the first religious Community. "Between the pages of the gospel, so fresh with simple and powerful emotion, and the chapters of Canon Law, where the rules of religious life are written down in a style precise and dry, lie about nineteen centuries of practice . . . but the essence of the thing has not changed."[5] Ever since the dawn of Christianity, there have been persons who bore witness to Christ by the observance of poverty, chastity, and total dedication to Him.

Certainly it is more than mere pious fancy that makes us see in Christ and the college of the apostles the first example of religious communal living as an integral part of the Church He was to found. Although neither the gospels nor the New Testament as a whole gives any instances of women who received publicly the call to follow Christ, yet we know that they did follow and "minister unto Him" during His public life.

Deaconesses and Virgins

The Acts of the Apostles and various epistles are studded with the names of women who served the Church in one capacity or another: Priscilla, Phoebe, Dorcas, Evodia, Joanna and others. As their numbers and works increased, they were given official status

---

[5] M. J. Nicolas, O.P., "Christian Perfection in Religious Life," *Religious Sisters* (London: Blackfriars, 1957), p. 6.

in the Church as deaconesses, a term not always clearly distinguishable from "widows." The work of deaconesses was similar to that of deacons. Their services were confined to their own sex. They visited and nursed the sick, gave alms to the needy, and assisted the dying. Under certain circumstances they were privileged to carry the Sacred Host to the very ill. They served also as catechists preparing women for baptism. The role of deaconesses in the Church was highly esteemed, and the title was given only to women of impeccable reputation who, as a mark of trust and as evidence of the need of their services, were sent far and wide on their appointed tasks.[6] Deaconesses would seem to represent, rather loosely, it is true, the first of the four stages of evolution in the religious life for women.

The second stage of officially Church-connected women was that of virgins. Pius XII, in the Apostolic Constitution *Sponsa Christi,* says:

When virgins came to constitute not merely a certain class of persons but a definite state and order recognized by the Church, the profession of virginity began to be made publicly. . . . The Church, in accepting the holy vow or resolution of virginity, inviolably consecrated the virgin to God and to the Church. . . .[7]

In the same Apostolic Constitution, His Holiness traced the evolution of virgins consecrated to God to the beginning of monastic life for women, in which the state of virginity was completed and confirmed by an express and explicit profession of the counsels of poverty and strict obedience.[8]

Need of the Church for Religious Women

Since in this chapter both the nature of the religious life and its relevancy to the Church are being considered, it is pertinent to note the Church's concern for it from apostolic times. Although Canon Law refers to religious life as a "state of perfection" and Christ

---

6 F. X. Funk (ed.), *Didascalia et Constitutiones Apostolorum* (Paderborn, 1906), I, Chs. 57, 58. Cf. also Ch. 28, 6ff.

7 Sacred Congregation of Religious, Apostolic Constitution, *Sponsa Christi* (New York: Daughters of St. Paul, 1952), p. 12.

8 *Ibid.,* pp. 13–14.

implies it as the foundation of a religious vocation in His invitation to the rich young man—"If thou wilt be perfect"—the concern of the Church did not stem exclusively from a desire of fostering greater perfection in certain pious individuals. Rather it stems from a recognition of the *need* the Church has for groups or Communities of such individuals. They are essential to the Church, not in the hierarchical or sacramental order, but in the moral, historical order, so that Christ's commands may be fully carried out. "Our Lord recommended the evangelical counsels, consequently there must be always some members of the Church who observe these counsels; otherwise the Church would not be fully in accord with the wishes of the Redeemer. Very few persons outside the religious state can and do observe the evangelical counsels, hence the religious state is necessary in its essence."[9]

In its essence. How this essence has been preserved through the four evolutionary stages of religious life—changes from deaconesses to virgins, and (as we shall see) from cloistered orders to active orders—should be kept in mind in these days where "adaptation" is looked upon by many as something new in the life and history of religious Communities. Historical perspective is needed to see that they have survived far more radical changes and adaptations in the past than are being proposed and put into effect today.

Enclosure a Need of the Times

The third stage in the evolution of religious life for women wishing to dedicate their lives to the service of the Church through the keeping of the evangelical counsels was the monastic life of strict enclosure. For more than a thousand years, roughly from the 5th to the mid-16th century, the cloister was the only Church-approved form of life for women who wished to consecrate themselves by vow to God. The thinking of those days demanded for every woman a "man or a wall," for woman had to be sheltered and, if need be, defended. She had to be protected by a man or by the Church. The law of enclosure was so strict that a violation of

9 Finan Geser, O.S.B., *Canon Law Governing the Communities of Sisters* (St. Louis: B. Herder Book Co., 1939), p. 19.

it meant *ipso facto* excommunication. Possibly some stirrings of "new winds" emanating from new forms of religious life for men entered the cloistered walls of women. It is precisely when these fresh winds might have been forcing a gentle entrance that Pope Boniface VIII issued in 1298 the Constitution *Periculoso,* making enclosure a general law for all nuns.[10] Thus the spirit of the times for the next two and a half centuries closed and bolted the monastery door. Religious life for women meant solemn vows and papal enclosure.

The laws of the Church were upheld by the laws of the land, so that a cloistered nun could not, even in a civil sense, leave her Community, marry, or inherit property. But cloistered nuns had, even as they have today, a duty towards mankind, an apostolate to pray and do penance for the world from which they had withdrawn. One might say that the cenobitical life replaced the hermitical because men needed to have witnesses in their midst, in their daily milieu, rather than out in the desert. Such witnesses were the monasteries of both men and women. They did not differ in essence—however much they differed in form—from the active Orders of today. Father Tilliard asks, "What, then, is the main thing which distinguishes us as religious in the midst of the entire human race? The answer to this is not to be found in terms of a special kind of activity, but in terms of *sacramentality*. By our very condition we are *signs*. In the inmost essence of the Church we are an expression of the absoluteness of God."[11]

The Apostolate of the Cloister

Cloistered life had its own form of activity other than prayer and penance. The nuns engaged in intellectual work, which their state not only fostered but required. In most monasteries, lay nuns were responsible for the domestic work of the house, leaving the choir nuns free, not only for Divine Office, but for study, writing, and the fine arts of music, painting, illuminating of scriptural and religious texts which are priceless treasures today. Sewing, in their

10 H. J. Schroeder, O.P., *Canons and Decrees of the Council of Trent,* Original text with English translation (St. Louis: B. Herder Book Company, 1950), p. 220.

11 J. M. R. Tilliard, O.P., "Religious Life, Sacrament of God's Presence," *Review for Religious,* XXXIII, No. 1 (January, 1964), 7.

hands, became a fine art, as witness the centuries-old vestments which are now the pride of countless cathedrals. The time spent by the nuns in these "active duties" contributed to their growth in sanctity, since they required the full functioning of the intellect and will, with supernatural motivation assured. In passing, we might say that, had there been no Abbess Hilda in the late 7th century, there might never have been a Caedmon, the inspired writer of scriptural verse. Had there been no Mechtildis, there would have been no St. Gertrude in the early 14th century, a woman of such rare intellectual ability and profound scholarship that she is unofficially classed as a theologian.

But cloister walls, however buttressed by ecclesiastical and civil laws, could not withstand the natural law of evolution which, being of nature, is also of God. Gradually, in answer to a need of the times, the nuns began, formally and informally, the teaching of girls. This was done with no violation of the law of enclosure and presumably with no mitigation of the prayers, penances and vigils prescribed by rule. In view of the carryover of this to our own day, one wonders how many nuns looked dubiously upon this teaching of girls as something that detracted from the holiness of their state —something which interfered with the vitality of their religious exercises. This is no idle conjecture; it has prophetic implications for today's apostolate.

First Attempts at Uncloistered Orders

A complete break with existing patterns of conventual life—in form but not in essence—was made in the 16th century. That period saw the first attempt at what today are termed "active" Orders of women: Again, this form of religious life was a response to the needs of the times. The social upheaval following in the wake of Reformation, the confiscation of monasteries and abbeys which had served as relief stations for the destitute, the deprived, the sick and the helpless, wars that had exhausted the revenues of the rich and noble, and which had left whole countries blighted, multiplied beyond reckoning the needs of the poor. The hierarchy, the clergy, the Church needed a bridge of communication between them and the suffering multitudes. Women, it seemed, with their instinct to console, to mother, to bring intuitive understanding to problems of the spirit—only women with the will to give of themselves unreservedly could be this bridge.

It was much easier to see the crying need for this bridge than to implement its erection. Angela Merici saw it in 1544, and envisioned an uncloistered Order with teaching and the service of the poor as its chief objectives.[12] Hers was a grand vision, but the time for putting it into effect had not yet come. Her plan was violently opposed by the traditionalists among both the clergy and the laity. St. Angela's Community—the Ursulines—after a brief but tremendously successful "active" life was forced to adopt the cloister with all that it implied. That modifications and adaptations in the Ursuline rule were to come later did not solve the problem of the immediate needs of the times.

The next serious attempt at a breaking through of enclosure for women was attempted by two notable persons very much attuned to the needs of their day: the gentle Bishop of Geneva, Francis de Sales, and the indomitable Jane Frances de Chantal. The Order they proposed to found was to be called Our Lady of the Visitation. As its name implies, the members were to visit, relieve, and give corporal and spiritual aid to the sick and poor in their homes. Both would-be founders of an uncloistered Order for women possessed great personal sanctity and powerful Church and State connections. Yet, these were unavailing to bring their plans to fruition. The Visitation Order was founded as a canonically enclosed Community.

The First Uncloistered Order

Other efforts were made to meet the needs of a society whose social and economic problems seemed to cry aloud for solutions that only groups of consecrated women, free from the responsibilities of home and family life, could provide. The laity had responded magnificently; men and women both were engaged in ameliorating the agonizing condition of the poor. But the times called for a consistent and continuous service incompatible with the vocation of laymen. So strongly was the mentality of the times entrenched in the traditions of monasticism, especially in the belief

---

[12] Sister Monica, O.S.U., *Angela Merici and Her Teaching Idea* (New York: Longmans, Green and Company, 1927), p. 306.

that women could not survive in sanctity out of the cloister, that these valiant efforts proved unavailing.

Success was to come, however, through Vincent de Paul, a peasant-priest of France, and his co-worker, Louise de Marillac, a widow of noble extraction. Through the exercise of what Cardinal Suenens calls "patience and pious cunning,"[13] they established in Paris in 1633 the first uncloistered Order of women—the Daughters of Charity of St. Vincent de Paul. They would not be considered religious, in the strict 17th century sense, he tells them in his first conferences with them, but "good girls of the parish . . . whose only cloister would be the streets of the city; their only chapel, the parish church; their veil, holy modesty; and their only enclosure, obedience."[14]

Even today in an age pleading for *aggiornamento*, for change and adaptation to meet the needs of the times, it is difficult to imagine anything so radical as this abrupt transition from forms of service that were safeguarded by canonical enclosure to the works of mercy performed in the market place in the very heart of the world. Humanly speaking, Vincent was greatly aided by the esteem in which he was held in court and in Church circles, an esteem which may have begun with recognition of his personal sanctity but which was continued and supported by his shrewd ability in human affairs, his perfect sense of timing, and his powers of organization. No one knew better than he the appalling ignorance and poverty of the people; and along with his love for those people, he rightly assessed the ultimate effect that their sufferings, if disregarded, would have on both the Church and the State.

Aims of the Active Apostolate

By a bold stroke Vincent and Louise advanced their unenclosed Community on four fronts simultaneously: health, education, social welfare and foreign missions. No human misery, no social need would be foreign to them. No work of teaching or nursing of the poor would be rejected as "not in their constitution"—hence, their help to the people, and reflexively to Church and State, was

[13] Léon Joseph Cardinal Suenens, *The Nun in the World* (Westminster: Newman Press, 1963), p. 39.
[14] *Rules of the Daughters of Charity of St. Vincent de Paul*, Ch. I, II.

so diversely demonstrated that all elements of authority, ecclesiastical and lay, came to accept it, first *de facto* and, after considerable hesitancy, questioning, and open opposition, *de jure*.
The desperate and all but despairing physical and spiritual needs
of society, combined with the fearlessness and vision of one man,
effected the coming into existence of women engaged in the active
apostolate of the Church and of the world, dedicated to God by
the vows of poverty, chastity, obedience, and service of the poor.

With a viewpoint that would do credit to today's emphasis on
preparation—both personal and professional—for the active
apostolate, Vincent and Louise urged the Sisters to study. In a
conference under date of August 16, 1641, he said to the assembled Sisters: "It is necessary for you to apply yourselves to study,
my dear Sisters, because it is one of the two reasons for which you
have given yourselves to God: the service of the sick and poor, and
the education of youth."[15] In an exchange of letters between the
two founders at the same period Louise speaks of enrolling the
Sisters with the Ursuline nuns to be educated as teachers. With an
even more remarkable foresight, Vincent de Paul, in his conferences on the rules of the new institute, set forth plainly that there
was no intrinsic dichotomy between prayer and active service of
the neighbor. Work was to be considered a continuation of prayer;
when the call of duty interrupted meditation, or even morning
Mass, such an interruption was to be considered as "leaving God
for God," and the soul was to remain undisturbed.[16]

Active Orders Multiply

The breakthrough from enclosure to active apostolates having
been accomplished, religious Communities of women dedicated to
the service of the neighbor in the world multiplied. In these new
Communities enclosure in the strictest sense of the word was
definitely eliminated. Members might now leave their monasteries
for "good works" as charity dictated. But the weight of cloistral
tradition was still heavy, and the common notion persisted that
women must be "protected." Founders of new Congregations

---

[15] *Conferences of St. Vincent de Paul to the Sisters of Charity*, Vol. I, trans.
Joseph Leonard, C.M. (Westminster: The Newman Press, 1952), p. 39.
[16] *Ibid.*, p. 38.

thought it necessary to retain many of the monastic rules and regulations to insure a sound religious life to undergird the active apostolate, and thus to safeguard the Sisters from "contamination" of the world. Certain parts of the convent were designated "cloister" to indicate "private"—that is, prohibited to visitors. In these new Congregations prolonged Community exercises, fasting, night vigils, physical penances and other practices of self-denial were part of an exacting horarium which served as a framework for the exercise of the spiritual and corporal works of mercy in behalf of the neighbor. The Sisters themselves, coming, for the most part, from homes where frugality and self-discipline were an essential part of family life, and living in a society that exerted none of the modern pressures of today, embraced this laborious life with love. They saw nothing extraordinary in a religious vocation that demanded constant self-sacrifice; it was a challenge they accepted joyously and from which they drew the rich rewards of peace and a deep-seated contentment.

Their works of mercy—whether teaching, nursing, care of orphans and abandoned infants, sheltering wayward girls or giving the poor material relief—as well as the spirit in which these works were carried on, drew many recruits, and soon the apostolate of the foreign missions was undertaken with the same zest and zeal that characterized all the other activities of the active Orders. Their services to the Church in all fields and on all fronts gathered such momentum that the Sisters became indispensable to the active apostolate of the Church. They well earned the tribute to be later written into the Code of Canon Law: "The religious state, that is the firmly established manner of living in Community, by which the faithful undertake to observe, not only the ordinary precepts, but also the evangelical counsels, by means of the vows of obedience, chastity and poverty, must be held in honor by all."[17]

Sisters in the United States

Early in the 18th century the United States, as a missionary field, attracted Spanish, French and Belgian priests, who, as an essential part of their plans to Christianize the native Indians and preserve the faith among the colonists, established schools for the

17 Canon 487.

dissemination of Catholic doctrine. They were shortly followed by Sisters from European Communities eager to share in the work of teaching and saving souls. The Discalced Carmelites, who confine their apostolate largely to contemplation and penitential prayer for those engaged in active missionary labors and other services of the Church, were the earliest of the most strictly enclosed Orders to reach America. There they served—and continue to serve today—as powerhouses of prayer and petition for the spread of God's kingdom on earth.

Also preceding the strictly active Orders came cloistered nuns such as Ursulines, Religious of the Sacred Heart, and the Visitandines, who include teaching in their apostolate.[18] They were quickly followed by Sisters founded for the active apostolates of the spiritual and corporal works of mercy. Many of these Sisters were blessed with highly cultivated minds, but it was evident that zeal was more highly prized than scholarship as a prerequisite for missionary endeavors.

They were to learn in the not too distant future, as did the Sisters who came to the United States in the wake of immigration from Ireland, Italy, France, Germany, Poland and other countries, that the New World would set great store by secular learning. The spread of religion in America could take place only within the framework of schools, designed at first to give but a rudimentary education, but destined to evolve into elementary and secondary schools and colleges which would be accorded a prestige undreamed-of in the early pioneering days of missionary effort.

Native Communities in America

As the 19th century passed the halfway mark, it was recognized that European religious Congregations could not continue to supply the rapidly growing needs of the Church in the United States. Under the tutelage of farseeing bishops and priests, native Communities came into existence in rapid succession, so that today there are in the United States some four hundred Motherhouses of native Communities or of Congregations who still maintain inter-

18 Elinor Tong Dehey, *Religious Orders of Women in the United States* (Rev. ed., Hammond, Indiana: W. B. Conkey Co., 1930), pp. 4–8; 115–127; 150–51.

national ties, but who, to all intents and purposes, regard America as their homeland.[19] Most of the American-founded Communities came into being for a specific need, mainly education; but they extended their services to social and charitable works as demands arose. A vast network of schools, hospitals and social institutions conducted by Sisters spread rapidly, as the population of the vigorous new country pushed westward and trails were blazed from the Atlantic to the Pacific Coast.

Throughout the 19th century and, roughly speaking, until after World War I of the 20th century, the missionary spirit was still strong in the Church and in religious Communities. It was kept alive by memories of their immediate predecessors and by the steady push of the Church westward. The Sisters exercised unremitting zeal in ministering to the needs of Catholic immigrants who, from 1840 on, had arrived in almost overwhelming numbers. These immigrants were, for the most part, destitute, disoriented, and baffled at the customs and culture of a strange land. The church and school—which, thanks to the wisdom and foresight of the early American hierarchy, had almost everywhere been built simultaneously—were familiar harbors where the newcomers could feel safe. In a word, life centered around the parish, home and school.

Uncomplicated Life of Sisters Prior to World War I

This made for a comparatively simple, uncomplicated mode of existence. In keeping with their monastic-oriented rule, and under the direction of European clergy saturated with 17th-century ideals of piety strongly tinged with formalism, and even Jansenism, the Sisters followed an order-of-the-day studded with periods of prolonged vocal prayers and multiplied religious exercises. Their spiritual reading ran heavily to such works as the *Imitation of Christ,* Rodriguez' *Christian Perfection* and unexpurgated editions of Butler's *Lives of the Saints,* all of which constantly emphasized the dangers of the apostolate in a wicked world

[19] *The Catholic Directory of 1964* lists 749 different Communities in the United States, pp. 897–901; and 400 Motherhouses, pp. 922–955.

and the safety to be found in the rigid adherence to rule and custom.

Yet the Sisters' innate common sense and their instinctive spirit of devotedness dictated the knowledge that the second part of the great commandment could not be divorced from the first. They were constantly dealing with ignorance, poverty, sickness and bearing witness to Christ amid His suffering members. This gave them the stamina and courage to maintain, with joy, a balance between the neo-monastic demands of communal living and the heroic labors of the apostolic life.

The Church and Religious Life

There is no real difficulty in seeing the relevancy of the religious life of women to the early Church of America; no praise can be considered excessive for what the Sisters accomplished. It is quite generally conceded that the Church owes its position in the United States today, a position unique in ecclesiastical annals, to the parochial school system of which Sisters, with their pastors, are the heart and soul. Small wonder that Pope Pius XII should have said on so many occasions: "The apostolate of the Church today is scarcely conceivable without the cooperation of religious women in works of charity, in the schools, in assistance to the priestly ministry, in the missions."[20] These same sentiments have been frequently expressed by Pope John XXIII and Pope Paul VI.[21]

20 Quoted by John J. Sullivan, S.J., *God and the Interior Life* (Boston: Daughters of St. Paul, 1962), p. 92.

21 Cf. Pope John XXIII, *"Il Tempio Massimo," Letter to Women Religious,* July 2, 1962 (Washington, D.C.: National Catholic Welfare Council, 1962). See also Pope Paul VI (while Archbishop of Milan), "Address to the Women Religious of Milan," February 11, 1961, trans. Sister Marie Valentine, D.J.M., *Sister Formation Bulletin,* X, No. 1 (Autumn, 1963), 1–6.

2

Relevance of Religious Life to Society

The relevancy of women religious to the Church as pointed up by Pius XII, John XXIII, and Paul VI in various allocutions is not difficult to see, since women have been closely associated with the life of the Church from the very beginning of religious Orders down to our own day. What was not so easy to see in the early efforts of their missionary labors in the United States was their relevancy to an alien society in the new world, a society almost entirely Protestant, and hostile to the spiritual ideals of the Sisters, one to which the very notion of the religious life was almost incomprehensible. In the small colonized communities of Puritans, life was influenced by a hard-core Calvinistic seriousness that thought of this world mainly as a warfare against sin and corruption. The joyousness and laughter in the face of hardships made Sisters in particular, and Catholics in general, a suspect people—"papists"—subject to a foreign power and a threat to the new life the first settlers sought to build in the young republic.

This spirit of hostility and suspicion pervaded the public schools of the times and made even Horace Mann, forthright anti-prayer man that he seemed to be (because in his youth he had seen too much harshness in religion), work untiringly for more happiness and less rigor in the education of youth. What Horace Mann was to recommend to the Massachusetts School Board in 1843, Catholics had enjoyed from their very beginnings in the United States. The great creative reformer of American education set forth as one of his seventeen recommendations: "The employment of more women teachers [should be sought] on the grounds that they are by nature more sympathetic and better adapted to deal with the elementary pupil."[1]

Women Teachers Preferred

Religious women teachers are not only "by nature sympathetic" but are supernaturally motivated towards their pupils and their profession. When, as were the Sisters of those days, they are in love with their teaching apostolate, they can endure cheerfully both the privations that accompany a pioneer existence and the yet sharper trials stemming from misunderstanding and deep-seated prejudice. In these circumstances they become persons valuable to the Church and of the greatest service to society. Such were the Sisters who, in obedience to the bishops and pastors, laid the foundation for the parochial school system of the United States.

The system developed from the strong, reiterated statements of the hierarchy who, for justifiable reasons, could not accept the public schools of America, so patently unsuitable for Catholic children because of the proximate danger to their faith. The spirit of anti-Catholicism, so pronounced in almost all of the original colonies, had been passed on, scarcely diminished, to the entire new nation. Responsibility for the free, tax-supported schools rested first with local civil authorities, but was soon centered in the State. Hence factors such as anti-Catholic textbooks, religious bias on the part of teachers, and compulsory participation in Protestant prayer services varied from one locality to another, but conditions were serious enough to cause the bishops of the United States to take an adamant stand: Catholic schools for Catholic children. This was adopted as a national policy, proclaimed in the First Plenary Council of Baltimore in 1852, re-emphasized in the Second Council of 1866, and developed as final in the Council of 1884. The solemn pronouncement was that every pastor was required to build and maintain a school; that parents were obliged to send their children to the parochial school unless dispensed therefrom by their bishops for very serious reasons.[2]

1 Frederick Eby, *The Development of Modern Education* (New York: Prentice-Hall, Inc., 1953), pp. 554–555.
2 Roy Deferrari (ed.), *Vital Problems of Catholic Education in the United States* (Washington, D.C.: Catholic University of America Press, 1939), p. 62.

Sisters in Teaching, Nursing and Social Work

Since schools were of primary concern to the Church, it followed that the apostolate of teaching was considered the chief work of the early Church in America, and the Sisters so engaged were ranked as second only to the priests who guarded their flocks with untiring pastoral zeal. However, during the entire period of the 19th century, but most particularly in the era that preceded the Civil War, much interest was manifested in the sad social conditions that existed among the lower-income groups, which included most of the early immigrants, who were desperately in need of help. The severe adjustments that had to be made to a strange land, with the attendant problems of anxiety, malnutrition, loneliness, and poor living conditions, had brought on epidemics of fever and a variety of physical and mental illnesses, especially among children. These miseries called attention to needs that even religious prejudice could not ignore.

It was the Sisters who served in time of war—Sisters on the battlefield, winning the undying respect and admiration of the soldiers; Sisters who, in those early days when lay nurses were not held in high repute because some among them led disorderly lives, became not only the "angels of the battlefield" but the angels of wards of hospitals, where the talent they showed for administration and bedside nursing caused the lay authorities to ask for direction and help in managing their secular hospitals.[3] Indeed the Sisters came to be loved and trusted so much that the authorities of the Philadelphia General Hospital (then known as Old Blockley) asked the Catholic Sisters to come in and restore order. The Sisters took control in the midst of an epidemic of typhus and cholera. They restored the hospital to order and sound organization, then returned to their own Catholic hospital. From the 18th century to the present, Catholic hospitals have had a phenomenal growth in the United States, a growth that had its inception in the early immigrant years when the Sisters, with little professional training but with great zeal and "educated hearts," served the sick in the historic epidemics of the 19th century.

[3] Gladys Sellew and Sister M. Ethelreda Ebel, O.S.F., *A History of Nursing* (St. Louis: C. V. Mosby Co., 1955), p. 252.

Growth of the Catholic Schools

But it was the schools that claimed attention everywhere, and by the standards of those days the school systems had but little reputation for learning. Though the curriculum was still very simple, religion first and foremost, the three R's, Bible history, and spelling, yet, within the limits of the few books at their disposal, the teachers enthralled their pupils with stories and tales from the great books, and this, in turn, engendered a desire on the part of the pupils to learn to read, especially about their own country.

Sisters continued to come from the teaching Orders of Europe. These, as well as the native Communities which from 1809 continued to be founded through the zeal of bishops and priests, gave to the Church a great reservoir of dedicated teachers on which to draw for each new parish that came into being. But the supply of Sisters, even as in our own day, was always short of the demand. This, combined with the poverty of the majority of the Catholic population, held back the rapid expansion of the Catholic schools, although there was a small but continuous increase. Yet the numbers do not seem unimpressive. By 1887 there were 2,697 schools, quite a few of which had been in existence since before the First Council of Baltimore. Five years later the number had grown to 3,482. In the 1920–30 decade, the Catholic elementary schools had increased from 6,551 to 7,293.[4] It would be interesting to speculate here as to the immense financial saving the Catholic schools contributed to society as taxpayers, by necessitating fewer public schools.

The Catholic Academy

The picture of the increase in secondary schools and their steady development along lines of the modern high school today is not so clear-cut as the one we have of the growth of the parochial school. Before 1852 there were 116 Catholic secondary schools under the title of "Academies" founded as isolated private schools. As economic conditions improved, the social climate

---

[4] J. A. Burns, C.S.C., and Bernard J. Kohlbrenner, *A History of Catholic Education in the United States* (New York: Benziger Brothers, 1937), p. 145.

called for more extensive education, so high schools, whether parish-owned as a kind of extension of the parochial elementary school, or the religious Community-owned Academy (asking a higher tuition) came into being as part of the evolving Catholic School System of Education. By the turn of the century Sisters were teaching in the cities of the industrial East, and in the smaller towns of the industrial South. They followed closely the expansion of the nation and of the Church in its westward march, dotting the Midwest with Catholic schools and establishing them in the far West, close on the heels of the gold-seeking Forty-niners.

Professional Preparation of Sister-Teachers

This expansion, however, was not as yet to take its toll of the professional preparation of the Sister-teachers. Self-education, independent study, the tutorial system—and other methods we think of as new and profitable today—were really the only way the Sisters studied and prepared themselves for their professional duties in those early days of our country. Many of the Sisters coming from Europe were well-educated; many of the native Communities had among their members young women who had attended the best schools of the day. The times, unlike our own, allowed for more leisure in which to study. The method followed was simple: In each school there were one or two scholars—Sisters, recognized as born teachers, with a predilection for teaching. These Sisters coached inexperienced teachers both in content and in the techniques of presenting lessons in an interesting manner. Curricula in both the elementary and secondary schools were un-crowded: a few subjects taught well was a procedure that gave time to the more basic disciplines such as fundamental arithmetic, reading, grammar, religion, spelling and composition in the grade schools. The Academies were more ambitious: here, "Logic for Young Ladies," literature, the classics in translation, history, mathematics and religion formed young minds to true culture.

The problem was, however, that comparatively few students went beyond the eighth grade. Those who completed the eighth grade were surprisingly well-grounded in the rudiments of a sound education; those who finished the Academies bore the unmistak-

able stamp of culture. This gave the Catholic schools a definite
prestige and the nuns a reputation for superior teaching. More
and more, the Sisters were becoming relevant and necessary to the
flourishing republic they had helped to found.

The Sisters' Contribution to Society

It is tempting to describe all of the activities in which the Sisters
engaged as they continued to grow in numbers bearing witness to
Christ before Catholics and non-Catholics alike. One source relates
that, despite the native Orders that continued to organize from
1809 on, 74 European Communities are listed as sending members to the United States between the years 1833 and 1913.[5] But
the scope of this book does not permit us to say more than that
the apostolates on the fourfold front: education, health, welfare
and missionary labors among the Negro and Indian, continued to
be those which brought the Sisters closer and closer to the people
as they approached the 20th century. They entered this century
sure of their goals and sure of the means of attaining them. These
means were relatively simple because life, as compared with
society today, was relatively uncomplicated. The tremendous
forces of questioning and searching, the eager unrest now stirring
the country, had not as yet been awakened. The Sisters were
spiritually serene, emotionally satisfied, and professionally secure.
The fourfold works done by them were clearly delineated by the
Church as their sphere of influence, accepted unquestioningly by
the Sisters, and approved whole-heartedly by the laity. Schools,
hospitals, orphanages, shelters for the homeless dotted the
country from the Atlantic seaboard to the Pacific, and from the
Great Lakes to the Gulf.[6]

The life and works of religious women constituted a rich tributary to the mainstream of national life, quite in keeping with the
national role of women in general. Working wives—out of the
home—did not, as yet, constitute a class, nor did career women
constitute a category. Women who agitated for the right to vote

5 Sister M. Salome, "The Hierarchy and Education, Studies in American Catholic History" (unpublished Doctoral Dissertation, Marquette University, 1933).
6 *Ibid.*

demanded political equality with men. They were dubbed "suf-fragettes"—a term hardly complimentary in those conservative days, and, truth to tell, not precisely complimentary in our own day, although we appreciate the hard-won triumph of political equality that was to mark the success of their cause in 1920. The earlier, less ambitious American women of those days found an outlet for their energies in running Church bazaars for the benefit of the parochial schools, conducting bake sales, and—on a higher scale by some standards—became officers in the Altar Society and Women's Sodalities. Such were the times of the very early 20th century within which context the Sisters must be understood.

Concern with the Needs of Mankind

It was in terms of this context that Sisters were concerned with the needs of mankind without, however, becoming deeply involved with the roots of those needs. It might be said of the times that Sisters answered symptoms of human injustices and denial of rights without getting at the grass-roots causes. Their role, as then interpreted, was to teach, nurse, engage in all of the spiritual and corporal works of mercy, and above all, to preserve and spread the faith. Their contribution to studying and solving the needs and problems of society consisted in the leadership they gave in good works. New ideas did not generate readily nor did they spread rapidly. Mass media of communication were not yet in evidence, and modern means of transportation were still in the experimental stage. No system of highways linked all parts of the nation. States, cities and towns were self-contained, separate, each with its own interests.

Such also was the position of religious Communities; each school, hospital, orphanage or other institution in which the Sisters served was a unit. These units leaned heavily on the past and on adherence to tradition to give them security. In a word, the atti-tude towards society which Communities maintained was not unlike that of the United States towards the rest of the world: service, good will in abundance, and—isolation.

This isolationism, a national policy since the War of Independ-ence, was felt increasingly as the new nation entered what might be called its adolescent stage. Adolescent-like, having thrown off the political yoke of the Mother Country, it was also determined to change any social, cultural or educational values or systems that stood in the way of its self-expression.

Public School System

Education was one of the areas where this desire for self-expression was felt earliest. The system of European education with its high regard for the intellectual, its great emphasis on religion—the first nine colleges established in colonial times were all church-related—and its frank fostering of class distinctions was deemed unsuited to the needs of a young, vigorous republic.[7] So, although the nation's Founding Fathers were, for the most part, of the social elite and intellectuals in their own right, educational ideals in the new world changed rapidly.[8] Only twenty-six years elapsed between the presidency of Thomas Jefferson, founder of the University of Virginia, and that of Andrew Jackson, the backwoods military hero.

The public school system of education had always held to three principles, as it does today: education for everybody, freedom from federal control, and separation of Church and State. But though the public school system had principles, it lacked pattern. What was held acceptable and useful in one section of the country was deemed unsuitable for another. The pattern of the common school was slow in evolving to what the country has today. The first compulsory school-attendance law, enacted in Massachusetts in 1852, was not universally accepted until 1918. Little emphasis was placed on secondary education;[9] in fact, occasional suits were brought by some of the States testing the legality of using tax-funds for education beyond the elementary schools. These suits were always defeated, but they serve to point up that in the early days of our country, neither public nor private education was promoted on an education-for-its-own-sake principle. In each case

[7] Eby, *op cit.*, p. 403.
[8] *Ibid.*, p. 559.
[9] H. G. Good, *A History of American Education* (New York: The Macmillan Co., 1956), p. 251.

it was sought as a means towards a utilitarian end. It was, first of all, necessary as a means of livelihood; to be poor was the great social sin. It was required for good citizenship, for a citizen should be able to read, study and debate the laws he helped to make and under which he lived. It was thought also to be a panacea for civic ills; it was considered as an answer to juvenile delinquency and dependency.

Thus there developed very early in our history the ideal of the American "common man"—honest, industrious, friendly, brave. If his formal education had not extended beyond the elementary grades, that added rather than detracted from his stature. Nothing is so prized even today, as part of our culture, as the self-made man who has risen from rags to riches by his own effort. But the common man had to be successful—success being measured by the amount of material goods he had acquired, the military prowess he had displayed, or the political position to which he had attained. It was a bleak atmosphere for the intellectual.

The First World War

Both private and public schools were to feel the terrific impact made upon the United States when, abandoning both insularity and isolationism, America was obliged to join forces with Europe and enter the First World War. This world conflict ushered in a new era of national life, leaving no area—social, economic, educational, political—untouched. The trends set in motion by these changes were to be radically accelerated even before an uneasy armistice of scarcely more than twenty years would usher in a second global war. Education was the first area to be affected.

Expanding industry called for better-educated employees. The experience of our armed forces—soldiers, nurses, and other army personnel in their military assignments—played a large part in the stepped-up educational programs. The war had sent countless numbers of our citizens to far corners of the world, hitherto unknown to them even as geographical entities. They had been brought into close contact with thousands of peoples of other cultures and outlook. Friendships had been formed, a mutually respectful exchange of views had enlarged the mental horizon of our boys and girls in over-seas service, and this taught them, as no classroom under whatsoever gifted teacher could, that education had an intrinsic value which had nothing to do with making money or preserving one's faith.

The Horatio Alger image of the typical successful American—from poverty to power—gave place to a revival of an image more in keeping with that of Horace Mann. The United States, in examining its internal resources, found that it was as poor in scholars as it was rich in dollars. With something of horror it learned that our soldiers in 1917 showed a median of sixth-grade education, and there was an uncomfortable feeling that this quite possibly represented the nation as a whole in the field of learning. To the American mind this called for change, and in keeping with one of the outstanding American traits, it called for change in a hurry. Education was in the saddle.

Higher Standards in Education

The first goal was to substitute the secondary-school diploma for the hitherto socially acceptable eighth-grade certificate, and insofar as was possible to encourage all girls and boys, irrespective of talent, to complete high school. Compulsory-education laws, long on the statute books but enforced with varying degrees of laxity, now commanded attention. However, as such laws had been for the most part framed with a view to ensuring an elementary education, they did not cover attendance in high school. Child labor laws, generally setting fourteen as the age at which a boy or girl might be gainfully employed, reinforced the compulsory-school-attendance laws. This allying of laws for school attendance with those prohibiting or limiting child labor again points up the fact that education was looked upon as a means to ends—the first of which was greater earning power. That schooling should bring increased social status and personal satisfactions and form moral, natural and civic virtues was taken somewhat for granted; but the improvement of one's economic condition was still the primary consideration.

Educational forces, then, worked continually towards promoting the completion of high school as the minimum ideal. Particular emphasis was placed on the preparation of teachers, and higher standards were set for schools all over the country. Regional agencies for the accrediting of high schools, in existence before the turn of the century, began now to enforce policies with regard to teacher-certification and physical improvements in school construction, equipment and academic programs. At the same time the upgrading of educational requirements was felt in other fields, especially that of nursing.

The greatest impact came when the State and regional accrediting agencies demanded baccalaureate degrees as the minimum requirements for teaching in high school, with major and minors in the special fields of instruction in secondary education. For the elementary-school teacher, second-class certificates would be granted when half the college program was completed, with the understanding that the baccalaureate degree would be earned as soon as possible.

Baccalaureate Degrees Required

It is difficult now, in a day when it is as common to see Sisters on the campuses of both Catholic and secular universities as it is to see children romping in our elementary-school yards, to imagine what a bombshell the idea of Sisters seeking baccalaureate degrees was to the religious Superiors of most Communities. To those who operated colleges, a little experience with Sisters studying at the Catholic University as early as 1911 gave some idea of what higher education might do to enrich and broaden the intellectual horizon of Sisters whose contact with learning had been more or less limited to summer sessions or so-called "Normal Schools" held each year at the Motherhouse. The more progressive among these had the additional advantage of hearing noted professors give lectures or six-week courses at the annual Motherhouse summer sessions. But the State and regional accrediting agencies that made college degrees for teachers (and, a few years later, for nurses) mandatory had somewhat the effect of an earthquake in the hitherto tranquil lives of the Sisters in the immediate pre- and post-World War period.

The States did not, however, ask the impossible of Sisters. Indeed they could not, since public school teachers were scarcely better off in professional preparation. Most of them began teaching with little more than two years of Normal School work plus the State Teachers' Examination that gave them temporary certificates. Some of them had even less than this.

The common requirements towards meeting State and regional accrediting standards were (1) successful teaching experience based on from five to fifteen years; (2) post-high-school professional training; (3) work towards completing two years of college, for the elementary-school teacher and, in the case of high-school teachers, the faculty should have at least one member holding a college degree; (4) evidence of steady progress should be such that in a reasonable time all faculty members would possess the baccalaureate degree with majors covering all subjects taught in the secondary-school curriculum.[10]

Since beginning teachers could not qualify with more than a high-school transcript, it took many of them more than twenty years to earn the coveted degree—coveted because the reputation of the Catholic schools was at stake. Older, more experienced, nuns finished sooner and held the fort, as it were, until the minimum quantitative requirements were met.

But the whole educational process of the times became a rush for credits, seen as a necessary expedient, but a fact that was to militate for many years—indeed even to the present day—against a love of knowledge for its own sake and an appreciation of the life of the intellect through which man comes closest to a love of truth and an understanding of God.

Dangers and Difficulties in Higher Education for Sisters—1920–1940

Considering the circumstances under which higher education was pursued—late afternoon and Saturday morning classes throughout the school year, and a six weeks' session during the summer—probably it was impossible for the Sisters to view it as

10 Bureau of Education, *State Laws Relating to Education:* Enacted in 1920 and 1921, Bulletin No. 20 (1922), pp. 103–110. Compiled by Wm. R. Hood, Specialist in School Legislation.

anything but penitential. Given the anti-intellectualism of the times, along with the accent in spiritual reading on the greater chances for salvation of the lowly monk at the foot of the pulpit than of the learned theologian thundering forth salvific rhetoric, it does not seem strange that few Major Superiors—and few Sisters, for that matter—saw in this requirement of extended education any inherent aid to growth in holiness, except as it might call for the practice of the virtues of obedience and self-denial.

Rather, the dangers were seen as great and as varied as the difficulties that beset putting this educational program into action. The dangers were pointed out as apt to affect the religious and social aspects of conventual living. What, for one example, would be the result of the necessary break in convent routine and order when Sisters had to leave their classrooms at three-thirty to be in class at some local university two, and sometimes four, afternoons a week till six or seven in the evening? What would be the physical strain of rushing, by public transportation, to reach classes on time, returning late for supper, with delayed vocal and mental prayer to be "made up"? Where would be the time for class preparation for the next day's work, not to speak of the study and reading assignments for university work? Since time had to be found somewhere, what was more likely than to dispense with Community recreation and to secure permission for retiring an hour or two later than usual, especially when research papers were due or final examinations were at hand?

What religious deficiencies would result from prolonged dispensation from certain spiritual exercises of rule? What loss to the social or "family" life in the convent would accrue from shortened or omitted periods of Community recreation? These were only some among the many anxieties that plagued Major Superiors as they sought to render to Caesar his just demands while rendering full service to God in spirit, even though the letter had sometimes to be denied.

The difficulties were many, not the least among which was the staggering financial burdens that had to be borne by even the smallest Communities with meager resources. Miraculously they managed somehow, at a time when the usual "salary" for religious teachers was thirty-five dollars a month, supplemented by income resulting from well-managed, highly competent music and art departments. Other difficulties lay in the location of schools in small towns far from universities, so that attendance was limited to summer sessions; the alien atmosphere of college classrooms peopled by seculars, and occasionally by professors who considered the Sisters "strange" and who betrayed their religious or ethnic prejudices by going out of their way to introduce into their lectures irreligious and even atheistic views.

On the whole, however, this was a relatively rare experience. Most of the professors and students in Catholic and secular universities alike were fair and courteous to Sisters everywhere— yet the experiences of those days were a far cry from the friendly give-and-take of equality today.

Growth of Catholic Women's Colleges

The decades from 1920 to 1940 saw thousands of Sisters attending colleges and universities all over the country, but for many Communities the financial burden became more than they could bear. In an era when college tuition was less than a third of what it is today, some Communities, sending four hundred Sisters to summer school alone, were spending close to thirty thousand dollars a year on tuition, books and fees, exclusive of transportation, board and room.

Few people connect this economic fact with the phenomenal growth of Catholic Women's Colleges conducted by Sisters during this period. Sixteen junior colleges and forty-four four-year colleges for women were founded by nuns between 1920 and 1938.[11] The nuns (surprisingly good business women as their networks of colleges, schools, hospitals and social agencies throughout the United States testify), thought thirty thousand dollars a year could do double duty in providing the now mandatory higher education for the members of their own Community while still answering another insistent need of society; a growing insistence since the close of World War I: a college education for girls who had completed high school and wished to enter the

11 *Directory of Catholic Colleges and Schools in the United States* (Washington, D.C.: National Catholic Welfare Conference, Department of Education, 1938), pp. 89–121.

teaching profession or to increase their earning power in one of the many avenues that post-war industry was opening up to the better-educated.

Post-War Emphasis on College Education

As is a matter of history now, all the professions stepped up college requirements after the war: better supervisory and executive staff positions went to nurses with collegiate degrees over and above the once coveted R.N. Dietetics, once a not too significant part of a nurse's education, was now becoming a profession in its own right requiring an academic degree; pharmacists, medical technologists, librarians, teachers of skill subjects such as typing, cooking, sewing (and even high-school athletic coaches) were required to have degrees, and their salaries rose accordingly.

Undoubtedly this brought American literacy to new heights. Whereas the First World War showed the median of soldiers to be a sixth-grade level, the draft for World War II rated the entering G.I. as ready to begin his junior year of high school. Where once the law made a free eighth-grade education possible to every citizen, the current ideal is the completion of junior college.

Practical vs. Ideal Objectives in Education

Much as we would like to believe that the concept of the "common man" is not incompatible or inconsistent with that of the scholar or the intellectual as an American ideal of the educated man, it has to be admitted that economic gain motivates more men (and even women in growing numbers) to pursue higher education. Although the status symbol of a college degree is a strong influential factor with men as well as women, granting a kind of social prestige contradictory to the American idea of the "common man," it is second in importance to the economic goal. This contributes to that phenomenon one sees in every college: students who clearly lack scholastic aptitude persisting in futile efforts to earn a degree, all counseling to the contrary.

It was a practical ideal of a sort that animated Sisters in earning a degree—the very practical ideal of qualifying themselves for their work. Just as the times make the man, the conditions of an era greatly influence Sisters too, and unless they are much on their guard, these influences are greater and more subtle than one would think. Getting the degree became the dominant motive, getting the necessary credits was the all-important goal—but the knowledge gained was far removed from the philosophy of true education that seeks to unify all knowledge and fit it into a scheme of life built upon the recognition that education forms the whole man and reaches into every element of his being—physical, emotional, intellectual and moral.

Although this ideal was accepted in theory, actually the Sisters were motivated more by a fear of non-acceptance by the accrediting agencies than by a desire for true culture. This led to the all but inevitable step, consonant with the over-specialization of the day, to delimit the intellectual field as much as possible to an intense professional preparation which, in the nature of things, could not completely rule out the subordination of religious formation to professional efficiency.

Effects of Over-Professionalism

Throughout the more than twenty years that followed the regulation that all Sisters attend colleges and universities, Major Superiors worried about its ultimate effects on the religious life of each Sister following the irregular and anything but scholarly road towards completing degree requirements. The over-all feeling was one of dissatisfaction. The first strong fears of the unknown had been allayed, yet hopes had not been fulfilled. No significant loss of fervor had been noted; success at studies had not turned the Sisters' heads. Community loyalty had not diminished. But where was a visible growth in maturity; where was a noticeable increase in leadership—a leadership that would make for a more intensive witness to Christ among the laity? In a word, where were the positive results one would expect from the advantages of higher education?

The transcripts earned qualified the Sisters to teach in elementary schools and, in their major and minor subject-matter fields, in high schools. But what was the Sister's background in theology?

in Scripture? Wisely enough, the Major Superiors were not pleased with what education had failed to do for the Sisters—and the Sisters themselves were none too satisfied. Most of them hoped to be relieved of the necessity of further study, and were more than eager to return to the regularity of Community life. Having proof that higher education in itself did not militate *against* a Sister as a Sister, Major Superiors looked to see what it had done *for* her. Did higher education itself remain as external to a Sister as the degree parchment on which her name was inscribed? Were the net results merely the satisfying of accrediting demands? Should there be no corresponding returns to the Sister herself as a woman, a religious and a teacher? Surely, superiors thought, the time—sometimes as much as twenty years—spent in study should result in more than the acquisition of techniques for their profession. They reasoned that there should be a marked spiritual and cultural impact.

There was discernible in the Sisters, *as Sisters,* a marked growth in physical and spiritual stamina, as there always is when one has met any challenge that obedience, loyalty, and love of one's Community require. The gauntlet of getting a degree had been thrown down twenty years ago; the Sisters had gone into the lists, and now, victorious, could show their younger comrades that nothing was impossible to God and correspondence with His grace. But this result seemed attributable more to the hardships attendant on higher education than to the education itself. As a matter of fact, in the majority of cases, the experience seemed to have destroyed rather than nurtured any love of learning. In plain words, *relief* that the "ordeal" was over seemed to be the predominant—and the *expected*—note. The degree was valued to the extent that it represented hard work and was the passport to teaching credentials. That it represented a truly appreciated intellectual experience, few Sisters of that era would agree, save those who were scholars by their very nature. But for them, the method employed was a travesty they accepted because—given the times—there seemed to be no other way.

The result, then, of the hard look that Superiors took at Sisters' education as it had been carried on from 1920 through 1940 was this: There were the gains noted in the preceding paragraph. But there was also an intangible something that could be sensed, but described only in negative terms. There was no discernible gain that could be ascribed as intellectual *growth* immediately traceable to higher studies; no notable increase in mental force or leadership ensued. Neither was there a deepened spiritual outlook, a more mature religious dedication, nor a more intelligent appreciation of the essentials of the religious life. These results stood out as deficiencies of higher education, as an indictment not of education *per se,* but rather of the method followed in the education of Sisters in their various religious Congregations.

While not only Superiors, but the rank-and-file of Sisters "pondered these things in their hearts," a doctoral dissertation dealing with these matters was published by Sheed and Ward in 1941 under title *The Education of Sisters.*[12] It was an appraisal of the results of twenty-five years of part-time attendance of Sisters in universities and colleges.

The Twenty-Five-Year Appraisal

The survey was nation-wide, conducted by personal interviews with Major Superiors, Mistresses of Novices and Deans of Sisters' Studies. It was far more extensive than a collation of data concerning the professional preparation of Sisters. It attempted, from personal statements of those most concerned, to gauge the effects of higher education, acquired in the manner used over a quarter of a century, on the five facets of a Sister's life: The religious, the social (Communal living), the intellectual, the professional, and the apostolic. The value of existing programs was measured against their success in integrating all these elements. The study brought out the growing sense of inadequate return from university work in many religious Communities and led to the strong premise that it was not higher education *per se* that was so much at fault, but the manner in which it had been pursued by all the Sisters who could not attend college full-time—and their number was legion.

The Major Superiors, Mistresses of Novices, and others interviewed in the study showed amazing frankness, sincerity and in-

12 Sister Bertrande Meyers, D.C., *The Education of Sisters* (New York: Sheed and Ward, 1941).

sight. They evidenced a tremendous courage, too—a courage which can scarcely be appreciated today, when public criticism of the Church, its works, and of those things once held sacrosanct, elicits praise and makes for a popularity equated with intellectual honesty and vision. But in 1940 such frankness could easily have been misconstrued as disloyalty towards both the Church in general and the religious life in particular, even though all identification of persons and Communities was conscientiously avoided. This honest, intelligent appraisal of educational practices was accompanied by a deep and earnest soul-searching effort to place responsibility for the present situation and point up the remedies that should be applied. It preceded by almost two decades the surveys to be made later by other qualified researchers who found the soil well tilled and prepared for their planting.

For here, together in one place in this 1941 Study, was the combined opinion of the Major Superiors, the Mistresses of Novices, and the Directresses of Sisters' Studies, analyzing and synthesizing, as it were, the results of their efforts to give the Sisters the kind of education called for by the State in order to qualify them for certification at the elementary, secondary, and collegiate levels of the academic world. In all justice, it cannot be emphasized too strongly that Sisters were their first self-critics, and nothing today can equal the candor and honesty with which they faced the appraisal of the problems attendant on Sister-education.

Community Isolation

There was a significant fact brought to light in the 1941 Study that was destined to play an important role in later developments within the Church and the work of Sisters in their various apostolates. This was the almost complete isolation that existed among religious Congregations in America, one from the other. Beset with many identical concerns, such as the State certification of teachers, the licensing of registered nurses, diocesan regulations for schools, and a host of problems in other areas where consultation among Major Superiors would seem to be of inestimable help, there was little or no intercommunication of hopes, ideas, or experiences.

There was, of course, cordial good will expressed between members of different Orders when they met in university classes or at conventions, but there was no thought of collaboration nor any attempt at a meeting of minds, particularly on the part of religious Superiors. This was to come later, and at the direction of the Church, when it began its program of *aggiornamento*.

Problems Preceded Progress

That they did not act immediately to correct the situations revealed by the study is evidence of the size and complexity of the problems. Progress might have come more swiftly had Superiors not been under immense pressure to send more and more Sisters into ever-expanding fields of service. Neither bishops nor priests could quite grasp the necessity of holding the young Sister back until she was fully formed, academically and spiritually, to enter the profession of teaching or nursing. To retain the Sisters for five years of collegiate as well as spiritual formation, to talk of educating the whole Sister, at a time when schools and hospitals were crying out for apostolic services, was tantamount to denying all assistance to the mobilizing armed forces of the Second World War. Progress would have been accelerated had there been, as there are today, adequate media of consultation and communication among the various religious Communities, or if Superiors had had, in 1941, the positive directives of the Church to guide them in the preparation of their Sisters for religious-apostolic work in the world. Each Superior was, in a sense, alone with the problem of educating her Sisters to bear witness to Christ in the fields of teaching, nursing and social work in a world growing daily more secular. Time was needed in which to think and plan; and their faith told them that help would come.

Meantime, the 1941 Study pointed up the need to bring bishops and pastors to see the necessity for withholding the Sisters for solid pre-service study. It proposed a plan, showing how an educational program could be devised within a framework, or rather on a foundation, of liberal arts studies that would fully satisfy all State and regional accreditation demands. It outlined an adequate synthesis of the religious, the social (the common life of the Sisters), the intellectual and professional ideals required by Community life. If organized and properly conducted, higher education would serve as a handmaid for continuous intellectual and Christlike growth. If, through an integration of all subjects taught in a carefully planned curriculum, professional studies were looked upon as a preparation for the apostolate—the works of mercy, teaching, nursing, social work—it would be a positive means of educating the *whole* Sister, not only as a fervent religious but as a competent apostle.

The Education of Sisters is now out of print and has been replaced by more recent surveys. But the thesis set forth in its pages of educating *Sisters as Sisters,* with its strong emphasis on integration as the cornerstone on which to build, and the keystone with which to bind, was to be adopted in 1954 as the basic principle of the Sister Formation Movement—a movement which, as later chapters will show, was to prove itself a providential instrument in promoting policies formulated by the Church to aid Major Superiors in devising programs for the religious and intellectual formation of their Sisters.

3

The Mind of the Church and Major Superiors

No more masterful, comprehensive and penetrating blueprint for education could be written than the encyclical of Pius XI on the *Christian Education of Youth*. It covers the essence and importance of education in all its varied aspects: those who have a right and duty to educate, the responsibilities of the respective parties, the nature of the person to be educated, and the qualities and preparation educators should possess. Published December 31, 1929, it was everywhere received with acclaim, read with interest, and widely discussed. It might well be said that in school circles, between 1930 and 1940, it was, among Sisters, the most frequently quoted encyclical. To it they turned to justify the reading of certain literature deemed controversial and, perhaps, unsuitable for adolescent minds. What high-school, not to mention college, teachers could not aptly quote:

. . . And if, when occasion arises, it be deemed necessary to have the students read authors, propounding false doctrine, for the purpose of refuting it, this will be done after due preparation, and with such an antidote of sound doctrine, that it will not only do no harm, but will be an aid to the Christian formation of youth. . . . In such a school moreover, the study of the vernacular and of classical literature will do no damage to moral virtue. There the Christian teacher will imitate the bee, which takes the choicest part of the flower and leaves the rest, as St. Basil teaches in his discourse to youths, on the study of the classics.[1]

[1] Pope Pius XI, *Christian Education of Youth*, December 31, 1929 (Glen Rock, New Jersey: Paulist Press, 1951), p. 32.

What college deans, high-school teachers and elementary-school administrators have not included in their faculty meetings, institutes and other talks to teachers the following pertinent reminder:

Perfect schools are the result not so much of good methods as of good teachers, teachers who are thoroughly prepared and well-grounded in the matter they have to teach; who posses the intellectual and moral qualifications required by their important office; because they love Jesus Christ and His Church. . . .[2]

And today, in this age of the laity serving side by side with religious in the conduct of Catholic schools at all levels, how modern is the note struck by Pius XI in praising "excellent lay teachers, in such large numbers . . . laboring with zeal and perseverance . . . in the direction and formation of youth."

What catalogue of Catholic colleges and universities of the period did not paraphrase, in their purposes and objectives, these quotations from Pius XI:

The proper and immediate end of Christian education is to cooperate with divine grace in forming the true and perfect Christian. . . .

Hence the true Christian, product of Christian education, is the supernatural man who thinks, judges and acts constantly and consistently in accordance with right reason illumined by the supernatural light of the example and teaching of Christ; in other words, to use the current term, the true and finished man of character.[3]

It would be difficult indeed to name any book on the subject of pedagogy that has had a wider appeal and has been more consulted than this encyclical of Pius XI, on the *Christian Education of Youth*. Yet, from the vantage point of Sister-teachers, one is forced to wonder why it has taken more than thirty years for Pius XI's statement, implying the need for a strong pre-service preparation of religious teachers, to be put into effect. In all honesty, it must be admitted that even today some Communities have not yet organized a satisfactory intellectual and professional preparatory program. The Pope is, by his office, the highest superior of every

2 *Ibid.*, p. 33.
3 *Ibid.*, pp. 35–36.

religious Congregation, both of men and women; and every Pope
has called for unsurpassed excellence in Catholic schools. However, bishops and pastors exercise a subsidiary authority that has
to be obeyed. Zealous bishops and harassed pastors, with echoes
of the Councils of Baltimore in their ears, urging upon them their
responsibilities, "Catholic schools for Catholic children," have
been calling constantly for more and more Sister-teachers for the
rapidly multiplying schools that have seen a phenomenal growth
since the end of the Second World War.

Parochial Schools Maintain Prestige

In spite of teacher shortage and the need for new buildings, the
Catholic schools have maintained great prestige, as evidenced by
the growing requests for new parochial schools and the overcrowded
classrooms of those now in existence, the number of which today,
in 1965, exceeds ten thousand. Non-Catholic as well as Catholic
parents seek to enroll their children in parochial schools.

One thing that helped to build up the prestige of Catholic
schools in the past was that they clung in large measure to basic
traditional subject-matter disciplines at a time during the '30's
and '40's when the public schools were adoring the strange gods
of progressive education and offering "life-adjustment" snap
courses to replace hard-core subjects of the traditional elementary-
and high-school curricula. In keeping with the rather easy standards set up by the life-adjustment philosophy of education, the
more "progressive" public schools of the day were experimenting
with permissiveness and freedom of self-expression, while the
Catholic schools were emphasizing the three r's, history, geography
and grammar in the elementary schools. The college-preparatory
program for the average and better students of the secondary
schools aspired to a kind of excellence that served them well
when the admission policies of undergraduate colleges had to be
met.

Neither Major Superiors nor the nearly one hundred thousand
Sisters engaged in teaching in the 1940–1950 decade felt entirely
reassured by the apparent success of their schools. There was no
complacency; rather, a divine discontent urged them constantly
towards improvement. Yet, almost on the eve of the Second World

War, Pius XII, successor to Pius XI, endorsed his predecessor's views on the success of Catholic education in America. In an encyclical to the Bishops of the United States, Pius XII wrote in the very first year of his reign:

It is with good reason that visitors from other lands admire the organization and system under which your schools of various grades are conducted, the generosity of the faithful upon whom they depend, and the vigilant care with which they are watched over by the directors. From these schools come forth a host of citizens, strong in heart and mind, who by reason of their reverence for divine and human laws, are justly considered to be the strength and the flower and the honor of Church and country.[4]

To the older and more experienced Sisters, these were words of encouragement and support; they received them with gratitude. But to the young Sister, new and inexperienced in the classroom, they brought a sense of guilt, of worry, of anxiety. For, with the war came, at least temporarily, a shortage of vocations, which in turn meant a further delay in the pre-service spiritual and professional education of the young teachers so sorely needed. Crowded classrooms meant problems which could be solved only if the Sisters were well-grounded in the subjects they were assigned to teach, and well-versed in the art of presenting them in an interesting manner through the use of modern techniques. By 1945 Pius XII noted this need in his stirring allocution to the Catholic Italian Teachers' Association:

. . . your formation must be complete. For this reason, it is not only opportune, but also indispensable that your professional, pedagogical standing—precisely because you desire to tend toward perfection in the supernatural order—be eminent, superior. You should always be up-to-date with the uninterrupted progress of ideas and methods. . . . It follows from this that both your personal life and your professional activity must be imbued with a supernatural spirit which, then, must flow out into those committed to your care.[5]

4 *Sertum Laetitiae,* "To the Church in the United States." Issued on the Occasion of the 150th Anniversary of the Establishment of the American Hierarchy (National Catholic Welfare Conference, Washington, D.C., 1939), p. 4.

5 *Education: Papal Teachings,* Selected and arranged by the Benedictine Monks of Solesmes, trans. Rev. Aldo Rebeschini (Boston, Mass.: Daughters of St. Paul, 1960), pp. 343, 344.

The Sisters felt that their formation was anything but complete, and the restless anxiety described in the preceding chapter continued to grow.

Influence on the National Catholic Educational Association

The National Catholic Educational Association of the United States provided a forum for presenting and discussing problems of teacher education. Its speakers had done much to keep Major Superiors aware of the pressing problems of pre-service education for Sisters, but the answers had a way of always returning to one point: "The bishops and pastors are worried about our schools. They ask for more and more Sisters before we can give them adequate training." In a memorable meeting of the association in 1949, Sister Madeleva, then president of St. Mary College, Notre Dame, Indiana, read a paper entitled "The Education of Our Young Religious Teachers." It was reprinted and widely distributed as a booklet under the title of *The Education of Sister Lucy*. It made a powerful contribution to the growing conviction that an integrated, pre-service preparation for Sisters for the apostolate, be it teaching, nursing, social work or anything else carried out by them as agents and representatives of the Church, was of prime importance.

The Education of Sister Lucy pointed out that, for the young religious, "her education as a teacher and her formation as a religious are completely compatible, complementary and can be prefectly synchronized." Sister Madeleva emphasized the priceless value of a vocation by the use of modern comparisons: "Lucy and her companions are our most priceless and irreplaceable materials in the whole world of education. Let us treat them with much more than the care and caution bestowed on centers of atomic energy. Let us keep them out of the categories of vacuum cleaners and Bendix washers."

Danger of Defections

Perhaps her most telling point in favor of full, pre-service education was scored when she said:

Then, there is the question of prudence. Should Lucy be educated before her Community knows that she will persevere? Nothing can possibly do more to undermine her vocation than to send her out to try to teach without adequate, often without any preparation. Nothing can so disillusion her in her Community as the dishonesty of assigning her to do in the name of holy obedience what professionally she is unqualified to do. Our secular accrediting agencies have been more than discreet and courteous in bearing with our practices in this matter. Our end does not justify our means.[6]

Major Superiors recognized the penetrating honesty of Sister Madeleva's words. Since Sheed and Ward's publication of *The Education of Sisters* in 1941, Sisters in growing numbers had been giving vocal and written expression to the same sentiments. Indeed, experience had borne out only too well that defections had resulted from imposing responsibilities on Sisters before they were either spiritually or professionally ready to assume them. More and more Superiors were coming to realize that to save and safeguard vocations was but a partial fulfillment of their duty. Their chief responsibility involved making the most of every Sister's potential by developing her natural and supernatural talents and abilities.

Role of the Local Superior

In less pressured days, much of a Sister's training in the religious life, following the novitiate, could be left to the local Superior. Her formal instructions in the spiritual life and her private counseling brought the young Sister to the true and continuous practice of the virtues special to her state. It was the local Superior, also, who often served as "master teacher," visiting the young Sister's classes, advising her as to classroom management. In the late afternoon or evening she gave individual help to these new and untried teachers, and even conducted formal classes in methods and devices for securing and holding the interest and attention of the pupils—the best answer to discipline problems.

[6] Sister M. Madeleva, C.S.C., "The Education of Our Young Religious Teachers," *National Catholic Educational Association Proceedings and Addresses*, 1949, p. 254.

Now, the local Superior is principal of the school, executive of many and varied offices: it is her duty to keep in touch with civic and social agencies, attend diocesan meetings and implement policies and directives from these more complex school authorities. Now, too, a large number of lay colleagues have a claim on her time, which lessens the hours she can give to counseling young Sisters, as was formerly done by less harassed administrators. This makes it a very real necessity that young Sisters come to the local Superior as completely prepared religious, well-grounded in the spiritual and social life of the Community.

At the same time, they must come as competent teachers, ready, able and thoroughly prepared to take the class assigned them. The local Superior will indeed always be their "mother" with a true and supernatural interest in her young charges, and she will continue to see that appropriate advantages in further study and professional competence are made available to them. On their part, the new teachers should come equipped with a modest self-confidence and a balanced sense of their professional abilities.

This—not so much ideal as downright necessity—is what many Sisters had been clamoring for as the only way to solve the problem of preparing young religious for their apostolate, whether it was to be teaching, nursing or social work. It would mean, as the more experienced nuns were insisting, retaining the young Sisters at the Motherhouse for a post-novitiate period, to study— and to be studied. Just as Superiors had always had a salutary fear of wasting, or not using prudently, the material goods of the Community, they now were experiencing a growing fear of not putting to the best use the far more precious resources of the Community, the Sisters. But looming large before them was the age-old problem: bishops and pastors were clamoring for more and more Sisters, some of them urging "on the job" training as sufficient for souls as dedicated as were the Sisters.

Certainly the plight of the bishops and pastors deserves sympathy, but satisfying these demands conflicted, in many instances, with the dictates of the conscience of the Superior who had to make the decision. Only the Holy See could break this impasse— and break it the Holy See did, but by the slow and always wise intervention Rome has used down the centuries. Nevertheless, it was to bring about a solution that would open up a whole new era of religious life.

*First International Congress
of Religious, Rome, 1950*

All reports, as well as all roads, lead to Rome. Reports of the anxiety felt by Major Superiors concerning their inability to answer the myriad calls for Sisters; concerning the "Sister shortage," resulting not only from a decrease in vocations but from an increase in defections; concerning the lessening in some countries of esteem for the religious life on the part of some priests and laymen; concerning the growing unrest and uncertainty as to the Sister's role in a rapidly changing society—these and other problems reached the Holy See. Pope Pius XII realized the need for prudent action. Through the Sacred Congregation of Religious, that papal office which concerns itself directly with the affairs of religious Orders of men and women, he convened the First International Congress of Religious in Rome, 1950.

By gathering together delegates from the whole world—four thousand responded to the invitation—the Holy See could determine which problems were universal and which had more of a national character. The over-all objectives, as then stated, were twofold: to establish a strong and friendly bond of unity among all Communities, and to treat of some of the more important internal and external aspects of the religious life. Frank presentation and free discussion were encouraged. The decline in vocations was common to all nations, with but few exceptions, and emerged as the root of many other problems that were to be considered.

With a forcefulness and directness which only the Sacred Congregation of Religious itself could exercise, the delegates were told that the shortage of vocations was not a cause but rather an effect of individual Communities clinging to antiquated customs, traditions that had long lost relevance and meaning to present-day thinking, and that in convents today a mode of life persisted that— internally and externally—was geared to other centuries. "Such things," speaker after speaker reiterated, were "obstacles both to attracting vocations and to retaining them." The Sacred Congregation of Religious, the delegates were told, would look favorably upon requests for any changes in constitution, rule, custom and ascetical practices that would modernize the spirit and works of the individual Community, provided that the essence of the religious life was preserved in all its purity.

Emphasis at this congress was placed on unity among Communities, especially those Communities engaged in the same type of works. Not a corporate union was asked, for Rome welcomes the existing variety and diversity now found among its dedicated servants; rather, a unity springing from friendly contacts and the sharing of problems and experiences was desired. This unity was essential to the far-reaching movement which the Church was initiating, since only concerted action could ensure success.

Mindful of the principle of subsidiarity, Rome expressed its wishes and suggested guidelines to follow, but made nothing mandatory, nor did it set a time limit for the accomplishment of any changes and adaptations. In deference to episcopal authority and in view of the differences in the culture and customs of individual countries and the varying degrees of impact made by social and educational problems, Rome decided that National Congresses of Major Superiors, planned, organized, and held at some centrally located city, might prove more useful and practical in attempting to solve the urgent problems now being presented at the First International Congress of Religious. Thus, the Congress of 1950 marked the beginning of a movement, Church-inspired and Church-directed, towards helping religious function more holily and effectively in today's world.

First National Congress of Major Superiors in the United States, 1952

This First National Congress of Major Superiors was convened in the city of Notre Dame, Indiana, August 9–13, 1952. It brought together the largest gathering of Mothers General and Provincials ever witnessed in the United States. At its opening, the delegates were told by the then Apostolic Delegate to the United States, His Excellency, the Most Reverend Amleto Giovanni Cicognani that: "His Holiness Pius XII has blessed this Congress with joy

and paternal satisfaction, and is watching it with great hopes."[7]
The direct interest of Rome was further indicated by the suggestion of the Sacred Congregation of Religious of certain specific
subjects to be included in the program. These subjects were the
identical ones with which Major Superiors had been concerned
for some years: "The Necessity of Special Training for Mistresses
of Novices and Superiors," "Ways and Means of Prolonging the
Formation Initiated in the Novitiate," "Training in the Positive
Aspects of the Religious Vows," "Special Problems in the Practice
of the Vows in Modern Times," "Theology for Sisters" and, above
all, the necessity of sound education for the various apostolates.
To these, the Committee responsible for the program added topics
equally pertinent and timely.[8]

Noted speakers discussed these and other problems connected
with the four fields of health, education, welfare and foreign
missions which were of interest to the nation as a whole, but
especially to the Sisters particularly involved in those areas as
part of their apostolate. All present were keyed to a sense of the
significance of the Congress and their personal responsibility for
carrying out its objectives.

These objectives were, in essence, the same two stressed at the
International Congress in Rome: unity and a sharing of problems
among Communities, and adaptation to the needs of the time. The
accent, frank and forceful, was placed on the former. Noting that
there existed what he called a reserve and reticence among
religious Congregations, one towards another, the Very Reverend
Arcadio Larraona (now Cardinal) said with touching sincerity
and earnestness:

It is sad to say that frequently religious congregations live and work
unknown to one another. Perhaps this is more noticeable among
Superiors than among the members. There is a tendency to act and to
think as though we were not all perfect Christians bound fraternally
to those who like ourselves are striving for religious perfection. Much
harm is done to the Church and to souls, and many worthy apostolic

[7] "The Religious in the U.S.A.—Past, Present, Future," *Religious Community
Life in the United States,* Vol. II (Glen Rock, New Jersey: The Paulist Press,
1952), p. 11.
[8] *Ibid.,* pp. 28–174.

works are hindered in their development by this regrettable lack of cooperation. By fraternal collaboration we can intensify our common action for the greater glory of God and thus accomplish work which would be impossible to the individual Congregation.[9]

With paternal understanding, this Prefect of the Sacred Congregation of Religious added that he fully realized that the reserve and reticence that had been so long an almost sacred tradition could not be abolished overnight, but the seed now being planted would, he knew, bear permanent and substantial fruit in a short time. The Major Superiors, listening to these words, recognized that the Holy See, through the Sacred Office of the Congregation of Religious, would be pleased if all Orders would take steps to eliminate the walls of secrecy and separation that had existed from early monastic times when complete isolation from the world made intercommunication not only difficult but unnecessary. Rome promised assistance in bringing about abundant means towards a closer cooperation and collaboration among religious Sisterhoods.

In another of his addresses, the Very Reverend Father Arcadio Larraona paid special tribute to the religious in America. "This Congress," Father Larraona said, "witnessed the largest gathering of Mothers General in the history of the Church. Religious in America are conscious of their mission, a world-wide mission," he reminded them, pointing up the fact that America accounted for one-fifth of all religious women of the universal Church. "Therefore a providential leadership is expected of you that will go forth and conquer, not only America, but the whole world for Christ."[10]

Epochal Movements in 1952

All of the educational problems worrying the Sisters of the United States were touched upon at some length at this epoch-making Congress of 1952. Sister Madeleva, C.S.C., spoke of the experimental program in theology for Sisters begun in the summer of 1942 and now, ten years later, of the thriving centers in the United States with noted scholars in theology making their de-

[9] *Acta et Documenta Congressus Internationalis Superiorissarum Generalium* (Rome: Editiones Paulinae, 1952), p. 303.
[10] *Religious Community Life in the United States*, p. 189.

partments the strongest in the college. Along with the most thoughtful, keen-minded students majoring in theology, this discipline, organized in proper sequence, was available to Sisters. This made it possible for Mistresses of Postulants and Novices to avail themselves of these opportunities—a suggestion needed and dwelt upon by the speakers of this Congress.

The words "formation" and "houses of formation"—new words in their new context—were being proposed, described and discussed, and although, as Sister Madeleva pointed out, these rich developments of the religious life were entering our convents by the "oblique route of education" this took nothing from the glad tidings. They were a veritable kerygma; and if taken at the fullness of their tide, would lead on not only to further fruitful discussion but to substance and endurance.

Some Prophecies and their Fulfillment

Other topics of interest filled not only lecture halls but corridors and common rooms. One paper, "Sharing the Sisters," offered a missionary promise of opening more Catholic and parochial schools if lay teachers were hired at the ratio of one lay teacher to every four Sisters. We well know the success of this suggestion, although it was thought radical and impractical at the time it was first proposed.

Another prophecy made at this 1952 Congress in the United States was that of overcrowded classrooms. For the forty or fifty children then representing unwieldy enrollments, eighty were predicted, and that is vastly too many in a class, especially in the lower grades. The fulfillment of this prophecy was surpassed when some pastors allowed as many as one hundred children in a classroom, until parents angrily protested and many teachers collapsed under the strain. But parents, in spite of these overwhelming problems, continued to recognize the priceless values inherent in a Catholic education even under the crippling difficulties that beset the parochial schools.

Where once in the early days of America it was the bishops who urged their priests to build first the school and later the Church, in the early 50's, and even now in 1965, it is the parishioner who says: "Father, build the school first with a basement or auditorium large enough to be used as the parish Church—but let us begin with a convent and a school so our children will have a Catholic education."

Such, then, in the 160 years of Catholic school education from 1792 to 1952 was its popularity with Catholic parents that they were most reluctant to accept any substitute. The parochial school had spread to all parts of the country and its influence was everywhere felt. One of its far-reaching effects was seen in all parts of Europe, most markedly during the years of the Second World War, when American G.I.'s impressed Europeans with their knowledge and practice of their faith, so evident in their attendance at Mass, even when it entailed great personal sacrifice—rising early, missing breakfast when distance delayed their return to the dining halls. Many lay people in Italy and France later commented on this to the writer, expressing special edification at the eagerness of G.I.'s to serve Mass when, as so many Europeans remarked, "I'm afraid our own young men had forgotten the formula."

But—returning for the moment to the 1952 Congress in the United States—the most often expressed foreboding among Sisters and a majority of school Superintendents was that the growing pressures on Major Superiors for more and more Sisters to fill the ever-crowding classrooms of the Catholic parochial and secondary schools would further delay the proper integrated formation and education of the Sister-teachers, to their own personal loss and a consequent loss to the Church.

The Knowledge Explosion in Academic Fields

The population explosion that followed hard upon the close of the Second World War not only filled to overflowing Catholic classrooms all over the country but created a constantly expanding reverberation of another kind that opened up new problems for the schools at the elementary and higher levels. This was the sudden and simultaneous explosion of knowledge on all fronts. The natural sciences took the lead and called for an updating of all the traditional courses in physics, chemistry, biology and mathematics, so that the expert teacher whose college courses dated back some eight or ten years found her various course syllabi obsolescent. Even teachers who possessed hard-earned masters' and doctoral degrees were obliged to return to the universities for almost completely new courses. Luckily, federal and foundation grants to defray rapidly increasing expenses were available for Sisters and lay teachers alike to acquire the new knowledges that became vital to elementary, secondary, and college faculties.

The social and behavioral sciences took on new stature from new discoveries, especially in depth psychology and human relationships; and, at long last, it dawned on Western peoples that for too long Eastern man and the history of his civilization had been ignored. It came as something of a belated shock that even ambassadors and military personnel had not bothered to learn the language, much less an appreciation of the culture, customs and mores of the countries to which they had been sent as representatives of a United States which professed, at least in theory, a desire to love and protect all peoples who were struggling against the poverty and deprivation that impeded their progress towards independence and freedom as men and nations.

Thus, courses in the natural sciences, social studies, Middle-East and Far-Eastern civilization, as well as the history of our nearer neighbors in Latin America, came to enrich Catholic school curricula. At the same time, television programs on rocketry and spacecraft put first-grade pupils ahead of their teachers in missile-mystery. All this opened up a new world of knowledge that made full-time study a not-to-be-delayed necessity for young Sisters and prospective entrants into the religious life who would choose teaching as their apostolate.

The Knowledge Explosion in Other Fields

At the same time that knowledge moved forward in academic areas it opened up new implications in the terrain of nursing and social service. These once narrowly professional fields became increasingly aware of the importance of a truly liberal education which would not merely add to the store of information possessed by all truly cultured people in the areas of history, literature, art, music, science and social studies, but would increase the power to think and to engender creative ideas. These seemed to be the necessary abilities to develop any profession into something beyond an organized body of skilled workers, and both nursing and social work were engaged in steadily pushing out the frontiers of creative service to mankind.

Since Catholic hospitals and social agencies were global efforts of the Church to reach and alleviate the miseries of mankind wherever found, it meant that here, too, the Sisters and prospective postulants to the religious life would need to be educated in a wide variety of professions undergirded by a strong liberal arts foundation interwoven with sound courses in philosophy and theology. No ordinary education would suffice for the Sister of today. Something special would have to be designed that would develop all her intellectual, social, spiritual and psychological powers into an integrated, holy, religious woman, mature, cultured and capable in the profession through which she would effectively serve God, the Church, and society. Such a program would need careful planning and a faculty of rare ability and dedication.

This problem was discussed at length at the National Congress of Major Superiors at Notre Dame in 1952. All agreed it would take prayer, thought and cooperation among the various religious Congregations. The desire for greater collaboration among Major Superiors was one of the most significant outcomes of the Congress. It enabled Superiors to talk freely about their common problems and to exchange ideas as to possible and practical solutions.

Congress of Major Superiors at Rome in September 1952

Scarcely had the National Congress of American Superiors in the United States concluded their deliberations in August of 1952 when Rome called together an International Congress of Major Superiors of the entire world in September of the same year —1952. The problems presented were of the same nature in general as those discussed at Notre Dame, Indiana, but with a different emphasis.

How best to educate the Sisters for their expanding roles in the fourfold apostolates of health, education, welfare and foreign missions received major attention. The need for Sisters to be well-grounded in philosophy and theology was universally recognized, and a plan for organizing Regina Mundi in Rome as a special center for educating Sisters in theology was the direct and prompt response from the Major Superiors from all countries of the world. More than three hundred Sisters, representing one hundred Orders from forty countries, have continued to study theology there since its establishment in 1952.

The Sacred Congregation stressed the interest it bears towards all that touches the religious Communities spread over the entire world. It spoke of having formed a Central Consultative Commission to follow up and coordinate the various activities, those especially which had for their objective the updating of the religious, cultural and professional-apostolic preparation of Sisters for their missions—teaching, nursing, social work. Almost every session mentioned the necessity of a union of minds in a joint effort to discuss their problems and defend their common interests.

Higher Studies Stressed

In proposing higher studies for those institutes of women whose apostolate required advanced education, the following points were put forward[11]

1. Arrangements should be made in every country for nuns to carry on higher studies under conditions approved by ecclesiastical authorities, and where possible, in Institutes attended only by nuns.
2. Higher studies are necessary for those destined to occupy positions of importance, e.g., those who train or teach Sisters, and these should be carried out in every country. For some chosen subjects Sisters might well study in Rome.
3. In countries where no special Institutes of Higher Studies exist, suitable for Sisters, they should be founded; where already existing, they should be used, encouraged and developed.

11 *Acta et Documenta*, p. 209.

4. Steps should be taken to found an Institute of higher religious studies in Rome (Regina Mundi) for nuns and women of all nations in apostolic work, and schools of other higher studies to serve as a model for such Institutes in other countries.

Referring to his fourth point, Father Larraona pointed out that since a large part of the program of deliberations to follow would return again and again to the urgent need for higher studies of religious, in order to prepare them for their apostolic-professional roles in the Church, he wished to assure the Sisters: "There is not the slightest intention or desire to interfere with the many excellent schools of higher culture functioning in your own countries and in various parts of the world."[12] These, he insisted, would find no "competition, but only help" from the proposed establishment of a university in Rome.

Although the problem of pre-service education for young Sisters was to be emphasized as a major concern that could not be delayed much longer, Superiors were reminded that other Community matters must receive attention before the root-causes of more serious but cognate factors concerning "Sister shortage" could be corrected. If the world is changing, it was pointed out by various speakers, so should the traditional attitude of Superiors towards their Sisters change. They should realize, they were reminded, that, under whatever pressures, *to make professional use of Sisters for the works of the Community before they had been well prepared in all spheres of their lives was to be guilty of the very activism against which they themselves warned their subjects.* A thoughtful "Examination of Conscience Concernng Religious"[3] was proposed, and the following provocative questions pondered:

1. Were the stresses and strains, resulting in physical and mental breakdown, not due to causes that could be remedied?
2. Was the rigid, impersonal novitiate training, possibly well-suited to the girl of fifty years ago, stultifying and harmful to the girl of today?

12 *Ibid.*, p. 23–87.
13 *Ibid.*, pp. 235–236.

3. Were the Sisters finding in religious government a likeness to that maternal love and fraternal charity which should mark the Christian home?
4. Were archaic customs and Community regulations presenting barriers to vocations and promoting defections?

These and other questions were presented by the various speakers at the International Congress of Major Superiors held in Rome in December, 1952. These same questions, asked by a retreat master in one's own country, might have excited doubt, fear, anxiety and frustration. Conducted publicly and collectively, with learned, sympathetic, and authoritative mentors at hand to resolve difficulties, suggest remedies, and keep all suggestions within the scope of Canon Law, the inquiry was an enriching and rewarding experience, bright with the hope of immediate fruits and full of new promises for the future.

The Juniorate

Father Larraona spoke of the Holy See's desire that each Congregation erect its own Juniorate, in which a period of from three to five years (at the discretion of each Major Superior) beyond the canonical year of novitiate would be provided for study. This added time of formation was to be allowed for the extra and individual preparation necessary to each Sister in view of the times and the needs of the future apostolate which would call for newer forms of services and closer, less supervised contact with seculars at the levels of children, adolescents and adults.

In speaking of the need for the Juniorate to follow either the canonical or second year of novitiate, Cardinal Larraona said:

Sisters in the Juniorate are in a kind of middle stage of formation, in which they are not subjected to the restrictions of the novitiate in all their rigor, nor yet allowed all the freedom of the perpetually professed religious. At the same time they are provided with an opportunity to integrate their general and professional education with the demands of their religious vocation.[14]

14 *Ibid.*, p. 276.

In the closing address Father Larraona spoke again of Juniorates stressing their need, purpose and form:

In the novitiate, the formation of the religious is begun . . . In the Juniorate it is continued though not with the detailed program of the novitiate year. . . . The Juniorate is intended to forestall the catastrophes which have sometimes befallen young professed Sisters who were sent into the active life without any transition period to prepare them for the special problems confronting them in that life. . . . In the Juniorate, they are provided with opportunities to *integrate* [Italics mine] their professional training with the demands of the religious vocation.

During the Juniorate, whatever form it may take, Sisters should be under the close-range guidance of experienced and capable religious. . . . There is no objection to the Juniorate lasting during the entire time of the Sisters' temporary profession. The ideal is a special house for those Communities that can provide one. The threefold aim of the Juniorate is formation, practice, probation.

The Sacred Congregation is ready to allow up to five years of temporary profession (or Juniorate), with the possibility of an extension of one year. No temporary profession can be extended beyond six years according to the present Code of Canon Law. . . . If a Sister has not succeeded in satisfying her Superiors as to her vocation during the period of postulate, novitiate and six years of temporary profession (or Juniorate), it is hardly probable that she will be able to provide this satisfaction in an extended period of probation.[15]

This pronouncement was a tremendous boon to those who heard it. Here, from the Secretary of the Sacred Congregation of Religious, speaking in the name of the Pope, Superiors received authority, which might be called a mandate, to withhold young Sisters from the apostolate until the spiritual and religious formation, begun in the novitiate, had been integrated with the intellectual and professional. Thus, a matter once open to debate was now made an obligation.

During the course of his allocution to the delegates, Pope Pius XII exhorted the Reverend Mothers on two points; first, their manner of government, which he said should be maternal and not such as would add unnecessarily to the sacrifices inherent in the

15 *Ibid.*

religious life. "You, as Superiors General, should be the first to breathe into the common life of your Sisters the warmth of family love."[16] The Pope then spoke, as he had spoken many times before, of the responsibility of the Mothers General for the complete preparation of their Sisters for the apostolate of the Church. His words were specific, clear, all-inclusive:

In the training of your Sisters for the tasks that await them, be broadminded and liberal and admit of no stinginess. Whether it be for teaching, the care of the sick, the study of art or anything else, the Sister should be able to say to herself, "My Superior is giving me a training that will put me on an equality with my secular colleagues." Give them also the opportunity and the means to keep their professional knowledge up-to-date. This is important for your Sisters' peace of mind and for their work.[17]

The words spoken at the 1952 International Congress of Rome, coming as they did from the highest authority in the Church, had a profound effect on the Mothers General. They felt at once challenged and reassured. The government of a Community is a weighty responsibility at any time. This responsibility was intensified in an era of rapid and often bewildering change, where society was making new demands upon Sisters, and where the novices, coming from that society, brought to Communities an analytical and even critical spirit quite different from that of preceding generations. Major Superiors, in touch with the world and alert to its needs, had been struggling with the necessity of bringing the services of religious women into line with the needs engendered by a society grown materialistic by reason of unprecedented prosperity, yet influenced by a secular humanism which could be directed into channels where the laity and Sisters could work together for a better world.

To do this, however, meant breaking down many barriers of time-honored tradition in the convent and in its way of life. It would mean digging to the root of customs and practices, to reach the original spirit which conceived them and to express that same spirit in ways more suited to contemporary times. This they had

16 *Ibid.*, p. 333.
17 *Ibid.*

prudently hesitated to do until such time as now—God's good time—when the Church not only authorized but urged them to act.

In regard to the preparation of the young Sisters for the apostolate, all scruples concerning a lack of zeal in withholding them from the mission field had been laid to rest. However urgent the pleas of regional bishops might be, the Bishop of Rome had personally told them that a planned and prolonged preparation should be given to every Sister; not only to lessen defections but to increase competent and worthy representatives of the Church in all areas of activity. Now they could, without qualms of conscience, refuse the requests of pastors for Sisters to staff new schools or to add to the number in expanding old ones. The Supreme Pastor had made clear where the primary, solemn obligation of the Mothers General lay. The obstacles that lay ahead, they were determined to overcome.

Cordial cooperation and collaboration among religious Congregations had been recommended. All realized that the other directives of the Holy See could not be carried out if this essential element of fraternal charity were lacking. One might say that the spirit of ecumenism had become strong among the representatives of nearly one million women religious ten years before the convening of Vatican Council II. The Pentecostal fire had descended, and though the Mothers General came from many nations, each had heard "in her own tongue" what the obligations were that their office laid upon them.

Fortified, enlightened, reassured, renewed, the Mothers General returned to their respective countries, cherishing the words they had heard from Rome and strong in their determination to put them into practice. No longer did each Community feel left to its own devices. *Ecce quam bonum* was their watchword. The Sacred Congregation of Religious had given the pattern for *aggiornamento,* had prescribed that higher education was essential for Sisters, and that this education should be given in an environment and under circumstances that would develop the spiritual and religious elements of a Sister's life as well as the intellectual and professional. This called for the organization of a post-novitiate, pre-service Juniorate. The Communities were left to work out the manner of doing this, each according to its resources or by calling upon the resources of other Communities in that spirit of cooperation and collaboration so earnestly urged by the Holy See.

Each Mother General knew there would be obstacles to overcome in putting the instructions they had received into effect; these would vary from Community to Community. There would be opposition arising from a misunderstanding on the part of those who had not been present at the Congress to hear in person the expressed wishes of the Holy See. This opposition would have to be met with fortitude, intelligent patience, and prayers. But *aggiornamento* was well on its way. The decade 1950–60 was to mark the greatest changes in the active Orders of women during their more than three centuries of existence. It may well be said that during this decade Major Superiors of religious Communities of women matched their predecessors of pioneer days in vision, courage and resourcefulness.

4

The Call to Aggiornamento

Vision, courage and resourcefulness were indeed qualities needed in the work that lay before the Mothers General as they returned from Rome to their various convents throughout the world. Reassured and inspired as they were by the Holy See's interest in their problems and progress, they were now, more than ever before, alert to the tremendous obligations and responsibilities which their office placed upon them in the governing of their respective Communities.

As they saw it, the Congress of Religious Superiors at Rome in 1952 had narrowed their immediate concerns to two grave problems: giving a strong, integrated, supernaturally motivated pre-service education to their young Sisters. This would result in the fivefold formation of each candidate to the Community: the religious, the intellectual, the social (Community living), the professional and apostolic training so necessary for the world of the 20th and 21st centuries. This, Rome had seriously impressed upon the Mothers General as a primary duty. But the Sacred Congregation of Religious saw, with the wisdom of centuries of experience with Church affairs, that the problem of vocation-shortage went deeper than any other of the many considered at Rome during the congress. This was the very *heart* of the matter, and Pius XII urged that the causes for the decline in vocations and the lack of perseverance of postulants and novices be first studied; then the question of pre-service formation could be considered. In the closing address of the congress, His Holiness said:

For your part, this is what we counsel:

Make sure that nothing in your (Community) customs, your manner of life, or your ascetical practices raises a barrier or causes loss of vocation. We have in mind certain usages, which were no doubt suited to the times and surroundings in which they were instituted, but are out of place today, so that even a good girl with courage, would find them an obstacle to her vocation.[1]

Examination of Community Practices

These words had indeed given the Mothers General pause. The rules and customs of their respective Communities, their way of life, their ascetical practices, had all been handed down to them by their founders and were hallowed by a long and honored tradition. Now they had been told by the Pope, the highest Superior of all Communities, the one to whom they ultimately owe obedience by reason of their vow, that these holy practices, which they and their Sisters had held sacrosanct, might constitute a barrier, not only to the attraction of girls to their way of life, but to their perseverance once they had embraced it. In a word, these time-honored customs might prove to be an occasion of a loss of vocation. These were words to be pondered. Nor did they stand alone as a statement. In an allocution to teaching Sisters at Rome, September 15, 1951, speaking of the need for adaptation, Pius XII said:

You wish to serve the cause of Jesus Christ, and of His Church, in the way that the world of today demands. Therefore, it would not be reasonable to persist in customs and forms that hinder this service, or perhaps render it impossible.[2]

The need of adaptation which Pius XII was to stress so markedly during the latter part of his reign preoccupied him from its beginning. During the first year of his pontificate (1939), addressing the Regular Canonesses of St. Augustine, he said:

---

1 *Acta et Documenta*, p. 333.
2 *Counsel to Teaching Sisters* (Washington, D.C.: National Catholic Welfare Conference Publications), p. 7.

You have remained and doubtless intend to remain faithful to the spirit of your founders. . . . But since a tradition of three centuries runs the risk of remaining inert or deficient in its application, if it is not revitalized by the breath of progress and adaptation, we are glad to see that while remaining substantially faithful to the origin of the Institute, the Congregation of Our Lady has assumed a new form in the twentieth century.[3]

And to the Sisters of the Assumption, May 19, 1946, he repeated the same theme:

Without doubt, religious habits and pious customs are of great value, but only when from one generation to another, they awaken, stimulate, support and further the personal life of faith.[4]

Action could no longer be postponed. The call to *aggiornamento* was clear, specific and far-reaching. Superiors were faced with making decisions and taking steps fraught with consequences not only for the present generation but for generations to come. The situation called for guidance from the Holy Spirit and prudent action on the part of Mothers General. There was need of informing the Sisters as to the attitude of Rome towards the updating of Community life, and time must be allowed for ideas to be accepted and assimilated. While each Superior knew that there would always be some excellent Sisters who would look upon even a minor change as radical, the vast majority of Congregations were made up of flexible religious who could be counted upon to welcome and even to augment with alacrity the new views brought back from Rome by the Mothers General. These latter were earnestly mindful of Father Arcadio Larraona's words in his closing address to them at the congress of 1952:

Rome wants this evolution to be without stress or shocks—a genuinely vital evolution, imitating the growth and development of a human being. Hence the usual procedure is to require that all proposed modifications be submitted to a General Chapter, and that the changes be approved, not merely by an absolute majority, but the moral unanimity of the delegates.[5]

---

[3] *Education: Papal Teachings*, pp. 292–293.
[4] *Ibid.*, p. 349.
[5] *Acta et Documenta*, pp. 272–273.

This remark alone made clear that Rome was asking for a well-paced evolution, not a precipitate or immediate revolution. To assure this evolution, many Mothers General promptly took steps to obtain the collective thinking of their Sisters by consulting each of them, following in this the democratic method of the Church. By questionnaire, by personal interviews and by group discussions they sought to ascertain the views and opinions of the Sisters as to what changes should be made for a true *aggiornamento* of convent life, and in what areas. The intelligence of Sisters runs above average,[6] and once obedience asked them to look at their life of work and prayer critically and objectively, to view their present practices and customs to which they had become habituated through long observance, and to give their frank opinion of them, in light of a 20th century world of rapid change and upheaval, they responded readily. Temperately, and with honest courage, they stated which rules, practices and customs seemed to aid or to deter their spiritual growth and which seemed to develop or to inhibit their religious spirit. Far from lessening their esteem for the religious life, this opportunity to think through their rules and customs, questioning their current relevancy to prayer and work, and above all to spiritual maturity, became a source of renewed fervor. But naturally there would not be unanimity of thought among the more than one hundred eighty thousand Sisters in the United States alone,[7] much less in the nearly one million Sisters involved throughout the world. Many of the United States' Communities had strong ties with Europe, and their missions were extended to all parts of the world. Sisters in foreign countries had to be consulted, lest changes fragmentize an Order. In many cases the changes had to be initiated in Europe, for many United States' Communities have Generalates there. At all costs the integrity of international Communities had to be preserved. This should be taken into account when the effort is made to equate promptitude with obedience.

[6] Unpublished studies of admission requirements and I.Q. of entrants, correlated with grades obtained in college and graduate work. Admission requirements set by the Church "average" intelligence. The norm used in studies was based on I.Q. of 100 as average.

[7] General Summary, Statistical Insert, *The Official Catholic Directory*, 1964, p. 1.

Reaction of the Sisters to Adaptation

From the information thus gathered within each Community, Superiors had patent evidence of the penetrating wisdom of the Holy See when it called upon Communities to make an examination of their "customs, manner of life, and ascetical practices." The suggestions received could be classified under a number of general headings, not always clearly defined into categories since, necessarily, one demarcation will impinge upon another. However, in order of frequency, most Major Superiors agreed that the following list represents the items that Sisters mentioned with a degree of emphasis that implied a certain urgency:[8]

1. Revision of horarium, so as to find more time for study and class preparation. (The need for more time is the most frustrating problem.)
2. Freeing of Sisters from household chores—cooking, sewing, and laundry—in order to allow more time for professional reading and class preparation.
3. Pre-service preparation of young Sisters, based on a sound knowledge and understanding of doctrine.
4. Introducing more liturgy and Scripture in the Sisters' prayer life.
5. Reducing vocal prayers to a minimum. They are distasteful to the American mentality. Mental prayer should be stressed, with a choice of subject matter in recognition of individual differences and levels of spirituality.
6. Updating of spiritual readings, with a choice of books for individual taste and opinion. Reading may be taken preferably in the Chapel, but each one should be allowed to read silently. The custom of one reading aloud for all in the Common room is to be abolished.
7. Permitting Sisters to take a more active part in parish life. Those who have time and zeal should be allowed to follow their own inspiration, guided by prudence and obedience.
8. Making clear, in the very early stages of formation, that the Church comes before the Community in our service, though stressing loyalty to the Community.

[8] 762 questionnaires filled out by Major Superiors, Mistresses of Novices, and rank-and-file Sisters served as the basis of this and other chapters dealing with *aggiornamento*.

9. Increasing Sisters' contacts in an apostolic way with the adult laity, and producing a more direct apostolate through expansion and extension of assigned apostolates, such as teaching, nursing, social service.
10. Abolition of rank in seating arrangements in refectory and Community room.
11. Modification (or radical change) of the Habit.

In all honesty, most Communities reported that many older Sisters found the ordeal of change a painful and frustrating experience. Naturally enough, practices that had been a help and source of inspiration, as well as a strong aid to character formation, could not now be readily recognized as militating against the good of a Community. Change is but too often seen as an implied criticism of the past. This is an error in thinking that calls for study. Change is not a criticism of the past, it is a recognition of progress: that new times call for new ideas. The view of change as a condemnation of earlier practices is responsible for resistance to many adaptations which life calls for. Small wonder, then, that resistance should be found among the older members who had built the Community to its peak of success and had given it stability. Nevertheless, the good of the Community was at stake, and indeed perhaps its continued existence. These older Sisters were quick to see with their Major Superiors that Rome, as always, had good reasons for asking for *aggiornamento*.

Since revision in the order-of-the-day (with its particular problem of finding more time for necessary apostolic work) was mentioned more frequently, and since a revision of the horarium was an obvious key to other changes, most Communities began their *aggiornamento* with modifying the horarium

Analysis of the Horarium

Communities, upon the examination of their prescribed order-of-the-day, came to see that most horaria were framed to meet the needs of an earlier era. The hours of rising and retiring seemed to have been regulated to make the most of natural light, when oil lamps had to be depended upon after dark. They were also

geared to a social climate when religious could take for granted
that the laity would regard the Sisters' daily schedule as something
which they would naturally take into account when there was
need to visit the convent to confer with a Sister on business of a
special nature. The whole parish knew at what time the Sisters
"could not be disturbed" either by visits or by phone. They knew
one could never call a Sister from a meal where spiritual reading
accompanied the breaking of bread. They knew that convent doors
were "closed for the night" at an early evening hour.

This semi-seclusion in active Orders, which in days past gave
an enhancing aura of mystery to the Sisters "and what they did
behind the convent walls," has become, in these faster-paced days,
an occasion of distinct annoyance, and even an irritating frustration
to seculars. Communities could now see that the revision of the
horarium had to take into account the hundreds of persons employed by the Sisters as their lay colleagues, in schools, hospitals,
and other agencies wherein they work side by side. These lay
people, in hospitals for one example, have—and justly so—their
eight-hour day and forty-hour week. For greater efficiency and
smoother collaboration some compromise must be worked out
between their schedule and the Sisters' sixteen-hour day and a
sabbath that only too often might rightly be termed a "seventh"
day of work. Above all, it was seen that a Sister's apostolate with
the laity should receive due consideration in the over-all horarium.

Superiors saw, too, that a not inconsiderable part of this sixteen-
hour day of the Sister is fragmented by Community exercises:
meals, prayers, recreation with the Community, spiritual reading,
and other claims on her time, just when she is needed most in a
hospital or in her office; an absence sometimes detrimental to the
apostolate, and most inconvenient to the lay persons with whom
she works. This fragmentation of the day was easily seen by the
Superiors, studying their horaria in the light of suggestions made
by hundreds of Sisters, as something in need of drastic change,
calling for close analysis, since it touched upon many other matters
more important than those connected with time schedules and
daily routine, although inextricably interwoven with the order-of-
the-day.

Problems Concerning Horaria

Foremost among these other important matters was the keen cognizance Major Superiors had of their responsibility for furthering the sanctification of each Sister by removing as far as possible those things which militated against it. On this count, revision of the horarium was plainly an immediate duty. From years of experience, personal communications, and maternal observation, Superiors knew well that meager apostolic sanctity can result from any practices that threatened the Sisters' peace of soul. They knew that Sisters, like most adult persons, are constantly faced with decisions as to which claims upon their time have the highest priority. Yet, they recognized the fact that unlike other adult persons, Sisters have an order-of-the-day, an integral part of their religious life, to which obedience, good order and the claims of communal living exact compliance. They realized from personal experience the questions that perplexed each Sister: Should answering the psychological needs of a patient be preferred to answering the bell for examen? Is it a lack of Community spirit that detains a Sister in the parlor, listening to the problems of a harassed housewife, when the other Sisters are at a meal? Should she offer her services as typist to a sorely pressed companion at a time which would require her to forego a half hour's adoration in the Chapel? Should a Sister absent herself from recreation when there is no other time to talk to the troubled parents of a delinquent pupil? Should she disregard the hour set for retiring to make an essential preparation for her next day's classes?

The answer would certainly be in favor of the act of charity or duty were these conflicting demands on a Sister's time unusual. But Superiors saw that they were of daily occurrence, in one way or another, and whatever the decision the Sister made, it would not leave her wholly at peace. Superiors appreciated the fact that such conflicts cannot be entirely eliminated, but they can be greatly lessened where the horaria have been revised and made flexible to conform to the needs of a 20th century religious-apostolic vocation. Many of the Reverend Mothers asked themselves whether a too strict observance of the horarium is emphasized beyond all proportion to its importance in a truly religious life, written, as it was, into a convent rule as it was lived one, two or three centuries ago. These rules derive their spirit, and even sometimes their very wording, from monastic observances and isolationism.

In analyzing the Holy Rule, for one instance, Major Superiors observed that not a few rules direct that such prompt obedience be paid to the bell calling from one exercise to another as to "leave even an alphabetical letter half-formed." Such obedience, they recognized, had meaning and merit in an era when monks and nuns worked in monastery scriptoria, free from all exterior social contacts and responsibilities save such as were consonant with monastic life. The manuscript with its half-formed artistic letter would not suffer from the abrupt exit of the illuminator. Today, when a Sister works with and for people, whose lives she is called upon to "illuminate" with the virtues of Christ exemplified in her own life, it is quite different. She cannot terminate an interview, withhold a service, or leave her typewriter (if it means causing an important letter to miss the mail) "because the bell rang." Yet, if spiritual readings, meditations and retreat masters hold up such rigid and unreasoning exactitude as the ideal, how can a Sister have peace in the apostolate? This was a question the Reverend Mothers pondered, for Rome had advised them to analyze all rules, customs, and even their Constitution, with critical insight directed toward change where change was deemed advisable.

Conflicts between Charity and Good Order

There was no wish on the part of Superiors to downgrade punctuality, which charity and good order require in congregate living, but they wanted to put it in proper perspective. They could see that a Sister leaves her duty, at the time of an exercise, for one of two purposes: To go to the Chapel to join her companions in prayer; or to join them elsewhere in a Community exercise. Needless to say, she should go promptly and happily, anticipating with joy what she is to do. But many Major Superiors have thoughtfully arrived at the conclusion that punctuality has been overemphasized as a virtue. "Sister X. is never late for an exercise" was an expression frequently heard, and considered a compliment. But now Superiors were analyzing its meaning. Is it really a virtue? Can a Sister engaged in the active apostolate never be late for an exercise and at the same time never neglect or ignore an opportunity to bear witness to Christ by some unscheduled service to her fellow man?

The apostolate, as all Major Superiors know so well, is so frequently exercised with such fruitful effects through the extra opportunities that a Sister sees and acts upon: The moody countenance of a student; the appealing look of a patient who has just said he doesn't need anything; the hesitant, apologetic question of a man concerned with his wife's health; the telephone call from a priest to ask if Sister would be interested in a project of his, or, it may well be, the unexpected, angry outburst of a lay colleague—these and a hundred other incidents are the occasions of rendering "plus" service, of "walking the second mile" recommended in the gospel. Superiors now found it difficult to reconcile this with "never being late for an exercise."

They realized that where the Community's attitude towards the "extra mile" is understanding and enlightened, a marked lessening of tension results. As a matter of fact, they well knew that Sisters will always answer these unforeseen calls on their time and never count the cost. In these branch houses where peace of mind is placed above punctuality by the local Superior and where regularity for regularity's sake is not a fetish, Major Superiors on their Visitations have found that the Sisters are not torn between conflicting demands. The result is a more fervent religious, truly dedicated to bearing witness to a Christ made more divinely human and attractive to a secular by one visibly in love with Him and ready to prove it by unstinted service to the neighbor.

To Labor Is to Pray

Pursuing their analysis further, many Superiors have been asking themselves whether there were an implied, if not an actual, dichotomy between profession and practice in the time-honored and readily accepted Benedictine motto: "To labor is to pray." A Sister dedicates her whole life to God with no reservations of time, of place or manner, they reasoned. Does it not then follow that if, at the time of a particular exercise prescribed by rule or custom, a Sister is engaged in an act of mercy—for example, counseling the doubtful or visiting the sick—this very act constitutes a form of prayer, of worship, of bearing witness to Christ, which the Will of God indicates for her at that moment? Should her peace of soul be disturbed with mathematical calculations as to how she can "make up" a spiritual or Community exercise before the bell summons her to another duty? Is it more important that a Sister "be counted" as present than that her work and prayer count for her? Hundreds of Sisters had admitted on questionnaires and in interviews that the greatest stress of their day arose from this source: If they are not present with the Community at a prescribed exercise, they must discharge the obligation privately at another time. In the meanwhile demands on their time continue, and many a Sister ends her day by striving to supply for several accumulated exercises missed through no negligence on her part. The result is acute spiritual indigestion. St. Vincent de Paul, founder of the first active Order, they recalled, had a dictum for it: "When you are called from prayer to serve the poor, my Daughters, you are leaving God for God."[9] This the Reverend Mothers could readily see. But the rule . . . the customs. Well, was it not the rule, the customs, Rome was asking them to study, to analyze, to make relevant to a new day with new demands? What a blessed source of peace obedience could be!

The Reverend Mothers continued their analysis: Since this matter of conflict between work and prayer loomed so large in the lives of Sisters, it would not be belaboring the point to ponder a further question. The Church teaches that through the communion of saints all share in one spiritual treasury. A man working in a downtown New York office can offer his work for a missionary in Africa to their mutual benefit, both being members of the Mystical Body. Does not a member of a Community, which is a special organ of the Mystical Body, actually share in the prayer offered by her companions when she is absent on another apostolic call, even as they, in turn, share in the merits of her good work, although they are not taking active part in it?

[9] *Conferences of St. Vincent de Paul to the Sisters of Charity*, I, p. 284.

For the Sisters, whatever their rank, to accept this view serenely, and truly to make work a genuine prayer, Major Superiors recognized, would require a strong basis of spirituality built upon sound novitiate training. How well they knew that it is a part of the "feminine mystique" to worry unduly about *petits détails,* as Abbé Dimnet[10] was wont to call them. "A man," as one Superior put it, "would never be so meticulous. That is why he enjoys greater peace and freedom in the service of God, paying tribute at once to the Divine Intelligence and to the sweet reasonableness God wants in His service. The Gospels show our Lord so much more appreciative of quality than of quantity. His attitude towards the Pharisees should warn us as to the priority He gave to the spirit rather than to the letter of the law. Why cannot women understand and accept it—and be at peace,"

In the questionnaires and interviews that serve as the basis of this chapter, the question of the need to "make up exercises" was pointed up by an incredible majority of Sisters as the most serious source of tension in their spiritual life and as a major temptation to doubt the hundredfold of happiness and peace promised to those who seek God above all values. Commenting on this subject, a noted theologian remarked: "It goes without saying that this problem will not be of daily occurrence where a Sister is faced with 'making up exercises of the common life' when she is absent through circumstances that require her presence elsewhere. These circumstances should be looked upon as the Will of God and as having equal value in His eyes with the exercises she has missed through no deliberate fault of her own. This is a concrete example of *leaving Christ for Christ*."

It calls for a deep spiritual maturity of judgment to strike a happy balance between feverishly "making up missed exercises" and seeing clearly, without anxiety or worry, God's Will in every circumstance that either gives one more time for uninterrupted prayer in the Chapel, or calls one to more apostolic activity somewhere else. In neither circumstance can be found a contradiction to His injunction, "Pray always."

It was plainly indicated that an appreciation of spiritual exercises

10 Ernest Dimnet, *The Art of Thinking* (New York: Simon and Schuster, 1928), p. 116.

will be increased and the fruits derived from them made more abundant if, in the horarium, such exercises are placed at a time when the Sisters are neither mentally nor physically overfatigued. A teaching Sister, for example, after a laborious day in the classroom, can hardly bring to meditation or to spiritual reading an alert and attentive mind if these exercises—or others—follow too soon upon the dismissal of classes. The switch-over from modern mathematics to the eternal verities, from chemistry formulae to an examination of conscience, requires a short interim for relaxation and the "shifting of gears," as it were. Ten minutes of "free time" might make all the difference.

"Getting exercises in," a term so frequently used by Sisters, should be the goal of neither the Sister nor her Community; rather, thoughtful planning should be given to scheduling prayer when, all factors weighed, Sisters will get the most out of it. Such is the thinking of many Communities who have found that this calls for a shortening, or even the suppression, of some minor practices, with a compensatory arrangement which takes the major exercises into account. Waiving the custom of having some pious activities—the rosary, visits to the Blessed Sacrament, novenas, litanies—in common, or delegating personal responsibility to each Sister for the fulfillment of these obligations when she is free from pressure, but with the understanding that there should be no scruple over their occasional omission for legitimate reasons, should result in greater fervor and a more genuine union with God. "What interests God," writes Canon Guelluy, "is my prayer translated into action."[11]

Practical Changes Necessary

Once the examination of horaria was in full swing, Superiors and Sisters alike were forced to smile rather wryly at what they found. They saw that in other fields, as their works and the range of their activity had expanded and increased in complexity, efficient steps had been taken to meet the changed situation. Buildings, equipment, methods, the professional preparation of Sisters, had all been brought into line with modern times. But until the Holy

11 Robert Guelluy, "The Call to the Supernatural Life," *Sponsa Regis*, XXV (April, 1964), 237.

See urgently recommended this inquiry, the horaria of Communities remained as they had been, in some cases, for centuries.

They faced the fact, somewhat belatedly, that it is highly impractical to impose an identical horarium on all. Identical Community exercises, yes. At the identical time for all, no. Many things need to be considered: the nature of a Sister's duty, her responsibilities, the number of lay colleagues with whom she works, the location of her office or department. In some large institutions one Sister's work may be within fifty feet of the Chapel or Community room, and another Sister's office a block away. These and other carrying factors needed to be taken into account. Some Communities, they noted, where twenty or more Sisters are assigned to a work in a branch house, have experimented with two or even three horaria, with highly satisfactory results. All horaria provide for the participation of all groups in the opening and closing exercises of the day. Order and cohesion can be preserved with gratifying efficiency when clear thinking and careful planning are concentrated on those areas thought of as the untouchables and the unchangeables until Pius XII, John XXIII and, later, Cardinal Suenens called so earnestly for *aggiornamento* in the religious life.

Hours for Meals

In discussing the matter of meals, a large percentage of Superiors agreed that with the exception of breakfast, being on time for meals is one of the great stresses and strains of a Sister's day; a situation contributing little to her spiritual, mental or physical health. Cafeteria service, installed in those houses which lend themselves to it, has solved the problem in many Communities. This allows for a time range which "takes up the slack" of unforeseen calls on a Sister's time and relieves her of anxiety on three scores: (1) that of leaving an apostolic work when her presence is necessary, (2) failing in promptitude, and (3) inconveniencing the Sister who is responsible for serving meals. This time range would also be a great boon to her lay colleagues. Lay people often postpone the presentation of important matters or the discussion of serious problems because "You had to go to dinner, Sister." There is a subtle effect on lay persons—perhaps not so subtle, either—when the Community's schedule, especially meals, takes precedence, save in cases of absolute emergency, of all other social and professional claims.

Taped Readings

In the refectory, some Reverend Mothers felt that there need be no infringement of the silence and recollection still required during meals in many Communities, particularly where taped spiritual readings (another helpful innovation) are used. This releases Sisters from reading aloud for the assembled Community, which usually takes a half hour of the appointed Sister's time. It has the further, incalculable advantage of providing *always* for distinct, intelligible, well-modulated readings, since the best Sister-reader can, at her convenience, make the recordings. These recorded readings can be repeated as needed to fit into the range of time allotted for meals. In addition, tape recordings allow for a wider selection of updated reading material, providing for increased variety. At times the reading can cover current matters taken from periodicals, papers and journals of opinion, on which all Catholics should be informed. Here again, Superiors agreed, is a means of widening the Sisters' apostolate, as they can later discuss these views and opinions with seculars, Catholic and non-Catholic.

Most Sisters, in answering one questionnaire, admitted that they know woefully little of the great changes going on in the Church. According to so great an authority as Father Elio Gambari, of the Sacred Congregation of Religious:

We have seen more changes in the past decade and a half than the Church has seen since the Council of Trent. . . . A revolution is going on in the Church today which, to my mind, compares in magnitude with the Industrial Revolution of the past.[12]

To which he added, most apropos of this topic: "We are made aware of and study what is transpiring in the Mystical Body of Christ, through our spiritual reading."[13] When during meals Sisters

---

[12] Elio Gambari, S.M.M., *Workshop in Instructional Programs in Spirituality*, College of St. Teresa, Winona, Minnesota, August 17–26, 1963.
[13] *Ibid.*

have listened, with calm and reflective minds, to refectory readings which are up-to-date, timely, and rich in content, they come from this experience not only better informed but physically, intellectually and psychologically refreshed and renewed.

It came as something of a surprise to many Mothers General that where refectory readings have been replaced by talk during meals, as a means of much-needed recreation, many members of Communities regret the change. In good-humored fashion Sisters remarked that, seated according to rank, one finds herself forced to talk with the same group of often completely divergent interests—or perhaps no discernible interest at all. The effort to initiate or participate in a listless conversation was far from relaxing, and "the good old days" when reading nourished the mind while the body was being refueled for the afternoon's work seemed to constitute an *aggiornamento* in reverse, devoutly to be wished, especially in this day when so many and such exciting books are available but time to read them is so limited. Many Superiors will smile at these lines, recalling how eagerly it had been recommended to bring about the *aggiornamento* of replacing reading with recreation at meals.

Hour for Retiring

The Industrial Revolution, accepted by historians as a milestone in the progress of Western civilization, and often compared in magnitude with the revolution taking place in the Church today, produced, until the last few years, but minor changes in the horaria of most Communities. As all Superiors will agree, industry might come and revolutions go without affecting one small Community routine. Scarcely more than ten years ago, an eminent prelate of a large diocese issued an order that no Sister was to be seen out of her convent after six o'clock in the evening. Other episcopal authorities repeated the same prohibition. By these orders night attendances at professional meetings were closed to them, as were also parish activities and personal contacts. The point is, not that the order was issued, but that it created no stir or questioning, since ten years ago Sisters would never think of being out after dark, except for evening university classes. The order was given, evidently, to eliminate some exceptional "abuses." An occasional parish activity, in which the Sisters participated in a limited capacity as keepers of order and counters of money, was still allowed. Once order (and money) were safely under control, Sister was expected (like the fabled Arab) to fold her tent and steal away. Now, changes have come about so quickly that night attendance at conventions is commonly accepted, and "live" appearance on educational panels on "late" television is received as part of the apostolate in the market place. These are the happenings of yesterday. What will tomorrow bring? This is a question each Superior asks herself.

Certainly it will bring about in a yet greater measure—for there has been considerable advance in this matter—the participation of Sisters in the affairs of society other than in their traditional roles. Pope Pius XII affirms that:

St. Teresa of Avila is a brilliant proof of the fact that the most active zeal can be closely associated with the quest for the riches of the interior life. That she herself attained to the highest perfection of the interior life is of course well known to all. But what may not be so well known is the fact that, far from spending all her religious life in quiet communing with God behind cloistered walls, the last twenty years of her life were marked by extensive exterior activity, fatiguing and distracting activity, the kind of activity necessarily connected with the personal establishment of thirty-two convents all over Spain, with the extensive travelling, frequent contacts with the world, the involvement in business affairs, which this entailed.[14]

St. Teresa herself, much criticized in later life for her controversial work in reforming old monasteries and establishing new foundations in all parts of Spain, was convinced that "good work in the world" need not necessarily interfere with growth in the interior life. Concerning the foundation of new monasteries, she writes:

. . . believe me, it is not length of time spent in prayer that brings a soul benefit: when we spend our time in good works, it is a great help to us and a better and quicker preparation for the enkindling of our love than many hours of meditation.[15]

14 Quoted by John J. Sullivan, S.J. (ed.), *God and the Interior Life* (Boston, Mass.: Daughters of St. Paul, 1962), p. 103.

15 St. Teresa of Avila, *Complete Works of St. Teresa*, trans. and edited by E. Allison Peers, Vol. I. (New York: Sheed and Ward, 1946), p. 26.

To the above may well be added the words of Pope John XXIII:

May those who are dedicated to the active life realize that not only prayers but works also can bring about a new course of society, which is nourished by the gospels, and in which all things work together towards the glory of God and the salvation of souls.[16]

That Sisters "may bring about a new course of society" depends upon the vision and wisdom of Superiors who plan horaria to which Sisters owe obedience, an obedience that will enrich their spiritual lives, yet not impede—save within reasonable limits dictated by health, strength and natural capacities—the exercise of an active and truly Christlike apostolate.

A Longer Day

In studying the needs of the apostolate, Superiors are certain that Sisters will no longer be cut off from all public evening contacts at eight o'clock or thereabouts. Since the preponderant number of Sisters in the United States are engaged in the teaching field, the necessity of being available to parents after eight o'clock at night exacts particular attention on this point. Major Superiors agree that parents, and other adults interested in pupils or the school, should be given reasonable time and opportunity to meet and consult with the Sisters on problems concerning home and school. These adults have home claims to which they must attend after working hours, so that any appointment prior to eight or eight-thirty will represent, in most cases, an insuperable inconvenience.

Reverend Mothers are well aware that parents, as noted in frequent articles in current educational magazines and school journals, complain rather openly that some parochial school teachers are unwilling to have (or attend) Parents' Clubs or P.T.A. meetings where an exchange of views between teachers and parents would clarify many misunderstandings left (sometimes with resentment) unresolved because of a lack of communication. Granted that a Sister is tired or busy, or both, in the late evening; yet, if she can dis-

16 *Letter to Women Religious*, p. 12.

regard this, what a world of good she can accomplish by being available to "talk things over" with Johnny's mother and dad! After all, how constantly parents have to listen to "Sister says," and more lovingly (and sometimes reproachfully) *My* Sister says. . . !" Small wonder parents desire an appointment, if only to gaze upon this paragon that Johnny quotes so often. Here is love in action; here is bearing witness to Christ, who can work miracles through a Sister willing to give, give, give.

The Evening Apostolate

Mindful of this, and of other activities to be taken up under another heading, a large number of Communities have found a satisfactory answer. Recreation, that period of group relaxation so necessary for the Sisters' well-being, the importance of which was emphasized by St. Louise de Marillac when she said: "Recreation is as necessary as meditation,"[17] is arranged to terminate before eight o'clock. In some Communities it terminates at seven. What individual Sisters will do after that hour will necessarily vary, but the time, Superiors believe, should be their own. There will then be a period for study, class preparation, or availability to lay persons who come on legitimate business—a blessed two- or three-hour period where apostolic services can be rendered for which the reward will be truly great.

In other instances, Superiors agree that time will have to be extended—to attend meetings, to confer with professional people, to make phone calls (many persons cannot be easily reached at an earlier hour), to conduct a study club, or to do some needed professional reading and extra preparation for the next day's class. The hour for retiring will necessarily vary even in the same convent and in different houses of the same Community, according to their specific works; but the horarium should be so constructed as to be always in accord with the health requirement of at least seven hours rest.

Most convents and institutions now try to provide private rooms for Sisters, so that a variation in the hour of retiring will incon-

17 *Instructions: St. Louise de Marillac,* Annals of the Daughters of Charity. Archives, Marillac Seminary, St. Louis, Missouri.

venience no one.[18] Where each Sister has her own meditation book, a reading of it as the last act of the day evokes a spirit of recollection and serves as a preparation for the next morning's period of mental prayer. When it happens, as it will at times, that a Sister's activities keep her up a considerable time beyond the regular hour for retiring, Major Superiors feel that some provision for additional rest and sleep should, when possible, be made the next day. Needless to add, Superiors will keep in close touch with the apostolic works of the Sisters so that neither their spiritual nor their physical health will suffer from an over-crowded schedule. As many generous Sisters remarked, in interviews and letters, regarding the danger of overwork: "Let's stop itemizing our overwork—what are we saving ourselves for anyhow?"[19]

Development of Individuality

One of the most profitable, and possibly unforeseen, results of *aggiornamento,* according to Major Superiors, is the development in Sisters of a keen sense of personal responsibility for their own sanctification. With an horarium set as fixedly as the laws of the Medes and the Persians, with no variation in time schedules of spiritual exercises, save for a dire emergency; with century-old traditions firmly entrenched in granite and stone, it took a hardy soul to develop true spiritual initiative. Few specific details are available, but it may well be that a considerable percentage of the girls who entered convents and went no further than the postulate or novitiate were living under excessive restrictions and baffled by antiquated practices that seemed meaningless to them. These defections may, then, have contributed no small share to the Sister-shortage complained of today.

These young girls could only chafe under what, to them, seemed trivial regulations and hampering rules; some irreverently called certain time-honored customs "silly." They saw stretching before

18 Personal interviews with Major Superiors, 1964.

19 This remark (or similar statements) that Sisters really make too much of "overwork" vs. the attitude taken by lay people whose days are more crowded, appeared in more than 80% of the 762 questionnaires that serve as the basis for this chapter. It points up the good humor with which Sisters view themselves and their numerous activities.

them—as one recently confided—a whole lifetime of endless petty
routines, long-drawn-out, tiring vocal prayers and quaint practices
that had no relevance to the practical and in their eyes seemed less
supernaturally significant than the work of the Peace Corps or Papal
Volunteers, which engaged in a kind of action they could appreciate
and applaud. So, feeling out of place in this milieu, they departed
from the convent disillusioned and deeply disappointed. This observation is meant as no defense of their reasoning, but it might
help in understanding Pope Pius XII's warning against holding on
to outmoded customs that may prove a barrier to even good and
courageous girls.[20]

A Mother General recently remarked: "Only now are we learning how many older Sisters have suffered an almost constant
frustration which they accepted willingly (but not always cheerfully)
as part of the cross they bargained to carry in following our Lord."
Recently a Sister, thirty years in religion, observed: "We used to
answer the Chapel bell at four o'clock each afternoon after school.
We had a full forty-five minutes of vocal prayer, litanies and
novenas, followed by a half hour of meditation. Most of us were
so dead tired after forty-five minutes of vocal prayer that we slept
during meditation, or sat there dazed, unable to drum up a single
reflection or affection. This was changed in 1953 to just a half
hour of mental prayer with all vocal prayer eliminated, and now
it's a joy to answer the bell for Chapel—I come out feeling like
a new person."

But the same Sister added: "If only we'd go the whole way on
aggiornamento! In the morning I drag myself out of bed too tired
to think. I get down to the Chapel where we say Matins and Lauds,
followed by a half hour of mental prayer and twenty minutes of
vocal prayers for the Church, the Community and benefactors, and
then Mass starts. By Communion time I'm lost in frustration because I can feel no fervor—only fatigue. Sometimes I kneel at
the Communion railing wondering if I can possibly please God
feeling as I do. Then we go to breakfast and are served in rank.
Since I'm near the end of my particular table, I'm served near the
last, and I practically choke with smoldering resentment—and
yes, let me be honest—with scruples because I'm in such a bad

<hr />

[20] *Acta et Documenta, loc. cit.*

humor every morning. Yet, I love to pray. What a joy and peace it would be if we just had meditation as a preparation for Mass. I could sing aloud with the best of them or join in hearty dialogue at Mass in all the glory of the new liturgy. And if we didn't waste so much time in the refectory serving by rank, life would be perfect." After a moment, she added: "But it's still a wonderful life, and thank God I can still laugh out loud at myself."

This was said with high good humor and did not sound as "frustrated" as it may in writing. Still, the lesson is there. Even older Sisters feel the waste of time and a certain ill humor at *petits détails* in the refectory and over-long prayers in the Chapel. Many Superiors report today that where rules and customs have been changed so as to have meaning in contemporary society, the Sisters bring to them an eager intellectual obedience quite different from the stolid acceptance previously practiced under the guise of virtue.

These dispositions are carried over into their work, to which they bring a new view. Their willingness to listen to suggestions and to delegate authority in their area is marked by that maturity and serenity one really expects from religious. Since unthinking obedience is not asked of them, they do not ask it of others. In these days, where Sisters everywhere work side by side with the laity, and are often outnumbered by them, this new manner of acting—this new "joy in the morning"—creates an atmosphere of cordiality and friendliness insuring no small bonus to the cause of charity and good human relations.[21]

By Their Fruits Shall You Know . . .

Major Superiors know they have nothing to fear in following the program of adaptation for which the Church is asking. In strongly recommending some changes, the Church has two objectives in mind. The first is that through a reduction of tensions and frustrations resulting from the restricting influences of certain rules, customs and exercises, there should be effected a true renewal in the religious life by increasing the fervent participation

[21] Questionnaires filled out by Major Superiors, used as the basis for several chapters of this book, especially chapters dealing with *aggiornamento*.

of the Sisters in all that pertains to it. Secondly, the Church desires Communities to remove anything from their practices that would seem to be foreign to the temper of modern times; or which might prove an obstacle in attracting new recruits to the religious life, or prevent their perseverance.

Certainly there are some exercises of piety which do not meet contemporary needs; some customs that have lost their meaning. Major Superiors are willing to study these with a view to their change or abolition. In commenting on this need for the abolition of certain practices, one Mother General remarked: "It is prudent to keep in mind that where one or several customs or rules are abolished, it is not necessary to replace them with others. One can often more tastefully adorn the sanctuary by what one takes out altogether than by what one puts in as a replacement. The idea of the Church is to strip to essentials, then multiply fervor and strict observance in these fundamentals. For some, however, there is a fear lest any diminution in quantity might effect a diminishing return in quality."

The analysis of answers to certain pertinent questions implied in the two objectives Rome had in mind in asking for changes would seem to offer satisfactory criteria for judging the value of suggested adaptations: (1) Do they effect a true renewal or increase of fervor in the religious spirit? (2) Do they conform to the spirit of the times? As an example, if reducing the time given to vocal prayers by one-half does not double the fervor of Sisters at prayer, then quite clearly the adaptation has failed of its purpose. If excusing a Sister from "making up" spiritual exercises does not increase her foresight in securing timely appointments or arranging her schedule so that such omissions become fewer, and punctuality is increased, then some other answer to her professed difficulty must be found.

If removing requirements of rank in the refectory and Community room does not increase fraternal charity; if it does not bring about better understanding between younger and older Sisters, maturing the young and making the old more tolerant, then the adaptation has been made to no purpose. Changing the method of holding Chapter should impel Sisters to greater eagerness for this exercise. The desirable end in mind, in trying to make this exercise more meaningful, was the revivifying of the spirit of humility and penance. This would indeed be a boon to the Sisters' spiritual life. If this boon does not result, then the adaptation or the method of adjustment was not the best that could be devised. The problem calls for a reappraisal.

For another example: fragmentation of the day has been a source of anxiety and frustration for many Sisters. If abolishing the multiplicity of exercises in common, which called for the use of much time in going to and from the place of assembly, has not resulted in a closer-knit, better organized day, leading to a more efficient use of time for God's honor and glory, then the well-intentioned adaptation needs to be re-thought.

In a word, after adaptations of the horarium and changes in other practices have been made, a careful scrutiny of the results of these adjustments is in order. If results show that the way has been cleared for a more fervent and meaningful fidelity on the part of the Sisters to the essentials of the religious life (to be spoken of in the next chapter), the adaptations have succeeded, for by their fruits they can best be judged. If adaptations as made now were to be considered final, it would be but a repetition and maybe a perpetuation of the old error of making tradition all but impregnable. Having been given the "go" sign by the Church, Superiors are wisely experimenting.

Some religious habits changed only a few years ago are again undergoing further modification. This is a wise and intelligent use of the Church's principle of adaptation. Doubtless the simplification of the Sisters' prayer life and the horarium will go through a series of modifications. Superiors, with the eager cooperation of their entire Communities, are wisely attuned to the "trial and error" method. There is no reason for any Sister to lose her peace of soul because change and experimentation have been introduced into the Congregation. This is a sign of health and vitality. If some adjustments have not proved helpful, they will be amended. If some have not progressed fast and far enough, they will be accelerated. It is well to remember the motto, "Nothing is final," or St. Teresa's dictum: "All things change; God alone is changeless"—and He alone should be, for He alone is complete.

Adaptations are recommended not to increase laxity but to

promote fervor. For instance, certain changes in Holy Mass have
shortened it, *not for the sake of brevity,* but that the faithful might
concentrate on their more meaningful participation. If the adaptations which have been made—and will continue to be made—have
as their purpose the return to essentials, the essentials of holiness
and fervor, none need be dismayed. A careful use of the proper
measuring rod will insure safety. "By their fruits you shall know
them." (Matt. 7:20)[22]

Where the "fresh winds of change" in the Church are allowed
to blow freely through convent corridors, we have a hardier and
a holier type of religious. It is the type of Sister which can result
only from an intelligent answer to the call of the Holy See for
aggiornamento.

[22] Unless otherwise indicated all biblical references will be from the Douay
edition.

5

Aggiornamento, a Means to Holiness

When the restoration of a great masterpiece of painting is undertaken, the process is a slow one and engaged in only by experts in the field. The first step is to determine the painting's authenticity. This done, the expert begins carefully to remove all overlaid painting and any additions made through the years, by later, grosser hands. The work requires infinite care and unlimited patience. Delicately the overlay is scraped away, bit by bit, with infinite caution in order that nothing of the original be damaged. Slowly the early masterpiece emerges in all of its original, incomparable beauty. It is there—the vision caught by one man (or one woman), at one time, yet belonging to all ages.

Restoration and Renewal

The restoration of the masterpiece to its pristine beauty is analogous to the restoration of the religious life, when accretions, in the form of added rules, customs, and practices, are removed; accretions, which multiplied with each succeeding generation, serve to obscure the original pattern. These accretions had meaning in their day, a meaning lost with the passage of time and the changes inseparable from progress. *Aggiornamento* seeks to remove this overlay of tradition, long since become irrelevant to the modern world; and to bring out in bold relief the original vision of the holy founder of each Community. This is the primary purpose of the Church-directed mandate for change: To rid all Communities of those non-essentials in the way of rules, customs and traditions that impede the Sisters in living the fullness of their vocation as their founders intended.

The essentials of the religious life are unchangeable, standing firm as a rock in the threatening sea of this world. Just as every great painting, regardless of the subject, must have lights and shadows, color and contrast, perspective and proportion, emphasis and focus, all used by a master hand to realize his vision, so all religious life, contemplative or active, has in common essential elements which are indispensable to its purpose.

In the preceding chapter reference was made to rules, customs and practices which might be termed the "overlays" obscuring the meaningful beauty of an original design as created by the founders and foundresses of religious Communities. This chapter will present those *constants* of the religious life which, one may say, were used by Christ Himself to portray a life of total dedication to Him. These constants are: a continuous striving for evangelical perfection and the profession of the vows of poverty, chastity, and obedience.

Prayer, mortification, self-denial, recollection and silence are also constants, as well as fraternal charity, zeal for the Community's apostolate and spirit, and (except in the case of secular institutes) Community living. That these essentials are adhered to today by nearly one million religious women throughout the world is a tribute to the drawing power of Christ. Even as they responded in His lifetime, so also they respond today, accepting the invitation to "Sell what thou hast and follow Me," not hesitating at the further condition, "Take up your cross."

The Spirit of Poverty

Though the essentials of the religious life are unchangeable in their substance, they are changeable in the accidentals from country to country. The application of them will certainly vary through the centuries, according to social and economic conditions. Poverty, for one example, will always be much more than a matter of permissions and possessions. Its underlying virtue is detachment, a virtue which frees a Sister from the complacency of possession and the torment of desiring. The poverty voluntarily practiced by a Sister in the 20th century will differ externally from that practiced by a Sister in the 17th century. The life of a missionary Sister in Africa will abound in privations which a nursing Sister in a United States hospital will never know. But both can say, with St. Paul, that they "have nothing" although they "possess all things" (2 Cor. 6:10), because nothing of the abundance the United States Sister administers is, in any way, her own.

The poverty practiced by mendicant friars in earlier ages—and to a certain extent in some European countries today—would bring the Church in the United States into disrepute. Thus a particular form of poverty, holy and helpful in some countries, would be repugnant and harmful in others. While it is the motive that gives supernatural value to the act, the taste, mores and customs of a country cannot be disregarded. It is recorded that a 17th century foundress, when seeking a house for her Community, said: "We must secure one that is not only humble and poor but which is obviously so. Otherwise, no one will contribute to our good works and the poor will suffer."[1] Today we know that the same motive that prompted that foundress to secure a "poor and humble house" in 1640 requires that her Community's institutions today in 1965 appear modern, substantial and efficiently operated if they are to attract benefactors.

As proof that prosperity and comfortable living do not necessarily lessen the spirit of detachment, we have but to look to the Sisters of numerous Communities now behind the Iron Curtain. Deprived by hostile governments of their houses, lands and all earthly possessions, of the right to wear a religious habit or to live in common, they are unperturbed and continue with cheerful hearts to aid and encourage others. It cannot be doubted that should the religious in our own country be subjected to a like ordeal—and who is to say, "It can't happen here"?—they would feel no personal loss, but in a spirit of detachment, like the first Christians, "would rejoice in being stripped of all they possessed," and carry on with crude instruments and improvised resources.

[1] Letter of St. Louise de Marillac in unpublished Annals of the Daughters of Charity of St. Vincent de Paul.

Chastity as a Way of Life

In electing to live a life of chastity, a Sister does so through complete love for a person—the person of Jesus Christ, God-Man. This does not render her indifferent to her fellow men, for it prompts her to love them as Christ loves them. No longer is it necessary, as it was in former centuries, to "protect" a consecrated virgin by walls and doors, gates and grilles, or to shut her off from all communication with the secular world. Pope Pius XII distinctly says:

We think it necessary, moreover, to warn that it is altogether false to assert that those who are vowed to perfect chastity are practically outside the community of men. Are not consecrated virgins, who dedicate their lives to the service of the poor and the sick . . . united intimately with their miseries and sorrows, and affectionately drawn to them, as though they were their mothers? . . . Indeed it is from that perfect chastity which they cultivate that priests and religious men and women find the motive for giving themselves to all, and love all men with the love of Christ.[2]

Chastity is no longer necessarily associated with withdrawal and seclusion from the world. Rather, strengthened by the love of God and the neighbor, it goes out to comfort and combat a world of unrelieved sufferings, of unrighted wrongs, of unheeded needs. The symbol is no longer that once used so frequently by spiritual writers and speakers: a lily blighted by the slightest touch, a mirror clouded by the lightest breath. Now it is a bright and shining sword with which a Sister, inflamed by the love of God, goes out to do battle for souls. Chastity is a many-splendored thing; it is active, not passive; it is warfare, not peace. This stronghold of strength and courage is expressed by Christ in the words of Matthew: "He that can take, let him take it." (Matt. 19:12) Chastity is, then, a gift for which full returns must be made to the Giver. These returns a Sister makes by engendering souls to Christ by the witness she bears to Him in whatsoever circumstances her apostolate places her.

2 Encyclical on *Holy Virginity* (Washington, D.C.: National Catholic Welfare Conference, March 25, 1954), p. 14.

The Concept of Obedience

Obedience will always be the *sine qua non* of the religious life. But just as chastity no longer needs moats and drawbridges, so to speak, to guard it, Major Superiors and Sisters have found that in the modern, complex apostolate of our day, obedience may be practiced differently, though the principle never varies. The principle of obedience is based upon the conviction that the will of God is made known to a religious through her lawful Superiors. This conviction gives to a Sister a true and lasting peace of soul. Far from checking her initiative or stultifying her personality—as a more narrow interpretation of obedience in other days often did —it contributes to the development of both. Since a Sister has been taught that the Community has a full claim on her intelligence as well as on her other qualities, she does not hesitate to use them.

Mindful of the parable of the talents, she is not spiritually misled into misusing those that have been given to her, be they one or ten. She knows that the Master will demand an account of all. It would be an unwarranted demand on Superiors, an unreasonable assumption, to expect that all initiative must come from them. The final approval and permission, yes. The original suggestions, propositions and proposals, no. In contemporary society the duties of almost any Sister are so specialized that no Superior can be familiar with all their varying details. The personnel with whom a Sister works, the interactions between departments and the repercussions of one department on another, and the outside contacts necessary to the work—all these lay upon the Sister an obligation not only to keep her Superior informed, but to suggest solutions for problems that arise.

A Sister free with the freedom that only obedience can give will readily offer suggestions and solutions, whether these lie in the realm of better physical facilities, additional personnel, or more frequent contact with outside agencies. The Sister will receive the Superior's decision, whether negative or affirmative, abiding by it with equal peace. For some, the older, more passive—not to say lethargic—attitude of an earlier era, when obedience was thought to consist solely in "I'm doing what I was told to do," will be difficult to renounce. But its passing, or at least its lessening, is not regretted by Superiors. Many have noted that where the asking of petty permissions has been eliminated, Sisters take a more mature responsibility for the administration of their assigned duties.

It will certainly require time for this larger idea of obedience, which substitutes responsibility for dependence, initiative for acceptance, and consultation for authoritarianism, to take hold of and vitalize the practice of this virtue in all religious women whatever their position. But it is only a correct and solidly intelligent interpretation of obedience as a virtue basic to each Sister's religious life and to the good functioning of every Community that can render effective the exercise of the apostolate today. It is so easy to confuse freedom with license, and generous permissiveness in government with a "mandate for change" without consultation or regard to the needs of other departments, so necessary to teamwork and smooth human relations. On the other hand, long habits of authoritarianism, bred into the bone and marrow by background and example, can render a Superior blind to the need to listen and learn, especially from younger co-workers.

The concern of Vatican II for the concept of subsidiarity at all levels of authority, from the Pope down through bishops, priests, religious and lay workers, should prove an excellent guideline in the effective use of authority and leadership today. The prudent balance between the exercise of authority and the practice of obedience is a decided part of the *aggiornamento* aimed at a restoration and renewal of the essence of the virtue of obedience and its relation to the religious life.

Liturgical Prayer Life

Fervor in the religious life is dependent upon prayer. The intrinsic meaning of the religious life lies in the relationship between God and the soul. It is grace which enhances the merit of all human activities. As noted in the previous chapter, many Communities had found a need for considerable pruning and suppression of vocal prayers and prescribed devotions that had been allowed to accumulate through the years. Where vocal prayers were reduced to a minimum, Superiors noted a growing and gratifying appreciation of mental prayers, thus giving meditation its essential priority in a Sister's prayer life. Introduction—in some Orders—of the Divine Office replaced the Little Office of the Blessed Virgin, so that at the Congress of Mothers General in Rome, 1952, Father Larraona could say commendingly:

Through the constantly growing liturgical movement, there is an increasing tendency among religious Communities to introduce the recitation of the Divine Office in the vernacular, instead of the Little Office of the Blessed Virgin. Needless to say, the Sacred Congregation is favorable in principle to all proposals which will insure deeper and richer participation of religious in the sacred liturgy since such participation brings them into more living contact with the Church.[3]

Here it was seen that to derive the maximum benefits from this living contact with the Church, a contact culminating in the Holy Sacrifice of the Mass, the hour of rising must be taken into account. This, by the majority of Communities, was set at a later hour, so that the Sisters came to the Chapel physically refreshed and mentally alert for the most important actions of their day: mental prayer or recitation of a part of the Office, as a prelude to assistance at the Eucharistic Sacrifice. This was in keeping with the admonition of Pius XII in *Mediator Dei:*

It is therefore desirable, Venerable Brethren, that all the faithful should be aware that to participate in the Eucharistic Sacrifice is their chief duty and supreme dignity, and that not in an inert and negligent fashion, giving way to distractions and day-dreaming, but with such earnestness and concentration that they be united as closely as possible with the High Priest, according to the Apostle: "Let this mind be in you which was also in Christ Jesus." And together with Him, and through Him let them make their oblation, and in union with Him let them offer up themselves.[4]

The limitations of nature, rather than lack of devotion, was in some instances responsible for the Sisters' assistance at the Holy

---

[3] *Acta et Documenta*, p. 274.
[4] *Mediator Dei, Encyclical Letter of Pope Pius XII on the Sacred Liturgy*, November 20, 1947 (Washington, D.C.: National Catholic Welfare Conference), pp. 31–32.

Sacrifice in a somewhat mechanical manner. Where the Rules of a Community called for a lengthy meditation—frequently having no connection with the liturgical season—read aloud by one Sister while the others listened; and when this was followed by the recitation of the Office or fifteen to twenty minutes of vocal prayer, it is not unreasonable to assume that a Sister's strength would be somewhat drained. In such cases, she could with difficulty focus her mental and spiritual attention on the Eucharistic Sacrifice, the sum and center of her day.

New Approach to Prayer

In Communities quick to grasp the inner meaning as well as to adopt the outer motions of the liturgy, the situation is now helpfully different. A new approach to meditation has been taken which allows for individual differences in this daily personal encounter with Christ through the use of the mind. In many Congregations each Sister is given a meditation book which follows the liturgical cycle, or she may select one of her choice. Vocal prayers have been considerably shortened and the accretions of litanies, novenas and extra petitions, added to satisfy the devotional tastes of former generations, dropped. This was done, not with the intention of minimizing prayers, but of intensifying prayer. One may or may not agree with Cardinal Suenens that the recitation of the Divine Office is not suited to Sisters dedicated to the active apostolate, but no one will question his statement that "The Holy Sacrifice of the Mass and the Communion which is its consummation, is the summit of the spiritual life of all religious."[5]

Primacy of the Mass

The Eucharistic Sacrifice is the great bond. It is not only a renewal of Christ's covenant with His Church but a renewal of each Sister's specific commitment to Christ in her Community. As Father Godfrey Diekmann writes:

[5] *The Nun in the World*, p. 118.

The Community Mass must mean the rededication of the Community to its specific role in the Church. It must mean the renewal of its will to serve in the manner that is specific to it. Each religious Community has its own spirit, determined by its founder, encouraged and perhaps adapted by the Church in approved constitutions. By participating in the Community Mass, the religious family publicly renews its dedication to the spirit of the Rule and to the will of the Holy See.[6]

Any changes, whether in horarium, prayer or other practices, which accent that primacy of the Mass in the spiritual lives of the Sisters, are not only commendable but essential. Those Communities that have focused on these have seen, according to their Reverend Mothers, a great increase in personal sanctity and fraternal charity. "This is the new Covenant in My Blood," said Christ to His apostles. The covenant was made with all those present, not with each individually. Where Sisters, when assisting at Mass, do so with a sense of shared, public, corporate worship, a sense of unity and a spirit of love impregnate their day. To see and to serve Christ in her fellow man, a Sister knows that she must first pray with Christ, and nowhere can this be done so perfectly as at the Eucharistic Sacrifice, the very heart of the sacramental system.

Holy Communion

The *aggiornamento* of the liturgy now stresses the central act of the Mass—Holy Communion—as the gathering of friends around the Eucharistic Table, thus changing the accent on sacrifice to an emphasis on familial, fraternal love. Nowhere is friendship more at home, "at-oneness," than in the breaking of bread. Even as, corporally, we have one main meal during the day, so it would seem to be more conducive to a steady growth towards perfection to concentrate on one main spiritual "meal"— the agape at the breakfast table—at the beginning of each day. These early morning hours offer the best opportunity for un-

6 Godfrey Diekmann, O.S.B., "Liturgy in the Life and Apostolate of the Religious," *Religious Life in the Church Today*, ed. Mother Mary Florence, S.L. (Notre Dame, Ind.: University of Notre Dame Press, 1962), p. 140.

disturbed communion with God, for, barring the unusual, Sisters are free from interruptions from the hour of rising until the close of thanksgiving after Mass.

With the tremendous increase in scriptural study among Sisters, with the liturgical movement constantly gaining both momentum and depth, with the conviction on the part of Superiors that Sisters should be versed in theology and Canon Law, we can with reason look forward to Sisters who have, by taking thought, added inches to their spiritual stature. This growth will result when every Sister interprets the bell for rising as a meaningful and joyous invitation: "Arise, and eat, for you have a long way to go" (3 Kings 19:7, Conf.)[7] and the reception of Holy Communion as her Community's corporate act of love of Christ and love of one another.

Silence Essential to Prayer

Closely associated with the practice of prayer as indispensable to the religious life is the need for silence as an essential means towards union with God. Silence, with its accompanying spirit of recollection, is a major factor in building a religious character; hence there is no Community which does not have both a rule and a long tradition specifying the observance of silence at certain times and places. Just as great paintings require shadow as well as lights, and space intervening between figures the more to emphasize them, so Sisters, whose lives are devoted to active works of mercy, must needs have the shadows of silence and the spaces of recollection to give those lives true balance. These are among the indispensables of the religious life.

Were there not a special merit in the observance of silence, all founders and foundresses would not have made it obligatory. How can Sisters mirror Christ to the world if they do not imitate Him in His silence as well as in His speech? in His withdrawal into solitude as well as in His mingling with the crowds? True, charity will always have priority, for charity is the universal commandment. Both are essential to the apostolate; hence the two can be easily reconciled. The uneasiness expressed by some Mothers General that the night activities now urged upon Sisters

[7] *The Holy Bible*, Confraternity Edition. Copyright 1962, The Confraternity of Christian Doctrine.

—in which a good number are already participating—might result in the abolition of the Great Silence, held sacred for so many centuries, has no foundation in the Church's views.

Not every Sister will engage every night in the particular apostolate that calls for outside activities. The two or three Sisters engaged in night Confraternity of Christian Doctrine work with adults, or other late evening apostolic work, such as Catholic Inquiry Sessions or Convert Groups mentioned by Cardinal Suenens, will all return to their convents quietly recollected, ready to immerse themselves in the Great Silence as a kind of well-earned reward for their labors; grateful even, to be far from the madding crowd, as they make a brief visit to the Blessed Sacrament before retiring for the night. Seldom does a need arise to speak for any length of time until after breakfast the next morning. Sisters who are heard, here and there, to favor the elimination of times and places of silence may have somehow failed to penetrate its importance in the formation of a strong religious character, and its daily contribution to the cultivation of self-discipline.

Silence is not a mere refraining from talking, it is an active listening to God. It is a means, a necessary means, to union with God, without which a Sister cannot reflect Him to the world. Just as every great artist or author needed regular times of silence and sometimes seclusion to complete his masterpiece, so also does a Sister need these periods of solitude to bring into bold relief the Christ-image in herself. As absolute silence is the highest tribute a throng can offer in the presence of a great person, so a Sister pays this tribute to the Great Personage in Whose presence she lives. "Be still," she says to her heart, "and listen to thy God." Silence is less a virtue in itself than it is the seed-bed for all virtues. How can the silence which humility, patience, charity, mortification, and a host of other virtues call for, be practiced as occasions require if a Sister has not previously disciplined herself to listening to Christ, virtue incarnate?

Intellectually, every Sister knows the absolute necessity of silence for deep, reflective study. It is through her intellect that she seeks to know Christ, and the search can best be made when all voices save one are stilled. Spiritually, it aids her to establish intimate friendship with Christ. As someone has said, "The highest form of friendship is that in which two persons can sit in silence and communicate perfectly." Socially, in her inter-Community relationships, the observance of silence at proper times and places is often the highest form of courtesy and consideration. If a Sister's companions are talking with God, or listening to Him, interruptions are unwelcome, unless the claim of charity dictates otherwise. Silence is most truly a social virtue when it is accompanied by a look of deep serenity on the face, and an atmosphere of tranquility.

Silence has its therapeutic value, too. In our tension-packed, nerve-jangling, anxiety-ridden lives nothing can afford a Sister such relief as a period when no social demand, not even the simple one of a passing word, is made upon her. Silence is not a manifestation of selfishness. It is time given for the building up of a Sister's spiritual stamina, as necessary to her apostolate as is the building up of her physical strength, for which we take, without compunction, time to eat three meals a day and at least seven hours for sleep.

Recreation

Every good life must be a balanced life. Therefore, it is not surprising that recreation should be mentioned among the essential means of acquiring religious perfection in the active life. It is the one Community exercise—outside of meals—where mere "presence" is insufficient for external compliance with the rule. In a condensed volume of the *Proceedings of the International Congresses of Religious at Rome,* in 1950, under the title: *For a Better Religious Life,* Father Vitus Gaiani, O.F.M. reports:

Recreation should truly attain its end, which is the real restoration of soul and body. Certain types of recreation, as for example, sitting around the Superior in conversation, are ordinarily not recommended. In certain cases it could be useful and agreeable to do some light manual work, to take a walk, or to play some games.

One should beware of vacations and furloughs lest in giving recreation to the body harm be done to the soul. Vacations should not be spent with the family or in houses of the laity, because the constant and prolonged contact with worldly persons—it makes little difference that they are relatives, friends or acquaintances—puts the soul in the frequent occasion of failing in its duty and of assimilating, little by little, the spirit of the world.[8]

In larger houses the Sisters may profitably separate into groups, each occupying itself with the relaxing interest the group finds attractive. In smaller houses, it would seem helpful if recreation should take such forms as would relieve the Superior from the responsibility of being the center of conversation. She, too, needs relaxation and a period of freedom from leadership. Where Superiors have taken the initiative in this matter, the purpose of recreation has been more pleasantly fulfilled.

Individual Differences in Sisters

While the religious vocation can, under favorable circumstances, develop and improve a Sister's natural endowments, it cannot basically alter them. To say that all Sisters should be apostolically-minded is one thing; to say that all are fitted for the same apostolate is unrealistic. Some Sisters are best fitted for, and make their greatest contribution to society by, working with children. These Sisters, it would seem, would best serve the Church by expanding their apostolate beyond the school or the institution in work devoted to children, since this is the apostolate God has gifted them for and where, it seems, they will make their greatest contribution. This will involve, according to circumstances, week-ending in camps, all-day trips to museums or other places of cultural interests, affording inner-city children opportunities they would never experience but for Sister's loving care.

Service to the less advantaged child has a thousand outlets for a Sister with a creative mind. She enables the children, as well as herself, to grasp and come early to appreciate the social doctrine of the Church in action. Many a nun gifted in this field would be a failure with adults. It can be frankly stated that if, from the first appearance of Cardinal Suenens' *The Nun in the World,* so much emphasis had not been laid by the readers on working with adults at night, a more speedy progress would have been

[8] *For a Better Religious Life,* trans. Patrick Shaughnessy, O.S.B. (Staten Island, New York: St. Paul Publications, 1962), p. 164.

made towards attaining many of the admirable goals His Eminence advocates so strongly. But with the misinterpretation of the book by so many Sisters, both Superiors and subjects, it seemed to mean that conservative religious life as they had known, lived and loved it, would, within a short time, be gone with the wind.

That no large-scale upsurge of night activities in the adult apostolate will disrupt the religious life a practical and typical example will show: In a convent of, say, twelve Sisters, scarcely half—perhaps four or five—would have the health, outgoing temperament, talents and abilities, to carry on an additional active apostolate fruitfully several nights a week. This is no reflection whatever on the other seven or eight Sisters, who are equally zealous, and are the intellectual, professional and spiritual peers of their more outgoing companions; and, it should be added, they are equally ready to adapt to the times. That their adaptation be truly fruitful, it should take into account the health as well as the gifts they have.

This is what St. Paul speaks of when, expounding the diversity of gifts in the members of the Mystical Body, he asks "Are all apostles? Are all prophets? Are all teachers? Are all workers of miracles? Do all have the gift of healing? Do all speak with tongues? Do all interpret?" (I Cor. 12:29, 30, Conf.) The conclusion is clearly that the Church is best served by each member using her gifts within a proper sphere of activity.

No Change in Fundamentals

So, even if the inspiring recommendations, not to say urgings, of Cardinal Suenens are carried out by all, the religious life will not be changed in its fundamentals. It is of the Church, and shares with the Church Christ's promise: "I am with you all days." (Matt. 28:20) In this connection it is most interesting—and enlightening—to read the sentiments expressed in a letter of Mother Janet Stuart, written in July, 1914. It might well have been written today or yesterday—or a tomorrow of the 21st century:

Of all virtues that religious can least afford to lose hold of in our times, that of hope seems the most needed. Dismal things are often said as to the future of religious life in the modern world. Some think that the existing Orders cannot keep their footing, that they will have to pass away and give place to other forms of good, "better adapted to the ideas of today." Those who know religious Orders from within cannot accept these dark prophecies. In many ways indeed it would seem that the world never had such need of religious as in our own times. The world is weary of vain endeavors to deal with its own hunger and emptiness of soul. It resents the assurance that religious have in the way of renunciation, the very thing which it vainly seeks in pursuing its own aims. Yet it is irresistibly attracted towards these centres of an "other-worldly" life. Fiction shows it, though it shows also how little the religious life is known. Poetry shows it, with a wistfulness that seems to long to understand more. Even bitter attacks show it, baffled as they are and striving again and again to blacken that which bears witness against them. Political violence or legal persecution affirms it more clearly than anything else. If religious are out of tune with their times, why not let them die out quickly as every worn-out institution dies?

But we know that there is a heavenly vigour in these germs and in these old, deeply-rooted stocks. We cannot fail to know that we have a message to give, and still more a power to exercise by prayer and sacrifice, which is a force that the Church counts upon beyond all earthly help. We know that saints are wanted to leaven the world, that there are saints already leavening it, but that, if religious are true to their vocation and spirit, they are in the very school where saints are made. And if we know nothing of the future it is for that very reason, that we may the more trust God not to let His work be in vain; and, if He allows some doors to be closed, it is to open others. For we believe that He makes no little account of all faithful devotion, and we cannot doubt that He has a use for every life which has dedicated its powers to His glory and service. Things do not clear up in this world; they are not definite, finished, explained and accounted for. So long as we seek such definite assurance and clear explanation we have not truly learned the religious life. It is tested by the uncertain and the inexplicable, its greatest certainties come of taking for granted things which cannot be verified in this life. It may be counted folly; it is an affirmation which can only be justified when the things of this world have passed away, but this affirmation is one of the most perfect and permanent professions of the Catholic faith.[9]

9 Janet Erskine Stuart, *The Society of the Sacred Heart;* Sixth Impression (San Diego College for Women, Alcala Park, San Diego, California), pp. 89–90.

These words, written more than a half-century ago by a very perceptive spiritual woman, words teeming with faith and common sense, and with a tinge of ironic wit, bring a strengthening reassurance to Sisters today.

Adaptation, a Commonplace in Religious Life

Adaptation is no new thing in the religious life. As a matter of fact, both as individuals and Communities, Sisters as a whole are remarkably adaptable persons. As individuals, they are called to adapt from one house to another, from one group of companions to another, from one type of Superior to another, and from one duty to another—within the range of their competency. An assignment may take a Sister from the Atlantic to the Pacific Coast, or from a crowded urban center to work in an isolated, rural environment. As for Communities as entities, their history in the United States is an outstanding example of adaptation to circumstances, conditions and persons. They operate under all forms of government, oppressive, neutral or supportive. This "built-in" flexibility derives its resiliency from their adherence to the essentials of religious living, among which is the sharing of a common life.

No Community, whatever be its age and austerity, is exempt from adaptations. Pius XII, speaking to a Congregation of Cistercians, said:

Religious Orders, even those noted for their antiquity, have carefully applied themselves to remove things, to accommodate other things by adaptation, and finally to change them altogether. And this is entirely in their praise because of the necessity to adapt the constitutions and rules, conceding that the first conditions of their foundations have been changed.[10]

Community Living

Life lived in common is an integral part of a religious vocation. In the Apostolic Age it was identified with Christianity itself: "And all who believed were together, holding all things in common."

[10] *Acta et Documenta Congressus Generalis de statibus perfectionis* (Rome: Edizioni Paoline, 1950), Vol. I, p. 16.

(Acts 2:44, Conf.) "Now the multitude of the believers were of one heart and one soul, and not one of them said that anything he possessed was his own, but they had all things in common." (Acts 4:32, Conf.) Closely integrated with the Vows of religion—which are the expansion and perfection of the Baptismal Vows—communal living has charity in its fullness as its goal. Community living is not mere group living, team action, dynamic "togetherness" or any other techniques used by secular groups to accomplish a given purpose. It is the voluntary association of persons who seek, by interpersonal relationships, within a given framework of order, and the fulfillment of an apostolate, not only their own advancement in charity and holiness but the advancement of the entire group.

Some *aggiornamento* in these areas, suggested in the previous chapter, would truly lead to making the common life *more* "common," or united: Some Communities that have experimented with changes have reported stimulating results. Among the changes was the disregard of rank or seniority in places in the community room and refectory. In place of long tables in the two latter areas, smaller tables seating from four to six have been substituted, and the Sisters are free to choose any place. This has the good effect of bringing older and younger members of the Community into informal contacts, leading to a better understanding and mutual admiration. It also enables the Superiors to mingle more with different members of the Community. Every Sister knows that often more can be learned about a Sister in a relaxed situation than in a formal visit to the Superior's office, or through the visit of a Superior to the Sister's duty. Since rank in Communities is now disregarded in approaching the railing to receive Holy Communion, it would appear to be in order to hold less rigidly to it in other areas of the family or common life.

Family Life the True Concept

Perhaps if "family life" rather than "communal life" were used to designate Community living, a better picture of it would be conveyed. True, a religious Community is not a natural unit as is the family, but neither is it an unnatural one, as so often depicted by authors, movie scenarios and cartoonists of "Little Nuns." Furthermore, it does not depend, except in the fundamental sense, on the supernatural for its joys and satisfactions. Primarily, the call to a religious life is supernatural, but the *living* of that life has its social, psychological, spiritual and other factors. The same awareness of mutual interests that draws banker to banker, musician to musician and mechanic to mechanic, draws Sister to Sister. Communal living brings first a meeting of minds on earthly values, and from this meeting springs a sharing of ideals, a communication of experiences, and the extending of mutual help and friendship.

Community life is not stilted, artificial or sterile. Sisters, even as other women, have advanced in literary, cultural and political outlook. In their interpersonal relationships they find stimulation, companionship and genuine enjoyment. True, this manner of life calls for discipline and self-sacrifice. But these austere virtues are necessary to the attainment of fraternal charity, the virtue given by Christ as the distinctive badge of His discipleship: "By this shall all men know that you are My disciples, if you have love one for another." (John 13:35) In these words Christ rated fraternal charity as even higher than charity for the poor, the suffering, the afflicted. Indeed, it is on the basis of fraternal charity that Communities carry on spiritual and corporal works of mercy, since without this love for one another Communities would cease to exist.

It is readily accepted that a man or woman should not be occupied with civic, social or business affairs to the extent of making family life impossible. In the same sense it would not be laudable for Sisters to become so engrossed with apostolic works as to leave no set time for prayer, rest and relaxation with their companions. A convent or a religious institution can never be the counterpart of a Woman's Hotel, providing food and lodging while each inmate pursues her individual program of activities. As Betty Prevender, former editor of *Today,* puts it: "We can never have an all-purpose nun living in her convent like a laywoman."[11]

11 Cf. Editorial in *Today,* XIX (March, 1964), 2.

Essentials Must Be Retained

It is with the retaining of these essentials of the religious life that the Reverend Mothers, those who have the heavy responsibility of guiding Communities during this epochal period, are most concerned. The Vows and the obligations flowing from them, a liturgical and scriptural prayer life, the observance of stated times for silence and recollection, Community living and fraternal charity—these are of the essence of the religious life. Changes and adaptations refer to accidentals. Many Major Superiors expressed the conviction that such adaptations as had been already effected were only the forerunners of greater ones to come. Precisely because their vision is clear in this matter, because they know that the call of the Church to Sisters for an expanded apostolate will bring them more and more into contact with seculars, with perhaps fewer human safeguards, Superiors realize that a special preparation is needed for young religious—a preparation deeper, broader, sounder than sufficed for their predecessors in the more simple life of even two decades ago.

Here, too, the Reverend Mothers had the expressed wishes of the Church in mind. They recalled that in the 1952 Congress of Major Superiors in Rome, a third state of formation, the Juniorate, had been strongly recommended in terms that were to all purposes mandatory. The Juniorate then may well be counted as a new essential to the religious life.

Planning a program, in accord with the wishes of the Church, required clear thinking and thoughtful prayer. That a number of Reverend Mothers were able to concentrate on the establishment of a Juniorate sooner than they had expected was due to a providential agency brought into existence in 1954—the Sister Formation Conference.

6

The Sister Formation Movement

The Sister Formation Movement, today nationally known and acclaimed, is co-sponsored by two associations of paramount importance to the Church: The Conference of Major Superiors of the United States and the National Catholic Educational Association (NCEA). It began under the aegis of the latter in 1954, two years before the Conference of Major Superiors of the United States was officially established as a permanent organization. The responsibility of Sister Formation to both of these agencies guarantees a mutual exchange of strengths, and assures maximum service from Sister Formation to the Church, to religious Congregations, and to society. For religious Communities of women, and all the works to which they devote themselves, it is now seen as an indispensable aid to further development, growth and inspiration.

Like all great historic movements destined never to be reversed, Sister Formation came into existence in response to a felt need shared by the majority of Teaching Communities in the United States. This accounts for the fact that during the comparatively short time of its existence it has attained to national stature, penetrating into nearly all parts of the United States and touching, directly or indirectly, all religious Communities of women, and thereby affecting, in one way or another, each individual member of those Communities. It has reached beyond national borders to function internationally. Its philosophy and its principles, its aims and ideals, its structure and its services need to be understood for what they are: a tremendous tool for the fashioning of Sisters for the service of God and of today's society.

Sister Formation Defined

What, then, is Sister Formation? It is a term used to express the absolute need for *integrating* the spiritual, social, intellectual and professional-apostolic preparation of a Sister for her fields of service in the Church. Its aim is to develop the Sister as a *whole* person, thus eliminating the dichotomy of the interior and the exterior life, of work and prayer, which gives rise to so many anxieties in a Sister's mind, and inhibits her full development as a woman, a Sister, and a professional person. Sister Formation has been given a detailed definition by one most closely associated with it and largely responsible for its rapid growth, Sister Mary Emil, I.H.M., President of Marygrove College, Detroit, Michigan, who says: "This [Sister Formation] rather unfamiliar expression was chosen to stand not only for the education of Sisters in a formal and informal sense, but for all of the influences, pre-service and in-service, which go to make a better religious and a better professional person."[1]

Organizationwise, the Sister Formation Conference—its full, official title—is a section of the College and University Department of NCEA, and a Commission of the Conference of Major Superiors of the United States. The former gives it professional status, and the latter insures the immediate interest and participation of those who have the desire, wisdom and power to effect changes indicated in order to keep Communities *au courant* with contemporary problems and to shape the services of the Sisters to meet ever-changing needs in school and society.

The invisible roots of the Sister Formation Movement reach back to the 1941 Study, *The Education of Sisters,* described in Chapter 2. Its tentative and first flowering as a formal association dates from the NCEA meeting in Kansas City, April 1952, where the preparation of Sisters for the teaching apostolate, with emphasis on the pronouncements of Pius XII on that subject, was the topic of a panel presentation. The discussion that followed brought out that, despite the overwhelming need for both spiritual and professional pre-service formation of Sisters, so widely discussed since 1940, little progress had been made. The inadequacies

---

[1] Sister M. Emil, I.H.M., "Progress Report on Sister Formation," *Sister Formation Bulletin*, Supplement (Summer, 1956), 1.

of pre-service preparation, so frankly admitted and deeply deplored at the Congresses of Major Superiors in 1950 and 1952, prompted a resolution to make a new survey of current practices and policies in this matter. All realized, however, that more than a gathering of statistics covering the desirable kind and quality of pre-service professional preparation was required. Consequently, the scope of the survey was broadened to discover what obstacles—such as lack of finances, unavailability of educational opportunities because of location, a want of understanding concerning the urgency of the situation, and other tangible and intangible barriers—stood in the way of adequate preparation of teaching Sisters.

The 1952 Survey of Practices and Policies

It was agreed that Sisters making the 1952 survey should also attempt to assess attitudes. Recommendations would scarcely be even minimally effective unless there was a conviction among the majority of Major Superiors that higher education was not something added to a Sister's life as opportunity permitted, but rather something essential to the fulfillment of a religious vocation which both justice and charity obligated them to provide.

A small group of Sisters, highly qualified for the work, volunteered for the task. It was not only of great magnitude but also difficult and delicate. Its success depended upon how well Major Superiors grasped the urgency of the need of pre-service preparation for teaching Sisters, how well they understood that the cause of Catholic education called for it, and their willingness to give information which, because of its character, was highly confidential. As results show, whatever fears the Sisters making the survey had on these points were fully allayed by the eager cooperation they received. They reported that on the part of Major Superiors there was no lack of vision or understanding of the need for giving the Sisters more adequate pre-service preparation. Indeed many recalled the 1941 Study and expressed the wish to establish a four-year basic program if and when the project could become possible through an increase of Sisters.

While the attitude of Superiors was most favorable, the statistical facts gathered by the Committee were the occasion for deep concern. Relatively few Communities were complying with the requirement of most States—although not equally enforced by all—that every teacher have a bachelor's degree before she was given a teaching assignment. Hundreds of Sisters were still beginning their teaching career after their first year of novitiate. This meant perpetuating the "vicious circle," noted in Chapter 3, of answering the "Sister shortage" with Sisters not only lacking professional preparation, but also without a firm rooting in the religious life, a theological understanding of a religious vocation, and the serenity that derives from competency in the duty assigned.

Under these handicaps Sisters had not only to teach, but also to become adjusted to Community living and at the same time to be faithful to a heavy schedule of spiritual exercises. In such circumstances, securing their professional education imposed a real strain on the Sisters and disrupted communal living. Girls were not readily inspired to follow a religious vocation that presented such an arduous prospect. Furthermore, the Sisters had no time for the unhurried interviews with girls or the contacts with them outside of school hours that had proved so productive of vocations in the past. Consequently, the ever-present "Sister shortage" continued and became acute. In a word, although there was good will everywhere evidenced, as shown by the 1941 Study, the picture in 1952 had changed very little.

The remedy for "Sister shortage" had to be a radical one; so radical that no Community working alone could effect it. While the survey, begun in April of 1952, preceded both of the two momentous Congresses of that year mentioned in Chapter 3, it served as a providential forerunner to both. The thinking aroused, the sharing of common problems, and the possibility of some unified action, gave the Sisters new hope and broadened horizons. These attitudes suggested the need for a common medium of communication for those who shared the responsibility for Sisters spiritually, intellectually and professionally. The survey committee, which had done its work well, was still intact and provided the nucleus for a new organization called *The Sister Formation Conference*.

Objectives and Structure

To establish and promote the wide objectives of Sister Formation was a matter not only for stout hearts but for keen intellectual ability and farsighted organizational planning. Sister Formation was blessed with persons possessing such qualities. Providence produced the right persons at the right time for the moment of significant decision. It would be impossible to list here all those Sisters who gave unstintingly of their time and talents to Sister Formation in its early days. But even a cursory reference to its history would be impossible without mentioning the name of its first National Executive Secretary, Sister Mary Emil, I.H.M.

Into the promotion of Sister Formation, Sister Mary Emil poured all her rare talents: a keen and disciplined intellect, a grasp of psychological factors, a sense of timing, the gift of convincing speech, organizational ability and—unlimited devotion. In the interests of Sister Formation, she traveled thousands of miles; speaking sometimes to hundreds of Sisters in metropolitan areas; again, to select groups of Community personnel; and, very frequently, to Mothers Superior of small, isolated Communities, to whom she brought light, encouragement, and suggested solutions for their educational problems. Through her untiring efforts, Sister Formation came to be known, understood and desired. There are many other Sisters who gave generous, unstinted zeal to the movement. One might ask, for example, if Sister Formation would have been possible without the support of the first Provincial Superior to encourage Sister Mary Emil when the horizon of hope looked bleakest—Mother Mary Philothea, F.C.S.P.—whose cooperation expressed itself in concrete deeds that called for a high degree of personal courage. There was Sister Ritamary, C.H.M., brilliant editor of the Sister Formation Bulletin. The names are legion of Sisters who dedicated their talents to this work for God and His Church. But above all, there was Reverend Mother Anna Marie, Mother General of the Sister Servants of the Immaculate Heart of Mary, and her Council, who gave Sister Mary Emil and Sister Xaveria full time to the service of organizing and administering the Sister Formation Conference, coaxing it from infancy to maturity.

Organizational Details

Convinced that the success of Sister Formation was inherent in its purpose, the founders so structured it as to insure understanding from within and growth from without. The first of these measures was to make membership *positional* not personal, limiting it to the Major Superior of a Community, the Mistress of Novices, the Directresses of Sisters' Studies and the President and/or Dean of Catholic Women's Colleges owned and operated by the various Communities. Invitations to meetings varied according to the topic of discussion. The Mistresses of Postulants were invited when the program was appropriate to their interests; when the erection of Juniorates was under discussion it was suggested that the Mistresses of Novices, Postulants and Junior Sisters attend. This insured the interchange of opinions and experiences, and a synthesis of recommendations for those persons charged with the guidance of Sisters, at different levels, during their formative years. The aim was to blend all of the areas of formation into one harmonious whole.

The second measure, framed to insure growth from without, was the setting up of regions based on those already established by the NCEA. Each region was, from the beginning, endowed with a great degree of autonomy, while keeping to the general guidelines emanating from the National Office, particularly as to the theme selected for the annual, sectional meetings. Sister Formation principles are not something imposed on the Sisters from without— as, for instance, State certification. Rather it is something that developed from within, as the vast majority of Sisters experienced a mounting sense of urgency with regard to greater sanctity in the religious life, and a desire to fulfill more completely their apostolic role in the Church. Underlying this sense of urgency was a strong conviction that a Catholic educational program framed for formation as religious and for competency in the apostolic vocation was essential to both.

Misunderstanding of the Movement

The very success of the Sister Formation Movement and the rapidity with which it spread caused opposition—so often a sign of the Lord's work—resulting in many instances from a misunderstanding of its goals and a misinterpretation of its function. Even today there are many among the clergy, Sisters, laity and educators who do not have a clear idea of what Sister Formation really is. To some, it stands merely as a plan to insure that every Sister will obtain a baccalaureate degree before being assigned to teaching, nursing or whatever the work of her Community may be. The idea—it was almost a principle—of "Education for the sake of certification and accreditation" does not die easily. To others, Sister Formation seems to be a program (which they vehemently oppose) for the "hothouse development" of young religious, impractical in theory and wholly unsuited to the conditions under which they will later work. Yet another class of "diehards" holds to the conviction that a Sister poorly prepared for teaching or nursing is better than no Sister at all; that the religious vocation itself will serve to cover—or cover up—a multitude of professional deficiencies. In addition, since Sister Formation was first concerned with the upgrading of Sister-teachers professionally, many still associate the movement exclusively with Sisters in the teaching field, excluding nurses and social workers. None of these concepts is true, but each contains a small half-truth upon which its adherents, all in honest error, make their unfavorable judgments and justify their adverse criticisms.

Sister Formation did not come lightly by its laurels. Thought-promoting goals, wholly in harmony with the directives of the Church, required explanation and interpretation to all classes of persons whom the Sisters' work affected: hierarchy, clergy, religious and laity. Within Communities, it not infrequently met, in its beginning days, opposition from both local Superiors and rank-and-file Sisters. The chief obstacle from without was expressed in this statement: "The idea is good, but this is not the time to put it into execution." The argument had a specious validity, for at the time Catholic schools were going through a tremendous expansion period, both on the elementary- and high-school levels. This expansion was totally out of proportion to the increase in religious vocations, so that the "Sister shortage" became more and more acute. Small wonder, then, that kindly disposed but harassed bishops and pastors argued loudly for the postponement of the plan of withholding Sisters from active service for full-time formation until the day (five years hence), when they could meet all professional requirements *before* being assigned to the schools.

Arguments against Sister Formation from within were based, first, on adherence to tradition, since Sister Formation stood for something radically different from "what we always used to do." To many it appeared to be a downright critical reflection on the older, experienced Sisters who had served the cause of Catholic education long and successfully, and with true dedication, bringing the parochial schools to a position of respect and confidence. In other cases, the in-service Sisters too, understandably enough, had a questioning and even a resentful attitude towards giving the members just entering the Community educational advantages which they themselves had received piecemeal, and at the cost of great hardships, over a period of many years. Opposition both from without and within failed to take into account two things: First, what had served past society, and served it well for a long time, would not serve it today because of the rapid changes of the past decade; changes involving family living, social values, educational aims, economic opportunities, class structure, etc. Second, the breadth of the training now required. The opponents of Sister Formation narrow their view to its formal educational requirements, to the obtaining of a degree before being assigned a duty. This is to denigrate the dignity of the religious vocation, which demands that the dimensions of a Sister's preparation for the apostolate take in all the essential facets of her formation: spiritual, intellectual, social and apostolic, in addition to the professional, that she may fulfill worthily the canonical mandate to do a specific work, given her by the Church.[2]

The Mind of the Church in the Formation of Sisters

It is this dignity of a Sister, a dignity deriving from her incorporation into the body of her religious Community—itself an organ in the Mystical Body of Christ—yet pertaining to her individually, that the Sister Formation program seeks to emphasize.

2 Elio Gambari, S.M.M., *Religious-Apostolic Formation of Sisters* (New York: Fordham University Press, 1964), p. 9.

Where the Community itself is aware of the uniqueness of each person, keeping in mind her formation within the framework of its Constitution and Rules wherein each Sister will be helped to attain that degree of personal sanctity determined for her by God, there will not be a forced flowering, retarded growth or premature blight. A Community conscientiously concerned with its obligations towards its young religious will accept the fact that the Sister Formation program requires time, a trained personnel, suitable environment, physical facilities, and—of paramount importance—a whole-hearted acceptance of the fact that the idea of Sister Formation originated in the mind of the Church and is now strongly recommended by the Sacred Congregation of Religious.

To inculcate this belief, this acceptance, the very cornerstone of Sister Formation, the first series of regional conferences, 1954–55, were planned around the topic of "The Mind of the Church in the Formation of Sisters." Once convinced that the principles of Sister Formation *originated* in the mind of the Church, Major Superiors had no further question as to their acceptance of the Movement. The obedience of the Sisters in the United States has always been outstanding, as has been attested to frequently by highly placed Church officials; it is the special strength of the American Sister.

Wisely, then, the group responsible for planning the program invited a number of priests whose Communities were composed of pre-eminent educators, Directors of Diocesan Seminaries, secular priests and brothers of teaching Orders, to present their own formation programs to the Sisters. For while the Church had repeatedly made strong recommendations for a prolonged, integrated pre-service education of Sisters, it had not legislated it into being. This lack, one learned speaker stated, was made up by "the principle of the analogy of law." After quoting extensively from Canon Law governing the education and formation of clerical religious, he did not hesitate to say that "the analogy of law" covered also the preparation and formation of Sisters.

Canon 490, which states that the provisions of the law in which religious are named in the masculine gender apply equally to women religious, unless the contrary is obvious from the context or from the nature of the matter involved, also justifies our use of the analogy of law in the matter of Sister Formation.[3]

This learned theologian pointed out that the courses of study prescribed for religious clerics were designed not only to prepare them for the priesthood but to deepen their spiritual lives and fit them for pastoral duties; hence there should be some application of these principles to the formation of religious women. Specifically, he called for planned courses in theology, in the Sacred Scriptures and in philosophical studies, adapted in content to the maturity and intellectual abilities of religious Sisters at the Juniorate level. Very pertinent to certain difficulties which the Sisters were encountering, and would continue to encounter, was Father Zimmerman's quoting of the prescription prohibiting the imposition on either professors or students of irrelevant assignments which would interfere with their duties of teaching or studying. He added: "This prescription can very fittingly be applied to institutes of religious women."[4]

Evolving Convictions through Regional Meetings

From such sources, for all spoke in a like vein, several convictions evolved: The period of training should be lengthened; Postulant and Novice Mistresses should have sounder training in philosophy and theology; sacrifices would inevitably have to be made to prepare and make available for formation programs Sisters who were best qualified by their religious spirit, psychological maturity and intellectual abilities to serve as instructors in the total formation process.

The next barrier to be hurdled, and one which even Rome could not eliminate by a *fiat,* was an inherent distrust of the intellectual. Because Sister Formation began in the field of education, it was now burdened with the misconception that it would promote the intellectual above all other elements in a Sister's life. Too long had it been held among Communities that for a Sister to be

---

3 John F. Zimmerman, C.M., J.C.D., "Ecclesiastical Directives for Seminaries and for the Education of Religious Men," *The Mind of the Church in the Formation of Sisters* (New York: Fordham University, 1956), p. 61.

4 *Ibid.,* p. 65.

both a saint and a scholar was a hard saying: "East is east and west is west, and never the twain shall meet." While there were some notable exceptions, too many Communities had inherited anti-intellectualism much as they had inherited Community customs. After all, many a convent garden had its Lourdes shrine, featuring the unlettered Bernadette at prayer, while one would be hard put to find a statue of the learned Teresa of Avila penning *The Interior Castle.*

To emphasize its strong interest in the spiritual, the Sister Formation Conference selected for its second (1955–56) series of regional lectures "The Spiritual and Intellectual Elements in the Formation of Sisters." As Sisters studied the matter, it became evident that it was the attempt and not the deed that did confound. Did not every Congregation have as one of its requirements for admission at least "average intelligence"? Surely this prerequisite is not included merely to insure that the subject will later perform efficiently some exterior work in the apostolate of the Community, but rather to make certain that the candidate will have sufficient intelligence to grasp the principles of the religious life as set forth in the Rules and Constitutions; to understand and apply spiritual instructions and readings; and to comprehend the obligations of the religious vows.

Furthermore, when considering the acceptance of a candidate, Superiors take note of the extent to which it may be expected that she can use her intelligence to reach a decision as to her vocation and to recognize and accept the consequences of this decision. Ordinarily, the candidate not only has recourse to prayer to help her determine on a state of life but seeks counsel of a confessor or spiritual advisor. She next assesses her own strengths and weaknesses, her personality and temperament, in making choice of a particular Community. She starts out on her search for total dedication through the full use of the intellect with which God has endowed her. In this age of anxiety she evidences intellectual maturity in the ability to make grave decisions. These are important points in her favor.

Spiritual directors of another age were wont to say to candidates for the religious life, "Leave your will at the door of the monastery." It is not recorded that they were ever told to leave their minds there too. In practice, Superiors have always held firmly that a good religious cannot be developed without the aid of a good mind; always excepting those rare cases (of which too much is made by way of example) in which grace acts directly and not according to its ordinary laws. Such action is no more to be expected in the spiritual formation of a Sister than are miracles to be counted on in the maintenance of her health without due precaution. Not mere theory but practical experience dictates the conclusion that the neglect of the intellectual and professional can be as detrimental to the development of a sound religious as neglect of the spiritual and social.

Integration, the Essence of the Program

Sister Formation principles hold firmly to the idea that the integration of the spiritual and intellectual should begin in the postulancy, continue through novitiate and Juniorate and be an ongoing process throughout the life of a religious. As the second institute (1955–56) continued, speaker after speaker emphasized the need for integration, and that "the integrators themselves should be well integrated." That is, that those chiefly responsible for the formation of young religious—Major Superiors, Novice Mistresses, the Deans of Sisters' studies, and all others in the formation program—should have the same goals and hold to the same effective means of achieving them. Each should know, understand and respect the role of the others. Instances were cited where the Mistress of Novices and the College Dean held different and even opposing views on the formation of a Sister. For a young religious to sense—if not actually to see and hear—this lack of harmony is a painful and confusing experience, harmful to both her spiritual and intellectual formation.

Influence of the Mistresses

To obviate this, the priest speakers insisted that Novice Mistresses should be selected, not alone for their good religious spirit and their record of having discharged generously and competently some administrative duty, as was usually the case, but also for their intellectual and cultural qualifications. This is required directly for the discharge of their duties, for their instructions should be theologically sound and doctrinally correct. In their counseling they will need, on the natural level, a knowledge of those social and psychological factors which differentiate individuals and call for personalized guidance. The greater the Novice Mistress' own intellectual preparation for her work, the more easily will she understand and appreciate that the intellectual virtues impinge on the moral, and the better prepared will she be to inculcate them both as a unit. Knowing that the will acts through the intellect, she will strive for excellence in the instrument, that the resultant action may be excellent. The Mistress, while keeping within the limits set by Canon Law for formal studies during the Canonical Year of Novitiate, will make clear to the novices that generosity, piety, devotedness and a great love of God can be manifested as genuinely and as discernibly in intellectual as in manual work.

Far from downgrading the intellectual, or incessantly warning against its perils, the effective Mistress will accentuate its disciplinary part in the fulfillment of a religious vocation. For one called to an active vocation is called also to the intellectual apostolate. The competency required in their apostolic and prayer-life as well will derive from a firm and well-ordered intellectual application to study.

It is the *attitude* towards study, which the Novice Mistress has a large part in forming, that will determine the peace or guilt feelings a Sister will have later in regard to how much time she gives to intellectual pursuits. If correctly formed, she will know that spending several hours in studying the nature and effects of the latest "wonder drug" is as truly serving Christ in the sick as if she spent the same number of hours at the bedside of a patient. Or when a teaching Sister devotes a whole Sunday afternoon to reading, to acquire information on the psychology of dealing with disadvantaged children, she will know that she has as truly served such children as when, in the past week, she had endeavored, with infinite patience but absolute futility, to cope with them in the classroom and on the playground. This intellectual approach to practical problems is, in the end, the more efficient, since it takes the teacher to the root of the problem, enabling her to avoid treating symptoms rather than causes. These are the principles Sister Formation seeks to inculcate in those who have the responsibility of developing the young Sisters from the Postulate through the Juniorate.

Far-Ranging Influence of the Sister Formation Movement

The annual (recently changed to biennial) regional meetings of the Sister Formation Conference constituted one of the chief media through which its principles, philosophy and purposes came to penetrate and permeate hundreds of Communities and thousands of Sisters in the United States. The regions of Sister Formation correspond to those of the NCEA, including the East, West, Midwest, South, Southwest and Northwest areas. Attendance of Sisters from all parts of the country (and this attendance included a large number of Major Superiors) was made possible with a minimum expenditure of time and money through careful planning.

Special sectional meetings for the three categories of Mistresses added to the value of programs offered, always well-organized and made attractive and informative by the high calibre of the speakers chosen to address the Sisters. Among these were priests with special experience in dealing with Sisters and the problems connected with their apostolates; occasionally Mothers General of rare executive ability and gifted with what might be considered prophetic vision were asked to speak. The Sisters gained a further bonus from their informal talks and discussions among themselves in lobbies and corridors. When one keeps in mind that the delegates all occupied key positions in their respective Communities, positions that made for great influence, one grasps the far-reaching benefits derived from these regional meetings. Representatives from large, medium-sized and small Communities met; useful information was shared and offers of services exchanged. Mutual help kindled growing hope, and Sister Formation became more and more a household word.

Corresponding to the growth and development of Sister Formation was its enlarged field of action and interest. As time went on, the in-service education of Sisters, in every field of the apostolate, was added to its scope. It sponsored Institutes of Spirituality for Sisters on different levels of authority. The *Sister Formation Bulletin* furnished readers with timely articles—some translated from foreign periodicals. It supplied reprints of talks on subjects of vital interest to Sisters, made available tape recordings to cloistered Orders both at home and in foreign countries. But always its chief purpose remained that for which it had been founded: to secure adequate, integrated, pre-service preparation of Sisters; a preparation which would form them spiritually, intellectually, socially (group living) and professionally for their apostolic vocation.

The number of Mothers General and Provincials attending the Sister Formation meetings steadily increased. Knowing the mind of the Church in regard to Juniorates, so clearly pointed up in the congresses at Rome, Major Superiors felt a strong conviction as to their necessity. As this feeling of conviction became more pronounced, the need for action became more urgent. The topic was discussed at length at the first regional meeting held in St. Louis, Missouri, in 1954, where the Juniorate was seen as basic to the whole concept of formation and all it sought to achieve for the Communities of the United States. However, many failed to grasp the first principles of the Sister Formation Conference, and thought its main *raison d'être* was to make certain that every Sister would receive her baccalaureate degree before entering the field of her apostolate. It was history repeating itself.

That is why the term "education," too limiting in its implication, came to be replaced by the word "formation," as embracing not only education—whether general, liberal, technical, or professional—but the total development of the person. Because this person is a Sister, full formation will necessitate educating her not only as a woman but as a *religious* woman, dedicated to God by the three vows of religion. This idea, as Rome had pointed out (and later offered *Sedes Sapientiae* as a guide), would mean a rethinking of the whole educational program for Sisters. It suggested that the Postulate, Novitiate, and the Juniorate be so situated as to form part of the Motherhouse, and should include a college, preferably for nuns only. An alternative would be that a house of studies (to be known as the Juniorate) would be built close to a college the young Sister could attend while following the full spiritual and social program of the Juniorate within her own community.

Initial Success of the Regional Conferences

The first regional conference of the Sister Formation Movement was held, as we have said, in St. Louis in 1954. The program emphasized the need for a strong, pre-service formation of every Sister, a formation that would include the spiritual, the intellectual, the social, and professional-apostolic with these facets of the Sister's life so integrated that the aim would be to produce the holy and effective religious. One of the outcomes of this 1954 meeting, preceded, however, by many years of hoping, thinking, and planning, was the opening of the Marillac Sister Formation College, St. Louis, Missouri in January, 1955.

In its conception, it embodied the very notions held up by Rome as ideals to seek: (1) the college was to be for members of religious Congregations only; (2) it would be the product of cooperation and collaboration on the part of many Communities, working together for the good of the Church; (3) the Sister students would be well-grounded in sacred doctrine: philosophy and theology would be the foundation on which the whole structure of general and special education would be built; (4) it would be a house set apart, as are the postulate and novitiate, but remain an integral part of the Motherhouse; (5) the faculty would be hand-picked with the formation of young Sisters in mind. The program would be of five years duration, including the Novitiate, wherein would be taught only such subjects as Canon Law permits. Summer sessions would supplement the regular curriculum so that professional credentials would also be assured.

In the early Spring of 1960, having graduated its first class of Sisters, Marillac College was, "with highest commendation" fully accredited by the North Central Association of Secondary Schools and Colleges; three years later, its department of nursing was accredited by the National League for Nursing, and labeled as one of the five best nursing programs in the United States. Marillac

College was a direct outcome of the Sister Formation Movement—
the first in the country.

Commendation from Rome

Under date of January 19, 1960, Valerio Cardinal Valeri, late
prefect of the Congregation of Religious, wrote a personal letter
of congratulation to the Provincial Superior who brought Marillac
College into being. We quote it in full:

SACRA CONGREGATIO
DE RELIGIOSIS

Prot. N. 2027/60   January 19, 1960

Dear Reverend Mother,

This Sacred Congregation of Religious has learned with great
pleasure of all that has been accomplished for the formation of
Sisters, at Marillac College, Normandy, Missouri, and offers its
sincere congratulations to your Province of the Daughters of Charity
on this foundation which corresponds so fully to the desires of the
Holy See.

In accordance with the mind of the Holy Father, this Sacred
Congregation has repeatedly recalled to Religious Institutes their grave
obligation to provide a complete formation for their members, from
the religious, apostolic and professional point of view. The renovation
and adaptation of the religious life depends in great part on the care
exercised by Superiors in this formation. And we have been indeed
happy to learn of the efforts that the Religious Families of the
United States have been making, with the assistance of the Conference
of Major Superiors and the Sister Formation Conferences, to conform
to the directives of the Holy See.

Especially do I congratulate you, Reverend Mother, on your having
conceived and created a unit as complete as that of Marillac College
where the program of formation is so well adapted to guarantee:

    (a) a deeper and broader spiritual and religious training and

    (b) a real and practical preparation for the Apostolate, through the
          technical and professional training required for the various
          activities to which the Sisters dedicate themselves, and through
          the conferring of the degrees prescribed by the civil laws.

Naturally all this demands great sacrifice both in the way of material means, and of time as well, in the sense that it means delay in sending the young Sisters into the field of the Apostolate; but these sacrifices will be amply compensated by the better work that will be done as the fruit of a more thorough preparation.

You are especially deserving of praise, Reverend Mother, for the spirit of charity truly worthy of a Daughter of Charity which has animated you in the Establishment of Marillac College.

For it is particularly gratifying to this Sacred Congregation to know that the College is open to all Institutes which desire to make use of its facilities, and that it has recourse to the collaboration of other Communities for the personnel of its Faculty, giving thus a concrete proof of the solidarity and spirit of cooperation existing among Religious Institutes.

Any initiative that is directed toward assuring for young Religious, even of divers Communities, a "milieu" reserved exclusively to them and where their religious and professional formation are made into an integrated whole, is particularly pleasing to this Sacred Congregation. In classes frequented by Religious alone, the technical training can be more easily fused with the religious and apostolic formation.

Most willingly do I bless the work that is being done at Marillac College, and I express my sincere hope for a constant increase in that spirit of fraternal charity which is already so evident there.

Faithfully yours in Christ,
Valerio Cardinal Valeri
Prefect

Reverend Mother Catherine Sullivan
Daughter of Charity
National Chairman, Sister Formation Conference
Marillac College, Normandy 21, Missouri, U.S.A.

These words of commendation from the Holy See were received as merited, not by one Community, but by all the religious Congregations of the United States, as letters and telegrams testified when it was published along with the accreditation of Marillac College by the highest regional and national agencies. It was indeed only with the cooperation and collaboration of the more than fifteen religious Congregations that contributed Sisters with advanced degrees to the faculty of Marillac College, that it was able to open its doors to nuns from all Orders and become an out-standing Sister Formation Center of the Catholic Church.

Other Responses to Sister Formation

For more than two decades the School Sisters of Notre Dame in south St. Louis had operated a high-calibre Junior College for the candidates of their own Order. These young Sisters, after graduating from the Junior College, would later go to other colleges or universities to complete their studies for the baccalaureate degree, some as full-time students, while others attended late afternoon, Saturday classes and summer sessions. The Notre Dame Community's response to Sister Formation was almost as immediate as was that of the Daughters of Charity of Marillac College, and as will be shown in the next chapter it now operates a senior college of Sister Formation in south St. Louis.

The Pacific Coast was to be the scene of the third Sister Formation College. In 1957, Providence Heights College in Issaquah, Washington, opened under the aegis of Seattle University. Through this institution it obtained accreditation by the Western Association of Schools and Colleges. This Sister Formation College has an interesting and original pattern. Four religious Congregations, within an area of thirty miles, joined the Sisters of Charity of Providence in planning a Sister Formation College in which the young Sisters of all five Communities would enroll for studies, returning by bus each evening to their own Juniorates located at their various Motherhouses. This college follows a special five-year program of studies known as the Everett Curriculum, a brief explanation of which follows.

Ford Foundation Grant

So well and favorably was the Sister Formation Conference known, and so esteemed was its position in the educational field, that in 1956 the Ford Foundation extended to it a grant of $50,000.00 for a significantly specific purpose: to gather together from all parts of the United States the top Sister educators in their respective positions and fields for the purpose of constructing a curriculum most suitable for carrying out the aims and ideals of Sister Formation. The construction of this curriculum may well be reckoned as one of the outstanding services rendered to Communities by Sister Formation. The grant was secured through the good offices of Sister Mary Emil, I.H.M., first National Chairman of Sister Formation and later its Executive Secretary.

The Everett Curriculum Workshop

Fifteen outstanding Sister educators, with consultants to act as resource persons, met from June 1 to August 30, 1956, at a Convent of the Sisters of Charity of Providence, Everett, Washington as the guests of Mother Philothea, Provincial of the Order. Three months of arduous, intensive work was scarcely sufficient to complete their assigned task. The work was carried on in workshop fashion, with sessions and consultations often extending far into the night. The Sisters knew they were working not for the present generation of Sisters alone, and for all those whose lives would be touched by their teachings, but for posterity. The entire Catholic school system, indeed the Church itself, would be affected by what they did. The purpose of the Everett Workshop was to determine—always with excellence in mind—which academic fields in general education should have place in a curriculum which was designed especially for Sisters.

Its chief and abiding value is best expressed in Sister Mary Emil's own words in the introduction to the final (printed) report: "It is not the purpose of the Sister Formation Conference to arrive at a single pattern of Sister education for all Communities. It was a purpose of the Everett Workshop to assemble and refine the principles which would have to be taken into account in constructing any pattern of Sister education. . . ."[5]

Herein lies its supreme value: it is an almost perfect springboard for adaptation by any Community to fit its individual needs. Philosophy and theology will form the sound foundation on which can be built the rich and enriching liberal studies that are the mark of the cultured woman, and which, in a well-planned cur-

[5] Sister Mary Emil, I.H.M. (ed.), *Report of the Everett Curriculum Workshop* (Seattle, Washington: Heiden's Mailing Bureau, 1956), p. vii.

riculum, can be pursued in logical sequence, followed by—or, more correctly, interwoven with—professional courses, to prepare the student for her future apostolic assignment.

Speaking of the Ford grant which made this gigantic undertaking possible, Sister Mary Emil says:

It remains to be said that the specific objectives of the research and curriculum construction for which the grant was sought and obtained were limited to a college curriculum for the education of Sisters. Every effort was made, however, to see the college education of the Sister as designed for one who is a special kind of student, with a special mission and dedication, and as taking place within the larger context of total and integrated spiritual and intellectual formation.[6]

Those Communities that were determined to give to their young Sisters the best possible pre-service formation eagerly awaited the long-heralded Everett Curriculum. That not all would find it possible, or even desirable, to adopt it *in toto* was foreseen, as the quotation above assures us. For example, Communities of multiple services had to meet demands not required of a single-purpose Community. But the substance of the Everett Curriculum is embodied in every college curriculum today where excellence is the goal.

Naturally there were problems other than the perplexing ones connected with the construction of college curricula facing the various Communities; problems of finance and personnel, location of the Motherhouse, the number of Junior Sisters, the revision of past programs and the updating of attitudes on the part of older Sisters towards pre-service formation of young Sisters.

These varied in depth and degree from Community to Community. But the universal problem facing every Major Superior was the prudent selection of that pattern of pre-service formation which would be most in accord with the wisdom of Church directives concerning preparation for its many apostolates; and would at the same time secure and preserve for posterity the special and unique spirit of her own religious Congregation.

6 *Ibid.*

7

Patterns in Sister Education

Of all the freedoms, privileges and prerogatives enjoyed by American higher education, probably none is so profoundly cherished as the right to be different. Variety is the spice of academic life. The wide diversity of teachers' colleges, professional schools, large complex universities, small private and state-owned colleges, institutes of technology, medicine and law are all evidence of America's belief in unlimited opportunity for the pursuit of truth by divergent paths.

Seldom will two institutions of learning, even in the field of general education, liberal arts or a special professional area, be found identical in organizational structure, administrative practice, curricular emphasis or in expressed philosophy, purposes and goals. Accrediting agencies are coming more and more to accept and even to applaud these differences where they exist, not for the sake of being different, but the better to implement and achieve the avowed aims and objectives of the institution.

This encouragement of non-conformity in practices and procedures for the surer attainment of stated purposes and goals has resulted in greater creativity in planning educational programs, especially in the small college.

Aggiornamento in Formation

In answering the urgent and repeated recommendations of the Holy See for the *aggiornamento* of each Sister's total formation, above all for a pre-service apostolic educational preparation in teaching, nursing, or social work, each religious Congregation has taken ample advantage of the variety of ways and means permitted within the framework of American higher education.

Each Community is eager to respond to the wishes of the Sacred Congregation of Religious that it provide adequate, and even excellent, academic and apostolic preparation for its young members and that it update also the advantages given to older Sisters on an in-service basis. But every religious Congregation cherishes the right to plan its program according to the individual spirit and works of its own Community with its unique constitution, rules, customs and apostolic ideals.

The Sister Formation Movement, through which much of this *aggiornamento* of studies has been channeled, has had the vision and the wisdom to know that this variety and diversity of program planning in the various Sisterhoods is as good as it is inevitable, for each Congregation will plan, not always *ideally* in light of what it *should* do for its members, but practically what it feels it *can* do in view of its present needs, requirements, possibilities, commitments and limitations.

When the Holy See recommended the establishment of Juniorates in all religious Communities, it was very clear as to *what* it had in mind—the *how* was left to Major Superiors. What the Holy See wanted was *aggiornamento,* the updating of the formation and pre-service education of the young Sister to the point where all young women entering the religious life would receive, not only a longer and sounder formation in spirituality, so necessary in today's hectic and materialistic world, but an intellectual and professional education equal to, or surpassing, that of the cultured lay woman who plans to enter one of the main service fields. This *what* that should be done includes every young religious having earned—as a minimum—the bachelor's degree before beginning her professional and apostolic work.

The Reverend Elio Gambari, S.M.M., speaking for the Sacred Congregation of Religious on "The Juniorate in the Mind and Directives of the Holy See," said at one of the regional meetings of the Sister Formation Conference in 1957:

The purpose of the Juniorate is to continue, consolidate and perfect the general and special religious instruction and at the same time to provide the professional education necessary for proper apostolic activity. The whole is to be animated and guided by a personal religious development which is the individual's response to the religious and professional training. The Juniorate should be so organized as to assure this triple formation.[1]

Underlying this directive is the assumption that each young person entering a religious Congregation after high school finishes a year of college as a postulant, while taking the first steps in the religious life and learning the social aspects of Community living. This period is followed by the canonical year of novitiate during which academic studies are severely curtailed, allowing for greater concentration on the liturgical life of the Church, the Scriptures, the history, constitution and rules of the religious Institute, and personal sanctification. The canonical year is followed by a three-year Juniorate, where academic studies are resumed, integrated with a continuing program of Christian and apostolic formation. The program culminates in the reception of a baccalaureate degree which represents five calendar years of preparation towards becoming a holy religious and an effective teacher, nurse, or prospective graduate student.

The Holy See recognizes that just as the strength of American education lies in its diversity, so the strength of Sister education may well lie in the variety of forms it has taken in answer to the directives sent out by Rome. Hence it is that spokesmen for the directives on Sister education issued by the Holy See are careful to stress the latitude allowed as to the time, place, length and manner of Juniorate formation.[2]

In general, the response of the Major Superiors to papal directives for establishing Juniorates for pre-service education has been as prompt and as generous as is always the case where obedience to the Holy See is concerned. As a matter of fact it is almost miraculous that so many Congregations were able to make the sacrifices attendant on major changes in Community edu-

[1] Quoted by Sister Ritamary, C.H.M. (ed.), *The Juniorate in Sister Formation* (New York: Fordham University Press, 1960), p. 10.
[2] *Ibid.,* pp. 10–17.

cational policy and practice. Even the very small Communities have tried to comply with the wishes of the Holy See for the updating of their formation and educational programs, so far as they can in view of the pressing problems due to the acute "Sister shortage" in all areas of the works of mercy.

This has been made possible in large measure by the generosity of bishops, pastors and superintendents of schools, who have made heroic financial sacrifices in hiring able lay co-workers to carry on teaching in the over-populated elementary and secondary schools of the country, as well as in our colleges and other institutions of higher learning. Major Superiors have likewise doubled and tripled the number of lay staff members in their hospitals and social agencies, so that Sisters can be given a longer pre-service formation in the religious, intellectual, social and professional facets of Community life.

As is only human, however, there are still some Sisters and priests who have not grasped the full significance of the Juniorate movement and the seriousness of papal concern for pre-service formation. They ask: "What is all this ferment about Sister education? There is nothing new here; we have always had the problem of educating our Sisters and we have been doing it for more than fifty years."

Like many half-truths this statement has a certain degree of validity—we have been sending our Sisters to college for nearly fifty years in order to qualify them for teaching and nursing certification; but we have been doing this on a part-time and in-service basis. It was a rare Community that could afford even two years of pre-service preparation, and until the Sister Formation Movement emphasized the directives of the Holy See, extremely few Communities gave their young Sisters an opportunity to earn the undergraduate degree with a period of practicum in teaching or nursing before entering the school or hospital apostolate.

Concern for Perseverance

Now all this, for most Communities, has changed to an amazing degree. Major Superiors have come to realize that the needs of the 20th, as well as the 21st, century will impose graver responsibilities on the young Sisters, and what may have been adequate, or at least expedient and permissible, for an earlier age will not suffice today. The young religious of the 20th century, however good and self-sacrificing, is eminently practical. While she is no less eager to serve the Church than her counterparts of the past, she is quick to ask: "Will I be thoroughly prepared for my assignment before taking up the work of teaching, nursing, or social work?" And when she is not, she is quite vocal, quite articulate about her need for adequate professional and apostolic formation. Where this need for complete academic and professional preparation is not supplied, the results can be traumatic.

A bishop who wishes to remain anonymous, but who was much concerned with defections of Sisters throughout the country in the early fifties had, in substance, this to say: Some effort has been made to determine why so many Sisters in the past decade have failed to persevere in their vocation. It is not easy to find the answer to this delicate question because so many factors—personal adjustment, character, care in screening candidates before they enter, and a host of other human debits and credits—enter into the picture. But in a certain area of the country some bishops pooled their findings as to the reasons Sisters give for leaving their Congregations. Many and diverse statements were made in this study which only served to becloud the real issue. But one significant clue emerged. Of all the reasons given—and they were widely divergent—there was one significant common denominator recorded by ninety-five per cent of the cases studied: "I did not feel that I belonged because I was neither academically nor professionally prepared for the assignment I was given in the Community's works."

It may be safely asserted that a Sister who is not competently trained for the apostolate she is assigned to will not be adequately trained in the religious life either, because both take *time* for maturation. The ascetical formation should proceed in close relation with the intellectual and the professional if the product of training is to be a truly integrated person.

Major Superiors, wise with the wisdom of the grace of office, and schooled in the experience that derives from dealing closely with human nature, know how important this integration of all the facets of a Sister's life is for her successful performance in apostolic activities. They know, alas, that the bright, intelligent young religious, at the close of her novitiate, is not mature enough to face the demands made by today's children in the classroom; nor is one year of study beyond the novitiate sufficient to equip her supernaturally, intellectually and professionally to work side by side with well-educated lay colleagues. They accept, in fact, that a Sister, by reason of her dedication and motivation, has a role different from, even though complementary to, that of her lay colleagues. In practice, they are sincerely seeking the best means of preparing their Sisters at all levels of competency, so that the immature religious will not too soon face situations for which she is not ready, situations which, through faulty reasoning, will cause her to seek refuge in the thought: "Since I can't manage the duty given me, maybe I don't belong in this Community. Maybe I don't have a religious vocation."

Pre-eminent Concern of Major Superiors

Anxiety about the peace of soul and serenity which are every young Sister's right, and which come only when the religious and intellectual security that results from professional competency is assured, continues to disturb Major Superiors. They have been doing some serious soul-searching to ascertain how they can give their Sisters the best education consistent with the ideals of their Order. This soul-searching has been aided by the questioning of many notable educators, as evidenced by their public speaking and writings. Dissatisfaction with education, though now acute, is really no new problem in the United States, as witness the countless books that deal with that subject, particularly teacher-education. The Conant Report[3] has done more than jolt the profession out of any complacency it may have felt. The author of *The Miseducation of American Teachers* tells us that: "We are probably no closer now to basing education, that most tormented of subjects, on anything 'objective' than mankind has ever been." He assures us that Aristotle indulged in a glorious rage against it

3 James B. Conant, *The Education of American Teachers* (New York: McGraw-Hill Book Co., 1963), pp. 127 ff.

and was frustrated because ". . . confusing questions arise out of the education that actually prevails."[4] The book abounds in quotations from authoritative sources on the inability of teachers to enjoy the pleasure of being intelligible.[5]

The Problem Restated

A rich program of Christian and intellectual formation, well correlated with the social ideals of Community living within the framework of the rules and constitutions of her Order, is the first part of a twofold requirement to be filled for every Sister's formation. The second part of this prerequisite is that it incorporate a full liberal arts education based on philosophy and theology, leading to a bachelor's degree. This program should begin with the first year of postulancy, and, allowing for the canonical year of novitiate, be followed by a three-year Juniorate in a Sister-formation college. In five calendar years, then, there should emerge a mature, holy and effective religious, ready for the beginning experiences of an active apostolate in teaching, nursing, and later graduate study, preferably at a large co-ed university.

This is no small order; it is the "what" that the Church is seeking, looking ahead to the complex society and the daring apostolates in which the young Sister will engage, once her formation period is completed. Then, more involved and varied experiences will become part of her active bearing witness to Christ in the market place of the world, to which service the Church is calling her, and for which the pre-service education is so necessary a foundation.

The "how" of achieving all this had to be thought through thoroughly and with objectivity by Major Superiors. To recognize the need for unqualified excellence in a first-class college where religious, intellectual professional-apostolic experiences can be so correlated with all the facets of a Sister's "Christian witness" that she evolves into a holy and effective religious is one thing; to implement this ideal is another. For the element on which the

[4] James D. Koerner, *The Miseducation of American Teachers* (Boston: Houghton Mifflin Co., 1963), pp. 1–21.
[5] *Ibid.*

Church places strongest emphasis is that the young Sisters shall live
in a Juniorate, apart from the professed Sisters where a full Community life can be lived, while pursuing this program designed to
integrate all aspects of their lives.[6]

Large Catholic Universities

As in the days when a college degree was first made mandatory
by State certification, most of the Communities turned to the
Catholic universities throughout the country, recalling the unstinting generosity with which the "men's universities" came to their
aid at what might historically be considered the most critical era
in Sister-education. At a time—perhaps too easily forgotten now
—when many religious Congregations of men were, by constitution
or custom, "not allowed" to organize or teach "mixed classes"
("mixed" meaning the presence of women on the all-male campus),
these priests found ways and means to provide classes for the
distaff students desperately seeking to comply with State and
regional accreditation requirements. Those prohibitions have disappeared from most campuses—but the gratitude of Communities
of women-religious remains undimmed.

However one looks at it, there are undeniable advantages in
attending large Catholic co-ed universities where distinguished
minds among professors and students challenge the Sister's powers
of critical thinking; where she can learn how men think, how they
provoke stimulating discussions. This is no small advantage indeed.
There, too, the best of library and laboratory facilities make work
a joy. In such a setting a Sister can not so much compete with
others (the possible disadvantage of which will be pointed up
later in this chapter) as fully exercise her own powers of judgment
and creative thought, independently of the quality of achievement
of those around her.

Yet there are many educators and Major Superiors who sincerely believe that, because of the variety of extraneous factors
that enter into this situation for a young Sister, these intellectual
contacts may more safely, usefully and fruitfully be reserved to

6 Arcadio Cardinal Larraona, "Foreword," *The Juniorate in Sister Formation*,
p. xi.

the graduate level. In the mind of this writer, such experiences, when built upon a solid *undergraduate* foundation of religious formation, are indispensable to advanced continuing education.

Catholic Women's Colleges

It is a matter of history that the Catholic women's colleges, too, were as eager as were the men's universities to help the Sisters when degrees were so urgently demanded by State and regional accrediting agencies; but they were fewer in number, at the time, and usually located in suburbs and outlying districts, planned more for resident than "commuter" students, which the majority of Sisters had to be. But these colleges showed a phenomenal growth in the years that followed the '20's and, where possible, the Sisters enrolled for courses, once the use of automobiles for nuns became common.

Born of the belief that "a woman should be educated as a woman," these colleges and their administrators and faculties today deserve to be enrolled among the forces that had a prominent part in the emancipation of women. Their contribution to America as a whole, and to the place and prestige women hold in the eyes of the nation, cannot be overestimated. In the midst of the lamentations of the prophets of doom who began early in this century to predict the demise of the Catholic women's college—once the universities accepted co-eds on campus—religious Communities quietly built more and more of them. And what has been their answer to the prophets of gloom of our own decade, warning against their demise, or absorption by the universities? Calmly they built larger and more beautiful residence halls, and continued to insist that a "woman should be educated as a woman"— and not as a man on men's campuses.

Many religious Superiors felt that this was a sound philosophy of education that could be applied to Sisters as women. These Major Superiors, especially those of Communities that owned and operated colleges, sent their young members into classes with the girls, assured by the presence of their own Sisters among the faculty of adequate supervision for the young Sister, and an excellent academic education. Other Superiors, mindful of the Church's insistence on Juniorate formation as an integral part of the intellectual, as well as the professional aspects that will play an important role in her future apostolic work, solved the problem by building a Juniorate on or near the college campus. Here the young Sister, under the guidance of a well-trained Mistress, could be formed to Community life, in an atmosphere of extended religious training, while, at the same time, giving herself to her present apostolate of study. For those Communities who own and operate colleges the plan is not only feasible but satisfactory.

Relevant Factors To Be Studied

However, a basic problem remained: a lay woman's college is essentially for lay women; and no matter how excellent in academic aspects, its aims and objectives are written with lay women in mind, and their education with its major purposes is bound—in justice—to receive greater emphasis. Still, for many Communities this has proved a satisfactory plan. Accrediting examiners have even pointed out that the competition that a religious group can furnish a lay group—and vice versa—might possibly be considered one of the major advantages of having Sisters on campus with college girls.

In the lead article of the 1963 Spring issue of the *Sister Formation Bulletin,* "The Local Superior as Spiritual Leader," Sister Annette Walters, a veteran psychologist in a woman's college, questions the wisdom—and the fitness—of trying to motivate Sisters by placing them in competition with lay people. "Even the most holy lay person has a vocation different from that of a Sister," she writes. "Sisters should be appealed to *as Sisters* with a deep intellectual and theologically sound interpretation of their role in the Church." One wonders—gratuitously perhaps—if comparisons or competition between lay people and Sisters might not beget a mind-set in a Sister, that a lay person is someone she must always out-shine or out-distance in some way. This would be most unfortunate in a day when it is so important, as will be pointed up in a later chapter, that lay people and Sisters work together in a spirit of shared partnership. A Sister's formation should include acceptance of the fact that a lay person will fill an administrative role in one of our own agencies, thus placing a

Sister in a subordinate position—as for instance, if a lay person should be made principal of one of our schools. We have with us the instance of men presidents in Catholic women's colleges, where in the past it was usual to find a Sister in the top administrative role. We can expect to find lay people in key roles in Catholic institutions of all levels of education and in institutions of various other works of mercy, early in the next decade.[7]

Need of Planning for Long-Range Goals

There still remain a large number of Congregations who do not operate their own college, and who still have the problem of carrying out Rome's directives concerning the importance of organizing Juniorate programs. Given the type of society from which girls come today, and the challenging apostolates they will later undertake, Major Superiors are impelled to think the whole problem through with long-range goals in mind. The thought of sending young candidates who have just entered the religious life, who are just beginning to understand what being a Sister means, into daily association with young lay people in an institution designed primarily for the education of lay women, gives pause to many Major Superiors. The young woman on entering the convent ceases to be a lay woman, she is now about to become a religious. If "a woman should be educated as a woman"—should not a Sister be educated as a Sister? She is a very special sort of woman, not necessarily more holy than a good Catholic girl, but certainly, as a Sister, different in attitude, viewpoints, and values.

Post-Novitiate Problems of Young Sisters

The first five years of a Sister's life are years of adjustment to many different phases and facets of the new life she has undertaken. She is deeply concerned with decisions and choices as well as with spiritual and academic progress. The novitiate has only cleared away the sand and rubble which must generally be removed before any digging can begin and the cement poured which will serve as the foundation on which to build a Christlike character.

[7] Neil G. McCloskey, S.J., *Catholic Viewpoint on Education* (New York: Hanover House, 1959), p. 105.

Almost any conscientious Novice Mistress feels that she has only made a beginning in the responsible task of setting the young novice on the right road toward becoming an effective as well as a truly holy religious. Much remains to be done before later roads can be traveled with confidence and security. Superiors weigh the beliefs of some educators that, since the young Sister is to live and work surrounded by lay people in her apostolate, it is important that she learn as early as possible how lay people think and what values they hold important. But the Reverend Mothers who deal with the post-novitiate young Sister know that she has yet much to learn about the religious life; much to weigh and correct in her own sense of values; and that she needs time to mature and develop a sound philosophy of life.

It is not surprising, then, that many Religious Superiors felt that the way to achieve this ideal was to establish a college for the young members of their Congregations so that they could be formed intellectually and religiously for the life and work of their respective institutes under their own immediate guidance, aided by Sisters who have proven themselves spiritually and intellectually competent. Where the Community was sufficiently large and able to provide faculty, facilities, and a sizable student body for a college comparable to other small undergraduate institutions recognized for their excellence, this seemed the adequate answer.

However, with what would seem to be more zeal than prudent forethought and careful planning, some Congregations have organized their own small colleges of Sister Formation and have found it next to impossible to establish a sound program of liberal studies with the necessary well-equipped plant, libraries and laboratories; and above all, sufficient enrollment to guarantee a proper academic atmosphere of study and intellectual activity, motivated by a well-chosen faculty with advanced degrees. As an example of how prevalent the idea is of Motherhouse Colleges as an answer to the serious and—let us say it—*sacred* problem of Sister Formation, the following statistics are noteworthy:

(1) Prior to 1952, before the Sacred Congregation so pointedly interested itself in Sister-Formation (and we can readily believe there were strong reasons for this updated interest),

there were 44 Motherhouse Colleges.[8] One-third of these have an enrollment of less than 38 students.

(2) Within the last 12 years, 52 Motherhouse Colleges have come into being.

(3) This means 96 Motherhouse Colleges are in existence with enrollments in 93 of them less than 55 students, a large percentage of whom are part-time.

(4) Only 69 per cent of these colleges have faculties holding M.A. or a professional degree as a minimum requirement.

Such small, poorly conceived programs can render a distinct disservice, not only to the Sister students involved and to their religious Congregation, but even to the Church, for regional accrediting agencies are not slow to criticize the institutions for lack of perspective and academic excellence. They deny them the approval and accreditation without which they cannot confer recognized degrees.

Criticism Made by Accrediting Agencies

The criticisms constantly pointed up—and often with undeniable justification—are: (1) Even where facilities are reasonably adequate, a too small enrollment makes a truly academic atmosphere impossible. (2) Too small a faculty renders difficult the achievement of an intellectual climate and a community of scholars, so necessary to any institution of higher learning. (This is calculated to make a strong and telling impact on the Sister student.) (3) There is too little contact with the mainstream of society. (4) Isolation from contemporary problems, insularity and inbreeding inevitably result from a too controlled and overprotective environment. (5) A few lay faculty members—well chosen—are needed to round out the experiences of an all-Sister student body.

These criticisms are valid. If they are not duly noted and the

8 *Official Guide to Catholic Educational Institutions and Religious Communities in the United States,* 1962, pp. 146–55, lists 93 such colleges, 49 of which came into existence within the last 10 years. As this book is being written 3 more such colleges have been opened; 2 are in the planning stage, and 2 junior colleges have been regionally accredited. Only 21 Catholic colleges and universities have been founded in the last twelve years as against 51 small Motherhouse Colleges in the same period. It is only fair to add that several of these small colleges anticipate closing and making other arrangements.

defects countered in a variety of ways, the graduates of "Sisters only" colleges could be too limited in their experiences to serve as effective apostles in the universal Church.

For example, only 3 of the 96 Motherhouse Colleges mentioned above are regionally accredited; Providence Heights, Issaquah, Washington, is regionally accredited through its affiliation to Seattle University. Notre Dame, St. Louis, is independently accredited by North Central Association. Marillac College, St. Louis, Missouri, the first and largest of these Sister Formation Colleges, is accredited by both the North Central Association and the National League for Nursing (which, as we have already noted, has pronounced the program of its nursing department one of the five best in the country).

These three colleges have avoided the outstanding criticisms made by State and regional accrediting agencies. For example, Providence Heights, Issaquah, Washington, has a large and impressively beautiful campus, an enrollment of 250 with 4 Communities participating in its program. It is operated, as we have said, by the Sisters of Charity of Providence. The college has a faculty which includes 32 Sisters of Charity of Providence, members of 7 other religious Communities, 1 priest and 1 lay woman.

Notre Dame, St. Louis, conducted by the School Sisters of Notre Dame, is at the moment constructing a new library; its fine arts and science buildings represent the importance the Community attaches to its Sister Formation program, which, at this writing, is restricted to the young members of the Notre Dame Community. Its 1963 enrollment exceeded 300. The Charter has recently been changed to permit the admission of students from other Communities, which will add not only to its enrollment but to those other, more intangible assets that will prohibit the insularity and inbreeding feared by accrediting agencies. Impressive grants have been made to an outstanding science department.

The present enrollment at Marillac College exceeds 400, representing 31 different religious Congregations among its student body. The Daughters of Charity own and operate the college, which is the proud possessor of one of the most unusual all-glass libraries in the country, housing more than 54,000 carefully selected books. The faculty consists of 26 Daughters of Charity, Sisters from 12 different Congregations, 5 priests, and a highly qualified group of lay persons—3 men and 3 women.

These three colleges represent three different adaptations of Sister-education, all in conformity with papal directives; and, having recognized the values accruing from the dedicated idealism of Catholic women's colleges educating women *as women,* they are committed to educating Sisters *as Sisters.*

Accrediting Agencies Encourage Quality and Variety

In the instances thus far cited one sees that religious Congregations in growing numbers are taking full advantage of the autonomy, freedom and variety—and, indeed, of the creative planning—not only permitted but encouraged and applauded by State and regional accrediting agencies. A word of high praise for these agencies might rightly find a place in this chapter because of their friendly cooperation, their insistence upon quality, and their very real interest in the growth and progress of Sister-education in the United States. Many college administrators can attest to the vigorous help and inspiration received from them, which made possible a variety of excellent programs in Sister Formation.[9]

The financial outlay required for establishing and administering an outstanding college, the manpower involved in educating and maintaining a gifted faculty, which is indispensable to an accredited college that continually strives for quality, and the annual operating expenditures necessary for full academic vitality, sorely tax the revenues of even the most flourishing Communities. Granted that no investment pays off so well in the essential well-being and stability of a Community as that which strives for the full formation and education of all the members thereof, yet the problem of finance is one of the many realities that cannot be ignored.

New Trends

The Church in this ecumenical age, calling for close cooperation and collaboration among religious Communities, shows a way to the solution of the dilemma. Colleges for Sisters only, where the

[9] Cf. Roy J. Defferari, *Some Problems of Catholic Higher Education in the United States* (Boston: Daughters of St. Paul, 1963), p. 163.

academic program is excellent and the milieu is that of religious orientation and intellectual appreciation, are possible when several or many religious Communities unite in contributing resources, staff and students. Emerging more and more as a pattern of total formation for Sisters, one to which Major Superiors seem to be giving serious thought as a solution to this problem of deep concern, is one which calls for even closer cooperation and collaboration of Communities so earnestly sought for by the Holy See.

It allows for the diversity and variety in higher education that is so dear to the American heart and, above all, safeguards the uniqueness of spirit and practices of each religious Congregation. Collaboration may be accomplished in a number of ways, and the creative minds of Major Superiors, at work on this idea, have already produced excellent plans. What their unlimited ingenuity will create in the future, the unprecedented achievements of religious Communities through the centuries give some indication.

What can be achieved in Juniorate programs by the cooperative efforts of a number of religious Communities is already exemplified in many sections of the country. Each educational structure has unique features growing out of different concepts of the way to implement the directives of the Church and their interpretation by the Sister Formation Conference and influenced by the needs and resources of the respective areas.

In the East, the proposed Sister Formation center at Trinity College, near which six Communities have indicated a desire to build Juniorates, offers the newest example in cooperative effort. In the far Northwest, Providence Heights College in Issaquah, Washington, has already proved the validity of its interpretation of the Everett Curriculum for the four participating Communities with Juniorates each located at their own Motherhouse within commuter distance of Providence Heights. In the Southwest the Dallas University project involves the cooperation of the university faculty and the Sisters that staff the Motherhouses built adjacent to the university campus. Most of the Sisters' classes are separate from the other university students'. The arrangement has been entirely satisfactory. Marillac College in the Middle West, the first multi-congregation program, has a student body representing thirty-nine States and seven foreign countries. There are numerous other developments either in full operation or in the planning stage.

A description of any one of these institutions would show the tremendous possibilities for Juniorate programs involving the co-operation and collaboration of many Communities.[10] These opportunities extend especially to the smaller Congregations for whom a Sisters' college restricted to their own young members would be an unattainable ideal. Because the writer is most familiar with Marillac College in St. Louis, Missouri, and because she is keenly interested in helping any Communities who would like to hear more fully what is being done in order that they may formulate plans of their own, consistent with the ideals of their institute, the Marillac program will be described in detail.

Sister Formation Program of Marillac College

At Marillac College several Motherhouses are within a ten- to fifteen-minute car ride. Several out-of-state religious Congregations have rented or bought large homes nearby, while still others are building their own Juniorates (some adding the second-year novitiate, others considering also the postulate) on various parts of the two-hundred-acre campus. The college is centrally located, and most of the Juniorates are close enough to allow for coming and going between classes.

The Holy See's significant desire for this kind of cooperation and collaboration of Communities is woven through every fibre of the purposes and policies of the whole formation program, of which the college is a fundamental part. The provision of these separate Juniorate buildings, each presided over by a Mistress, insures the privacy, and the living of a full Community life, so necessary for the development of a Sister in the particular spirit of her Order.

The Juniorate program, which emphasizes religious formation and Community-living, blends with the college program, which emphasizes the intellectual and the professional-apostolic in such a way as to make it possible for the Sister student to integrate all the facets of her formation and education into one harmonious

---

[10] Sister Rose Dominic, S.C.L., "Cooperation in the Use of Educational Resources," *National Catholic Education Association Bulletin*, LX, No. 3 (February, 1964), 18–31, describes many other plans.

whole. Too much emphasis cannot be given to the need for integration both within the academic curriculum of studies, the co-curricular activities, and the other areas that enter into a complete formation of the Sister as a person, as a woman, and as a religious.

Faculty for Formation Colleges

Needless to say, the teachers selected for a Sister Formation college should be gifted spiritually as well as intellectually, but above all they should be deeply impregnated with a sense of mission. By analogy they might be likened to natural parents who share with God in the procreation of children; for they share, with God and their Superiors, the responsibility of preparing members to carry on the life of the Community and its work. Within the religious Community of Sisters there could be no greater mission, no more noble destiny.

For such a college, for such a training, no sacrifice can be too great. The college must be a worthy instrument for its high purpose. No defect pointed up by regional accrediting agencies should be allowed to mar its function. Marillac College avoids the inadequacies which critics of the Sisters' colleges often point up, by the following means:

1. A sufficient enrollment helps to engender an academic atmosphere that bespeaks the pursuit of excellence.
2. Plant and equipment are generously adequate for study and research within due limits of the undergraduate program.
3. Faculty members are chosen with wide and varied intellectual background, a gift for effective teaching, and a dedicated sense of mission. This guarantees a genuinely intellectual climate.
4. Frequent field trips related to the various disciplines bring the students into close contact with contemporary problems; such as the practicum in teaching for future educators; clinical experiences for future nurses in hospitals and homes. For future social workers visits to municipal courts-in-session, to detention institutions for juvenile and adult delinquents, and to other welfare agencies. Other educational experiences are sought in the city's museum of fine arts, visits to scientific and industrial plants, and various cultural centers.

5. With permission of their Mistress, students on a voluntary basis, and under supervision of faculty members, spend a part of each Saturday and/or Sunday afternoon in a disadvantaged or inner-city neighborhood, studying social conditions, racial inequities, areas of defective education, housing and job opportunities. Thus, insights into these problems in the light of papal social teachings are available to every student.

Twofold benefits accrue from these last-mentioned activities: they are educational experiences and apostolic opportunities.

Guided Apostolic Experiences

These occasions of bearing witness to Christ in the market place are designed to perfect the apostolic facet of a Sister's total formation. But Major Superiors will understand all the significant implications in these experiences. They well know that this is an age of restlessness; some young (?) Sisters see the apostolate of teaching as too restricted, and the more distant field of "social work" exercises a strong attraction. Christ in the market place seems more glamorous than Christ in the classroom.

But experiences in disadvantaged neighborhoods—under the guidance of well-oriented faculty members—will teach the young Sisters that "going about doing good" in the steps of the Master, is, at times, a wearisome journey. When truly made for His sake and in His spirit, these visits shatter all illusions of glamor and restore proper perspective. Not the least of a young Sister's maturing experiences is to find herself the object of suspicion and hostility on the part of those to whom she goes so gladly to serve. It is not unusual that instead of being welcomed she is rebuffed. She will find it a trying experience to keep her patience in the midst of inordinate demands on one hand, or of unfriendly silence or skeptical contempt on the other. She may find her well-made plans, with every hour accounted for, disrupted by some family happening: a quarrel, an illness or an arrest. This may well have the subtle effect of making Community routine under which she, perhaps subconsciously, chafed, appear in a new and more inviting light.

While no unwise attempt is made to impinge upon the field of the skilled social worker, the young religious learns much from her informal contacts with those who live on a marginal subsistence level. She learns to give with simplicity, both of her time and such material means as she has available, without expecting gratitude. She learns to serve with humility, face to face with needs of which she never dreamed. She comes to realize that the poor have their pride which she must respect, and their privacy which she must not invade. So her apostolic work is a means of dispelling the notion that good will and sympathy are all that are required to fit her to deal effectively with those in need.

She will come to learn, perhaps as a by-product of those apostolic visits, that a job well done in every classroom will prevent many of the evils to be found in our inner-city ghettos. The task of the teacher is to make every citizen aware of his civic and moral duties towards his neighbor. The frustrations found in the laborious (but glorious) apostolate of teaching are well matched in every other apostolate.

There is no intention here of downgrading the extra apostolic mile all should travel in bearing witness to Christ in nursing, social work, teaching, or whatever the apostolate assigned by the Community. The implications here are for the "restless," and religious Superiors will appreciate that these problems can be prudently foreseen, and solutions for them included, in a Sister Formation program.

By-Product of Apostolic Experiences

A by-product, not sought directly but inherent in apostolic experiences, is the young Sister's increased appreciation of the well-ordered life of the Community which frees her from every social and economic worry and gives her a security that should make for a deep-seated peace of soul. Seeing how "the other half" lives, she will come to wonder at the munificence of the hundredfold that is hers for choosing God as her portion. Her own personal, petty trials will be seen in comparison with the sad realities of life that are common to the poor and underprivileged. She will become a happier and more understanding person in dealing with the troublesome child, the demanding patient, the frustrated adolescent, and the querulous aged or unreasonable adult. All these will become to her not "problem persons" but *persons with problems* —persons closely akin to those to whom Christ ministered and to whom she is called to minister in the spirit of Christ.

Thus it is fully evident that the apostolic element in a Sister's life needs cultivation, interpretation and development. The keeping of the full commandment to love God with one's whole heart and one's neighbor as one's self takes the same degree of formation and preparation as do the skills of a mathematician or of a creative writer. The author of *Love is Not Enough* had a point.[11]

Through the apostolic features of the college curriculum—that is, implementing the teachings of the papal social encyclicals with actual and concrete involvement in the needs and crises of disadvantaged neighborhoods—the student is kept in close touch with the mainstream of society. Regional accrediting agencies rejoice in this, for they see isolation and insularity and overprotectiveness as impossible in a program geared to bringing the Sisterstudent into contact with all the realities of our society as lived today. At the same time such a program tries to foresee the various situations in the future that will call for sound judgment and right decisions when the Sister's pre-service preparation is completed and her active apostolate begins. By this anticipation, helpful factors can be fostered and harmful experiences prevented.

Co-Curricular Activities

The Sister-students of Marillac College often comment on the opportunities for participation in varied co-curricular activities as being one of the most important sources of growth in personality and leadership as well as in the capacity for the intelligent acceptance of leadership.

They elect their own student-participation-in-government officers and committees. The Student Council organizes and directs college activities and is responsible for formulating and enforcing many regulating policies. Activities include such impressive programs as student organization and special patriotic assemblies: Devoir Day (paying its "devoirs" to the Board of Trustees, administration, and

[11] Bruno Bettelheim, *Love is Not Enough* (Glencoe, Ill.: Free Press, 1950).

faculty); Expression Day, including such widely diverse events as Morning Mass (following the Council's liturgical pattern) brunch, picnic, baseball and "track tournaments"; the class play, midyear Shakespeare Festival, planned to include five plays with casting, costuming and "props" managed entirely by the students.

Special Clubs—French, German, Literary, Creative Writing, Camillus (for R.N.'s only), Choral, The Cecilian Ensemble (orchestra) and others—are open to students, but they are limited to two choices.

The students take full responsibility for their own newspaper, photography and lay-out, visiting the printing firm, where they are introduced to the intricacies of press work; they write and edit the college magazine, take turns speaking at the podium, introducing guest lecturers; and serve as class officers—an activity which facilitates the coordinating of all groups from the newest Sister-students of the freshman class to the graduating group.

These co-curricular experiences help to conquer shyness, temper a too aggressive leadership, and develop latent powers for giving and sharing. Only in an all-Sister college could so many outlets be found for the exercise of active and dormant talents which will later be fully developed by their own Communities.

Cultural Co-Curricular Aspects

The cultural program that includes lectures, carefully selected operas, concerts, symposia, panels and literary experiences, such as book reviews, special readings, etc., are planned for more than their immediate objective of enriching and widening the students' intellectual and cultural horizons. With no obvious or forced intrusion, they carry overtones of the spiritual and social, invaluable to the Sister in her future apostolate. For example, one year a series of lectures on comparative religion was given by a priest-theologian with ecumenical vision. This proved tremendously useful in freeing the Sister-students from the shackles of inherited prejudice, fostering an open spirit. The next year the spirit was widened by having a series of lectures on the same topic given by ordained ministers of the different faiths. In this manner a young religious is greatly aided to work with genuine charity and understanding in our pluralistic society.

Book reviews and special readings by the authors themselves are experiences which the Sister-students are still young enough to describe as "thrilling." Not only to have listened to a well-known author talking about his books, or giving readings from them, but to be able to question and later to meet informally with him or her, adds greatly to a Sister's poise and sense of security in an adult, intellectual world.

By no means is it convenience that dictates the time of these cultural opportunities, which are generally placed at 7:00 to 8:30 P.M. There is here the thought of preparing Sisters for their future apostolate. In this age, and in this restless society from which a Sister comes, bearing its impress upon her, it is important that incorporated into a Sister's formation there be a sensible view of an occasional break in routine and all that is entailed in a Sister's being "out" participating in an evening event. Such occasions will later arise from professional meetings, parents' clubs, study discussions, and similar gatherings which necessitate a Sister's absence from her convent until late evening. When these events are introduced gradually as part of life's demands, the Sister comes to see that no more "glamor" attaches to a meeting scheduled for 9:15 P.M. than to one at 9:15 A.M. In this manner a restless desire for the unusual is appeased before it becomes a craving for "something different" in young persons brought up in an era of continual thrill-searching. Far from engendering and deepening a desire for "something different," these unusual occurrences are accepted by the Junior religious in an adult manner—and not as "forbidden fruit" which increases the appetite for the "different." Routine becomes relaxing and refreshing rather than restraining and restricting, once the Sister sees everything in light of her apostolate.

Thus will a Sister be well-grounded in her vocation—the first end of which is unlimited love for God and the neighbor; and the second end, the apostolate to which her Community is committed. This complete, integrated understanding of her vocation, learned early in her formative years, will bring a lifetime peace of soul which will carry her unshaken through inevitable temptations, trials and crosses; and bring a serenity which she will radiate within and outside her Community.

Long-Range Planning

The years ahead will be important for the education and formation of young Sisters. The trend seems to be towards regional Sister Formation Centers. With the type of education and formation these centers can supply, the next decade and a half could well see the Sisters of the United States as the best-prepared teachers and nurses in the country—and even in the entire world. For every Community today is more alert to the needs of the times than ever before.

Marillac College has been asked by many Communities to plan campus housing for future Juniorates. It is now studying housing needs, and, in that spirit of cooperation and collaboration with other Communities so urged by the Holy See, will welcome suggestions as to what might be done to accommodate more Sisters. The North Central Regional Accrediting Agency advised that the college could accept eight hundred more students than it now has without building one extra classroom.

This brings to mind the possible erection of a Convent Co-operative Apartment Building for the smaller Communities who may wish to send four, six, eight or twelve Sisters at a time. Each "Juniorate" apartment would be planned (perhaps by the college, or by some interested Community willing to share in the enterprise) as a completely separated convent apartment. Each would contain individual bedrooms, a community room, an oratory and Mistress's office, complete with private entrances. Chapel, cafeteria, launderette, parlors and reception rooms could be arranged for use in common. Each "Juniorate" could thus provide a separate Community life with proper privacy insured. Larger Congregations could build their own Juniorates, as so many have done or are now doing, suited to their size and needs. Foreign Sisters would be provided for within special "international" accommodations at the college.

Other such Centers will eventually spring up in the various geographical regions of the United States. If excellence, deriving from the spirit and wisdom of the Holy See's directives, is the watchword, there can scarcely be too many.

The once-felt fear that being too far from the Motherhouse might endanger Community spirit has greatly decreased. Marillac, as we have said, now has Sister students from thirty-nine States, and seven foreign countries. Summer and annual retreat periods spent at the Motherhouse take care of the unity and filial love of Community which the special formation encourages. Visits to the college from the Mothers General and Provincials facilitate inter-communication. But one of the real secrets of success lies in the appointment and preparation of the "just right" Mistress of Junior Sisters. Special times need special emphases: society and its varied needs require far-range planning. The different type of girl—"the new breed"—our day is producing, calls for *aggiornamento* in thinking and planning.

Among the 729 different Orders of women in the United States,[12] a welcome variety of thought will issue, in accordance with new directives from Rome. Keeping close to the Church's thinking, religious women will be well kept—for Christ, to and for whom they seek to bear witness in manifold ways, will always be with them. This is the premise and the promise on which each Reverend Mother and her Council will build.

[12] *The Official Catholic Directory,* 1964, pp. 922–955.

8

Role of the Intellect
in the Religious Life

One of the persistent accusations made against the Sister Formation Conference at the outset by persons who were vocal in their opposition but not at all clear on what the Movement called for was: "The Sisters connected with Sister Formation are intellectuals with their heads in the clouds and their feet off the ground. They overemphasize the intellectual and ignore the practical." For one who has worked closely with the Movement since its inception, this is a hard saying. What the Sisters connected with Sister Formation were then, and still are, most concerned about is that the religious and intellectual life of the pre-service Sister shall be so well integrated that it will deeply influence her Community life; that the intellect shall undergird the principles of fraternal charity, and so direct her professional life as to make it truly apostolic—a bearing of witness to Christ.

Meaning of the Word "Formation"

As we have already noted, the very word "formation," as opposed to the word "education," signifies a far greater concern for the total development of the Sister in all the spheres of her Christian, intellectual and Community life than for academic excellence alone. The intention is that these planes of living shall be so fused with her professional and apostolic life that the product of such formation will be a mirror of Christian holiness and an effective religious. Overemphasis on the religious element, without due concern to build on the intellectual, may well result in a person given to "devotional" practices rather than truly fervent. It could result in a religious quite capable of outward conformity, exact as to rule and custom and seemingly prayerful, but unable to bear with the slings and arrows of outrageous fortune and incapable of being purified by the suffering which every true disciple of Christ is bound to encounter in his journey through life on his way back to God.

It is the intellect, well-developed and conditioned to enter into every phase of life—religious, social, professional, apostolic—that insures, not an emotional response to life, but that precious ability to face reality which we often speak of as common sense. It is the intellect that must be developed if we are to see life on God's terms rather than on our own.

Giovanni Battista Cardinal Montini, now Pope Paul VI, when Archbishop of Milan, wrote in his 1957 Pastoral Letter: "Our main problem today is to re-educate the modern mind to think in terms of God." A profound utterance, yet so simple that its profundity may escape us. The main problem of the world, as the now reigning Pontiff sees it, is not in the field of international relations, nor in socio-economics, nor in adjustment to a technological age, but rather in the field of education. His use of the word "re-educate" implies a previous faulty education. To this, educators all over the world will subscribe, although they will differ as to where the fault lies. His Holiness is quite specific: "Man must be re-educated to think in terms of God." Such thinking is central thinking. It begins with God—man's primal cause—from which his thinking will extend in circling eddies to the circumference of his life, leaving no part of it untouched, whether he be statesman, farmer, banker, astronaut, business man, student, or teacher.

In urging a re-education, which will orient man to thinking in terms of God, Pope Paul VI is but phrasing anew St. Paul's reasoned appeal to the Ephesians: "There must be a renewal in the inner life of your mind; you must be clothed with a new self which is created in God's image, justified and sanctified through the truth." (Ephes. 4:23, Knox)[1] To be sanctified through truth

[1] *The Holy Bible*, trans. by Ronald Knox. Copyright 1944, 1948 and 1950, Sheed and Ward, Inc., New York.

we must find truth, and this is the work of the intellect. All education—religious and secular—has as its end to assist the intellect to find truth. But if the search for truth is divorced from God, who *is* Truth, it begins with a false premise; it is to attempt the journey of life with a faulty compass.

The part played by the intellect in the work of man's salvation has been for too long a time and for too many alleged reasons, downgraded. As Frank Sheed states:

> . . . salvation depends directly upon the will. If we love God, we shall ultimately get to God: we shall be saved. . . . But though in our relation to God the intellect does not matter as much as the will . . . it *does* matter, and it is too much neglected—to the great misfortune of the will, for we can never attain a maximum love of God with only a minimum knowledge of God. For the soul's full functioning, we need a Catholic intellect as well as a Catholic will.[2]

To speak in terms of relative importance does not rule out the fact that the less important is not only necessary but essential to the functioning of the whole. Thus it happens that the malfunctioning of a less important part of a machine—or of the human body, for that matter—results in serious malfunctioning, or even nonfunctioning, of the whole machine or of the whole body. What St. Paul said in his masterful summation of the relationships of the members of the Mystical Body can be applied to the faculties of the soul, and to the human person composed of body and soul; one part cannot say to another: "I have no need of thee."

Function of the Intellect

The will, therefore, has absolute need of the intellect. The function of the intellect when it is sufficiently developed, is to know, to judge, to understand. The intellect presents its "findings," as it were, to the will, which then chooses what it deems good, and acts upon its choice. There can be no act of virtue without the cooperation of the intellect. Hence the Christian life has need of the intellect to direct it. Obviously, a person with less intelligence than another can be a person of greater virtue, but to say that he *will* be is a *non sequitur*. In this connection, there is a lesson to

2 *Theology and Sanity* (New York: Sheed & Ward, 1946), p. 3.

be learned from the parable of the talents distributed by the Master to his servants "according to their several abilities." It is quite germane to point out that the servant who had received least from the Master fell under His displeasure, not because he failed to make as large a return in proportion as did his fellow servants, to whom more had been given, but because he failed to make any return at all.

The interdependence of intellect and will was emphasized by His Holiness, Pope Pius XII, in his radio message to the Fifth Inter-American Congress on Catholic Education, held in Havana in 1954:

Good teachers then, should have perfect human formation, intellectual and moral. For the teaching office is a lofty position which calls for intellectual discernment and goodness of heart . . . Good teachers need a professional preparation, at minimum above average, and better still, outstanding at all levels of instruction, and in each of the specialized fields.[3]

Such words are well calculated to destroy the long-cherished notion, held *de facto* if not *de jure,* of the antagonism between the religious and the intellectual.

St. Teresa of Avila, given unofficially the title of Doctor of the Church, was on sound theological ground when she said, "I would rather gather straws through obedience than build cathedrals through self-will." It is noteworthy, however, that not one of the saint's numerous biographers, profound or shallow, depicts her as engaged in straw-gathering; whereas the record stands that she founded seventeen monasteries for women, and with the help of St. John of the Cross, fourteen monasteries for men. Such occupations are rather akin to cathedral-building. No biograher shows where the reformer did not use to the full her spiritual powers of intellect and will in effecting the reform.

Anti-Intellectual Bias in America

That American Catholics inherited an anti-intellectual bias has been exposed and explained by the Church's friends and exploited by her foes; the truth involved in both attack and defense we can-

3 "Formation of Teachers," *Radio Message to the Fifth Inter-American Congress on Catholic Education*, January 12, 1954, D.R. 15, 563, St. Paul Edition.

not gainsay. What we can and should take cognizance of is the fact that circumstances have changed. What was true as late as a quarter of a century ago is not true today. With the amazingly rapid development of an alert and informed Catholic laity, following with intensity the liturgical movement, biblical studies, and papal encyclicals, and bringing the Church's teaching on social and family life into spheres of influence, the Catholic intellectual atmosphere has radically changed. The explanations once offered for Catholic anti-intellectualism are no longer valid. Monsignor John Tracy Ellis, in his historic, conscience-prodding treatise on *American Catholics and the Intellectual Life,* published in 1956, states in the closing pages of the book:

There is not a man of discernment anywhere today who is unaware that the intellectual climate of the United States is undergoing a radical change from the moribund philosophy of materialism and discredited liberalism that has ruled a good portion of the American mind for the better part of a century.[4]

Catholics have arrived at the full stature of accepted United States citizenship. They are involved in the quickening intellectual change. All indications are that the possibility pointed out and the hope expressed by Monsignor Ellis nearly ten years ago are now being fulfilled:

To whom, one may ask, may the leaders of the coming generation turn, with more rightful expectancy in their search for enlightenment and guidance in the realm of religion and morality, than to the American Catholic intellectual?[5]

Sisters above all are the gainers, in this changed climate. If the late Pope John XXIII opened a window in the Church to let in streams of fresh, invigorating air, his predecessor, Pope Pius XII, had done the same for religious Orders of women. Through papal utterances and urging, the role of the intellect in the religious life has been made clear, and its use mandatory.

This was sorely needed, for if American Catholics in general

4 Chicago, Illinois: Heritage Foundation, Inc., 1956, p. 58.
5 *Ibid.,* p. 59.

were educationally handicapped by their immigrant origins, the economic conditions and deep-seated prejudices of the day made intellectual development almost impossible. Religious, devoted to the active apostolate of the Church, had a difficulty far more radical to cope with. In a chapter of his book *Catholic Dimension in Higher Education* entitled "At the Sources," Justus George Lawler points out that in the Constitution of almost no active Order, either of men or women, founded since the 16th century, are the primary ends of the Order—the perfection of the individual through a deep love of God and fraternal charity—and the secondary end—the particular apostolic work of the Order (teaching, care of the sick, etc.)—treated as a unit. As a result, "Far from being regarded as harmonious aspects of a complete whole, or as reciprocally related causes of an organic unity, they are often conceived to be in opposition to each other."[6] This applies equally to the early Communities founded in the United States and is, perhaps, one of the reasons for so many Sisters failing to look upon their work, when dictated by God's will, as prayer. To labor is really to pray.

"*At the Sources*"

In the writings of the founders of early Communities, some of whom have been canonized, there are found passages which, while not unorthodox, are narrow and restricted. They were intended as warnings against excesses and conditions of their times. When these passages are taken from the context of both theme and times, they can be construed not only as anti-intellectual but also as anti-natural. Exceedingly pertinent is the fact that most of the Orders were engaged in the field of education and were bound by the traditions and attitudes they inherited. Nothing could have freed them from a grave (though unwitting) disservice to the Church, to their respective Orders, and to the memory of their founders save the word of the highest Superior of all religious: The Pope.

In one succinct sentence, Pius XII reconciled contemporary progress with filial piety: "Do what your holy founders would do *now* if they were living." Looking back, the members of

6 Westminster: Newman Press, 1959, pp. 54–55.

practically all religious Communities will discern that their
founders were not only innovators, but in many things revolu-
tionaries. This is true not only of the active Orders but of the
purely contemplative Orders as well, as witness *Three Religious
Rebels* by Dom Raymond. These "rebels" saw what their times
needed; they saw that action must be taken—and they took it. As
a companion sentence to the one quoted, religious were armed
with the words of His Holiness: "Serve the world of today as it
needs to be served *today*." One might say that the active Orders
of religious are the richest legatees of Pope Pius XII.

But, to come really to grips with the question of the contributions of the intellectual to the Christian life, let us admit that anti-
intellectualism goes farther back than conditions existing in early
United States history, and farther back than Community-inherited
ideas of 17th century Europe. It goes back to the first man's revolt
against His Creator. As a result of that revolt, man's will was
weakened and his understanding darkened. In plain terms, one
of the results of original sin is that man must earn his intellectual
bread, as well as his material bread, "in the sweat of his brow."
The man who gives testimony by his arduous intellectual efforts
to the maxim: "Knowledge makes a bloody entrance," is struggling
against the effects of original sin as much as, or even more than,
is the man who plows a field. Sloth is one of the deadly sins, but
rarely, if ever, do we hear it connected with the intellect. We
hear continuously from readings in ascetical literature, conferences,
and retreat masters of the dangers of intellectual pride. How often
is the warning sounded against intellectual sloth? Here may well
be matter of serious examination of conscience.

Role of the Intellect in Salvation

Christ Himself indicated the role the intellect must play in
salvation when asked the question: "What shall I do to inherit
eternal life?" His reply was, "Thou shalt love the Lord thy God
with thy whole heart and thy whole soul and thy whole strength
and thy whole mind." God demands specifically the service of the
mind, as well as that of the heart and soul, so that such service *is*
sanctity, for the essence of sanctity is doing God's will.

Far too long has the word "intelligent" held a praiseworthy, desirable connotation, while "intellectual" evoked something of the patronizing and tolerant, if not downright condemnatory. Certainly there are few Sisters who would not resent being told, "Sister, you are not intelligent," while there are (as yet) few who would recognize the full compliment in the comment, "Sister, you are an intellectual." Yet, an intellectual is not necessarily a person endowed with an extraordinary amount of intellect, but rather one endowed with an extraordinary capacity for hard, gruelling, continuous, intellectual labor. The adage "Genius is one part inspiration and ninety-nine parts perspiration" is not mere persiflage; it is a practical truth.

A Sister cannot be totally dedicated to the intellectual, inasmuch as she has made a total commitment of herself to Christ, and this includes more than just the intellectual. But she can and must recognize as a matter of course that professional excellence cannot be attained without a firm intellectual basis. Almost routinely the professions of nursing, teaching and social work (professions in which the largest percentages of Sisters are engaged) reject an applicant who is not in the upper third of her class. Qualifying intellectually does not insure acceptance, since personality, temperament and character are sometimes of even greater importance. It may be logically assumed that if these personal factors are satisfactory, the intellect has played a decisive role in developing them.

If Sisters who are principals of schools, directors of nursing education, and deans of colleges take the intellectual so largely into account in admitting students, it is not surprising that Major Superiors think it wise to give thoughtful appraisal when considering applicants for the Community, since the Church makes "average intelligence" a requirement for assuming the obligations of the religious life. It is true that the grace of God can act independently of human means, but it is equally true that such is not the ordinary way of Providence. "Not I, but the grace of God within me," said the indefatigable Apostle of the Gentiles, indicating how, in the service of Christ, he used both his enormous natural and his supernatural endowments. St. Paul sets the pattern for the integration of the moral and intellectual, in one's personal life, in social life, and in apostolic activities.

Pauline Spirit Needed

Sisters truly need a Pauline spirit to meet the demands of today's world, and providentially the directives of the Church to religious leave no excuse for not attempting to meet these demands. Pope John XXIII, in his *Letter to Women Religious,* prior to the opening of the Ecumenical Council, wrote:

Let all those who dedicate themselves to the active life remember that it is not by prayer alone but also by works that we shall obtain a new orientation of society based on the Gospel. . . . And since in the fields of education, charity and social work one cannot make use of persons not prepared to meet the exacting conditions of present regulations, busy yourselves under obedience at studying and obtaining the diplomas necessary to overcome all obstacles. Thus, apart from your professional competence, your spirit of devotion, patience and sacrifice will be better appreciated.[7]

Now is the acceptable time, now is the day of intellectual renaissance. Sisters can no longer, as individuals or as Communities, hide a disinclination for intellectual work behind the excuse of an American anti-intellectual climate, or kindred factors in their European origin. Their deeper doubts, their painful uncertainties as to the effect of their intellectual efforts upon their growth in holiness, should have been laid to rest by Rome. Never before in the history of the Church has the Holy See been so much concerned with the religious, intellectual and professional preparation of Sisters. Since 1952 the Sacred Congregation of Religious has continued its urgent and repeated directives for the establishment of Juniorates, where young religious will learn that no dichotomy between the intellectual and the religious life need exist. This is giving young religious an excellent start—or rather a start towards excellence. When enough of these young graduates of Juniorates have joined the ranks of those already in the field, newcomers should find that these graduates have maintained the

7 Pp. 12–13.

same high integrity, the same regard of learning for learning's sake, as well as for its use in the apostolate, the same attitude towards Christian ideals and intellectual scholarship which, in the Juniorate, they learned to associate with the religious life—and they must find them more abundantly.

To serve the world as it needs to be served *today* demands that we be competent to defend Christian ideas, Christian thought, Christian principles on every level. Fire must be fought with fire, and today we are at war with ideas and ideologies. The Church needs all of the intellectual power that it can summon. By acquiring such power, along with spiritual, social and apostolic strength, a Sister will develop and completely fulfill her religious vocation. This cannot be done without serious intellectual effort.

The Need for Discipline

The rigorous discipline of scholarly endeavor parallels the discipline of religious life itself. The first condition to make progress in either is the observance of silence. There is a symbolism found in the silence that reigns in two places of every Catholic College or University: The Chapel and the Library. In the former dwells the Incarnate Word; in the latter, live on the imperishable words of great thinkers and writers, as well as the temporarily helpful words of lesser minds. Both chapel and library require, for a fruitful visit, silence and reflection. The self-restraint of silence is required for study wherever it is carried on.

In the intellectual realm, silence means much more than refraining from conversation. It means concentration on the subject studied, a reasoned approach to it, seeking far more than the printed page presents, correlating it mentally with other knowledge, and restricting memory to its proper sphere of usefulness. The mind thus disciplined is the same mind the Sisters will take to meditation and to ascetical reading, which require the same intellectual effort.

Serious devotion to the intellectual life—not to be identified with the too facile "I love to study" frequently heard—requires, even as religious life itself requires, order. Order is not, as a proverb has it, heaven's first law, but it leads to heaven's first law,

Charity. The Sister must order her day, with due attention to all of the requirements of her life as a religious, so that she can devote her time tranquilly to the hours set aside for study. What is the most frequently heard excuse offered by Sisters for their neglect of—not to say aversion for—intense, intellectual occupation? "I haven't time."

A corrective would be for a Sister to make notes, actual notes— if she is in earnest in serving the Church with her intellect as well as her will—of what she *has* time for. A fifteen-minute telephone conversation that could have been concluded cordially in three; a half-hour's desultory discussion carried on through mere complaisance; the giving of prime time—time when one is most alert mentally and assured of no interruptions—to cleaning cupboards, arranging files, the doing of household chores that need not be done at the time; or taking time to complain that one has no time.

Then there are the larger delaying tactics of impulsively offering one's services for some inconsequential work, arranging for a demonstration of a new piece of equipment, suddenly remembering "I've put off going to the art museum for three months; I'll go today." Anything to serve as a justification for delaying intellectual work! Here is where spiritual stamina, derived from a life of self-denial, should come to life and action.

Devitalizing Luxury of Delay

Following the line of least resistance never yet made a saint or a student. The Sister who has a supernatural viewpoint will face a difficult mental task with the same spirit of faith with which she faces a difficult manual task, or other work of the apostolate, and she will not permit herself the devitalizing luxury of delay.

A highly successful business executive stated that he credited his success to adherence to the motto: "Do the hard things first." The crustiest customer was placed first on his list of appointments; the most difficult interview had priority on his agenda; the conference with his colleagues in which harassing problems had to be discussed was held as soon as possible after his arrival at the office. Doing the hard things first meant that they were attacked when he had his full, undrained mental and physical powers. Doing the hard things first increased his self-assurance, added to his courage, gave him a sense of freedom to face the less difficult things of the day.

A Sister's day is partially ordered by the demands of Community living—varying from assisting at Holy Mass to taking recreation—and the actual hours which her specific duty claims. But aside from these, a Sister can plan her day or her week—for some days are more routinely filled than others—so as to give the intellectual its due. Sisters who cannot find time for this should reappraise their motivation.

Perhaps in years not too far past, there could be found in religious Communities some justification for anti-intellectualism. But today, when the lines are clearly drawn so that either Christian or Communistic ideology must prevail; when Major Superiors are giving the finest opportunities to their subjects to assume leadership, not only in their own ranks but among the laity as well, no Sister can blind herself to the need for developing her intellectual powers. Conscience forces her to realize that she must, in a spirit of service to the Church, face and conquer the hardships of a dedication to study, even as her forebears conquered physical hardships.

Manual Labor Required in an Earlier Era

To meet the needs of their day the vanguard of Sisters in the United States had, frequently as an auxiliary to their particular apostolate, to chop their own firewood, milk cows, plow fields and walk miles of country road soliciting donations. These arduous tasks must certainly have interfered frequently with the horarium. In the annals of one such Community is found the following extract from a letter, written by the local Superior: "Since there are only four of us here, on wash days, two of us get up to do the washing at 3:00 A.M., while two Sisters stay in bed until 4:45 'to keep the Rule.'" Parenthetically, let us remark that we read with admiration such change of the horarium in favor of manual labor!

The present generation of Superiors have shown themselves worthy successors of their predecessors by giving much more than a nod of approval to such changes as the horarium requires in favor of intellectual labors. Those Sisters of an earlier era grew to giant stature in holiness, not because of the humbleness and the hardness of their tasks, but because of their response to what God demanded of them *then*. It is intellectual effort He demands of us now, and we cannot accept the comforts of a "push-button" age, which frees us from manual drudgery, without making a return of exacting labor in another field.

However, it would be a mistake to underestimate the part played by the intellectual in the religious lives of our pioneer Sisters. Most of them came with the intention of teaching, many had several generations of educational traditions behind them. Teaching was also the initial occupation of early American-founded Communities, with other works added as needs developed. If the integration of all areas of a Sister's life was not formalized as it needs must be today, it was there in fact. These Sisters laid the foundations for the expansion of their Communities, both in numbers and in works. But the techniques and materials used in laying the foundations of a building are not those used in putting in windows and doors. Not even the same artisans are employed for these different tasks.

The foundations of the Church and of religious Communities in the United States were well laid; succeeding generations added the superstructure. What are needed now are more windows and doors; windows through which may shine the teachings of the Church, not only in matters of doctrine, but in every area and interest of man's life; more doors through which an attracted, informed multitude may enter. It is the duty of today's Sister to do her work as well as did the Sister of yesterday, in order that there be Sisters for tomorrow.

No Conflict Between Reason and Emotion

Continuous concentrated intellectual effort contributes to emotional stability. Regrettably, there is no word in the English language to express an emotion except the word "feel." Psychologists make a nice distinction, but for the purpose of this chapter the usual equation will be accepted. Clearly, when a person says, "I feel comfortable," there is slight emotion involved. But when a Sister says, "I don't feel like studying," her emotions are aroused. She may have a dislike for a particular subject, she may fear failure. She may, through an aversion for any intellectual effort, employ certain defense mechanisms against it. Striving for excellence in the intellectual realm, she professes to regard as "worldly," and hints that Sisters who take every occasion offered to enrich their already broad and deep studies are selfish. Because the accrediting agencies or the State require it, she will obtain the degree or degrees that she must. Such a Sister may accumulate the necessary number of credits in much the same fashion as a man, obliged to go from one place to another, considers only the miles he covers, taking no notice of the scenery through which he passes or the people he meets. He arrives at his new destination as immature as he set out, and even proud that there has been no fundamental change in him. He has no desire to travel farther, and has no real desire to grow.

Maturation requires the discipline of emotions so controlled that they will serve but never dominate. Contrary to common opinion—or to an opinion commonly expressed—reason and emotion are not by their nature in conflict. The highest emotion, that of love, leads, when necessary, to complete self-sacrifice. But just as love, when directed to a noble object, something or someone superior to the person loving, enriches, so love directed towards something or someone else for its own ends is basically self-love, and impoverishes.

A so-called "love for study," lacking the proper motivation of a search for truth, as manifested by the Supreme Truth found not only in doctrine and dogma by way of philosophy and theology, but in science, mathematics, history, art, or any other subject to which man applies himself, is self-love. Lacking the proper motivation, one may enter the intellectual arena through ambition, the desire for prestige, or an eagerness for power that is one of the potentials of knowledge. The resultant intellectual pride must be attributed not to intellectual effort but to intellectual imperfection, and the ordering of a good toward an improper end, since such a person will have used his intellect through egocentric, and not theocentric, love.

That Sisters, like all intelligent beings, must love God with their wills they readily admit. But that their wills need to be vastly strengthened by development of the intellect, some have been slow to accept beyond a certain—what they term, practical—point. The duties assigned run the gamut from kindergarten teacher to college dean, from staff nurse to administrator of a hospital, from manager of a kitchen to director of a social agency. Whatever the duty, it demands, even as the love of God demands, the use of the mind as well as that of the heart, the strength and the will.

Difficulties Handicap the Intellect

The first difficulty in the way of worthwhile intellectual work is to overcome the inherent inertia which most persons, some highly gifted, have towards doing such work at all.[8] The great Samuel Johnson ordered his servants to tie him to his chair, before which he had placed paper and pens, so that he might be thus physically compelled to write. Sisters cannot resort to such means, but it would be interesting for each one to check on her activities when she does have the time, the solitude, and the place for study. She pauses to adjust the light, to regulate the heat or cold, to get just one more reference book, to dust an already dustless desk; she finds life-saving relief if her typewriter ribbon is a bit dim, thus furnishing a faultless excuse for delaying for another ten minutes the actual getting down to hard work.

Once the moment for real work has begun, she faces the next obstacle to be hurdled, the control of her imagination. But, the protest will be made, the imagination is a creative power which has given to the world the imperishable masterpieces of sculpture, art, literature, architecture. Before they came into existence, the Pietà was seen in a block of marble, an immortal painting in a woman sitting meditatively in a rocker, medieval cathedrals in stone and marble quarries, far from the site of the ultimate build-

[8] For an interesting chapter on time and its use in intellectual work see A. D. Sertillanges, O.P., *The Intellectual Life* (Westminster: Newman Press, 1960), Ch. IV, "The Time of Work," pp. 69–100.

ing. But any power, physical or mental, which can be used for great good can also be used for evil. It is a controlled imagination that will enable us to appreciate, improve and pass on our contemporary culture to posterity.

To verify the ramifications of imagination a Sister has only to review her too frequent experience at mental prayer. She listens to the subject read, or reads one of her own selection; before memory and reason can perform their proper functions, imagination takes over, creating images of persons, incidents, phases of the Sister's duty quite different from the subject of prayer, often quite divorced from reality. She reconstructs an interview with her Superior, and refutes with keen but respectful irony some remarks made to her yesterday. She accepts with gracious poise, *summa cum laude,* a degree towards which she is to start to work in the fall. She parries with courteous cleverness some out-of-place questions which she may be asked at evening recreation. The clock indicates the termination of meditation, and the Sister can say, with a nuance not intended by the pious writer who phrased it, "The time of meditation is all too short."

All are familiar with the havoc a free-rein imagination can work in a Sister's Community or social life. When "I think" is identified with "I imagine" the results are persecution complexes, jealousies, and breaches of charity. Many of the unpleasantnesses of Community living would be eliminated by the discipline of the imagination which serious, continuous, intellectual work requires, and in which the imagination plays such a dramatic role. This is only to say what Frank Sheed has said so unconditionally: "There is nothing to be done with the intellect until imagination has been put firmly in its place."[9]

Discipline of Memory and Understanding

A disciplined memory distinguishes both saint and scholar from the dilettante in their respective fields. Education by rote has long since passed into the discard. It is not so apparent that "rote" does not still play too large a part in a Sister's formation. In the beginning of the religious life, memory must of necessity precede

[9] *Op. cit.,* p. 12.

understanding. The postulant, ecstatically happy, miserably con-
fused or stoically calm, must use her memory to keep in mind the
time for exercises, places of silence, restricted topics of conversation, and all the details of acceptable modes of exterior conduct
which the Community requires. But the acceptable, stable, satisfactory religious cannot be formed by memory alone, nor can she
be judged to be virtuous because she remembers what she is told to
do and does it with such exactitude as to time, place and manner.
Unless she understands the *why* of what she is doing, she will never
attain to religious, intellectual or social maturity.

Knowledge, which is the end of study, requires for its acquisition
both memory and understanding. Without memory, there could
be no acquisition of knowledge; but knowledge without understanding would be but so much impedimenta. In the intellectual
field, memory and understanding must be teammates, which require
different handling. Memory must be held in check, its activities
confined to the intellect's immediate goal on which its undiverted
attention must be fixed. Contrariwise, understanding must be
prodded to sustained and arduous effort, until it has assimilated,
weighed, analyzed and judged what memory has fastened upon.
Connections must be established, cause and effect determined and
conclusions drawn.

It is immediately obvious that the directed teamwork of memory
and understanding which lead to convictions subsequently acted
on by the will are precisely those demanded by a strong, sustaining
interior life. The carrying over into the moral life of habits formed
in intellectual pursuits will be complementary to the carry-over
of Christian principles into the intellectual life. The result is a
Sister who after formation is no longer "hyphenated," Sister-
student or student-Sister, but one person, the integrated religious.

In passing it is well to note that a teacher, whether of nursery-
school children or graduate students, encourages the asking of
questions, deeming this to be an excellent sign of interest and proof
of a desire to know more of the subject and thoroughly understand
it. Would it not be well if the same interpretation were placed on
questions raised honestly and respectfully by Sisters, in the realm
not only of Community usages and customs, but of Community-

taught attitudes and policies, when such questions are directed to those responsible for their formation? Both subjects and Superiors gain by this form of uninhibited communication.

Better Rapport with Superiors

The Sister who is encouraged to seek reasons, the better to understand, gains not only by having her questions answered but by the establishment of a deeper rapport with her Superior. The Superior gains by experiencing the satisfaction of having settled a Sister's doubts. But she may also experience the far greater gain of having questions aroused in her own mind by the frank exposé of how matters—which she has for years taken for granted—appear to another generation of religious. She may be aroused to deep thought of the immediate and personal effects of the routinely made remark, "We live in a different world." The very creativity that doubt breeds may lead us to further and more creative experience.

There is yet another area in which the interdependence of the religious and the intellectual are involved, and that is the area of health. Here one must tread lightly and speak tentatively because the unpredictable elements of personality and temperament, of environmental and social situations, are involved. But it would be less than forthright to ignore the fact that "All this studying" is not infrequently cited as a contributing element in—if not the main cause of—a Sister's break in health, mental, physical, or both. "A sound mind in a sound body" has long been the desideratum of the natural man, and it is a desirable goal for the supernatural man. Physical health cannot be maintained without exercise; the same holds good for the health of the mind.

The growing number of ailments—from ulcers to asthma—which come under the classification of psychosomatic is proof of the need for helpful, complementary interaction of body and mind. Study, supernaturally motivated, does not mean merely, "I study because I am told to," though it certainly does include the all-important element of obedience. Having been assigned to study, the Sister is eager to find Truth both in the natural and supernatural order, and she finds that persevering study engenders an interest and enthusiasm which will have beneficial repercussions on her physical health.

Work cures the pains of work and those of the worker; it is the foe of annoyances, sickness, since it lifts us into a high region where the vexations of life and the weaknesses of the body find alleviation. The urge it rouses, the direction it gives to our energy, are an anodyne for worry and release us from wretched preoccupation.[10]

All this, of course, within the limits of good sense and good judgment. The Sister who studies through proper motivation and under proper guidance will maintain emotional balance. She will not expect too much of herself, which leads to frustration, nor too little, which results in boredom. But here is where she should seek counsel of her Superiors, who should be realistic in advising her. It requires perception and a sense of realism for Superiors to recognize when they have misjudged a Sister's intellectual, psychological and physical ability to carry on higher studies, and release her from a situation that may perpetuate frustration and strain. On the other hand, a Sister should be realistic in her own self-appraisal, and if she finds herself incapable of advanced study, or even of undergraduate work, she should represent this fact to her Superiors. Peace of soul, emotional balance and good physical health for each Sister will always take precedence in Superiors' judgment over success in studies too dearly paid for by both the Sister and the Community she hopes to serve.

Dangers of a Weak Intellectual Life

A weak intellectual life, like a weak religious life, engenders a sense of emptiness from which a Sister attempts to escape, consciously by the constant seeking of shallow pleasures, or subconsciously by the development of some form of socially unacceptable behavior which she attributes to stress of one kind or another. A modicum of stress is inherent in all purposeful work, manual or mental—making a pie or writing a dissertation.

When opportunity has been given for Sisters to develop in an

10 A. D. Sertillanges, O.P., *The Intellectual Life*, p. 249.

integrated manner, using all their skills and talents, they have a sense of achievement, an assurance of having made a real contribution to the common good. Such Sisters will be less vulnerable to mental illness, and better equipped to accept, as a salutary cross, those illnesses, chronic or acute, which have a demonstrable physical basis.

There is no phase of life—physical, mental or moral—which does not have need of the intellect to enlighten, develop and strengthen it. Where the intellect is not called upon to make its contribution in the measure that it should, undesirable results ensue: the religious life offers no challenge, for the apathy of routine and the habit of formalism take over. At the same time, the fruits of the Spirit of Wisdom: charity, joy, peace, patience, as well as the gifts of understanding and fortitude, are manifestly lacking.

These are some of the reasons why the intellect must have a large part in any sound Sister Formation program. Overemphasis here would be as detrimental as it would be in any other area of a Sister's life. It would create the same imbalance as any overemphasis on the religious, social and professional would. Too much stress on the intellectual is apt to make one anti-social; overemphasis on the social can make one frivolous, or certainly incapable of sustained intellectual and professional effort at excellence; overemphasis on the professional militates against a deep interior life. Overemphasis on the religious aspects of Community life will surely perpetuate the seeming dichotomy between work and prayer that can so confuse a Sister, otherwise truly concerned with being a good, well-balanced person. These are the dangers that the accent on *integration* in a Sister Formation program seeks to avoid.

Scripture tells us that the world is lost because no man thinks in his heart. This points up not only the need of the intellect in one's Christian life, but the role that thinking plays in the salvation of the world. It may well be that the young Sister's future apostolate in contemporary society could be summed up in the words of Paul VI, indicating what he regards as the most pressing need of today: to help modern man think in terms of God.

9

Religious Vocations
in Contemporary Society

Today, religious women are being paid the highest possible compliment by society—it wants *more* of them. Eagerly the Catholic laity, no small segment of society, ask that Sisters come out and walk more freely and frequently among them. One might say diffidently, with awe at the thought, that Sisters are being asked to imitate Christ when He emerged from the hidden life of Nazareth to begin His public life, sharing the common concerns of men. The world needed redemption, so Christ came and, by His life and death, redeemed it. Now, Sisters are asked to bear witness to that redemption by entering actively into the insecurity, uncertainty, turmoil and torment of contemporary society. As we saw in a preceding chapter, this calls for a sound practical as well as an academic foundation before the Sister is ready to return to the society so eagerly awaiting her services. That this society has left its impress upon her is undeniable; but it is an impress which Communities seek not to eliminate but to modify.

Never was the world so unsure of itself, and with reason. Man's whole civilization is threatened. Technology has outrun man's power of adaptation. Human science has invented weapons which will many times "over-kill," but man's moral sense has not yet overcome the obstacle of "under-love." Mass media of communication and of transportation have so shrunken the world that all men are neighbors—while few men are friends.

New Days, New Challenges

Small wonder, then, that Sisters, with their inner source of strength and security deriving from their dedication to Christ, are asked by the Church and by their fellow men to give more fully of themselves. At this moment, religious Communities face the greatest challenge of their history; a history going back to the days of Christ when He issued the invitation to those who would be most closely associated with Him, to do so in the way of evangelical perfection—the way of voluntary poverty, chastity and obedience.

The crowds pressed upon Christ and asked much of Him. The crowds press upon religious women today and ask much of them. No longer is the laity satisfied to have Sisters merely teach each generation from early childhood to adulthood; no longer is it content that they be ministered to only by Sisters' nursing skills; no longer is it willing to see Sisters restricted to a maternal role towards the foundling and the aged, the orphan and the lonely, the handicapped and the delinquent; no longer is it deemed sufficient for Sisters to teach catechism at home and spread the Faith abroad. Today, the laity wants *more*. It presses for Sisters to become acquainted with them and their families; to be conversant with their economic and political interests, their sociological and psychological stresses. Society wants Sisters to feel with them the pressures of interracial tensions, the burden of unfair labor practices, the contradiction of thirty-five million poor in the richest nation in the world.

What emphasizes this as a phenomenon is that it comes at a time when, with good reason, we are calling this the age of the laity. In fact, we have here the meeting of two phenomena, for the rapid rise of the laity to the position it now occupies in the Church is nothing less than astounding; at the same time, laymen want the Sisters at their side. To an extent never before known in the history of the Church in the United States, the Catholic laity is well-informed, interested and active in all that concerns the Church. Laymen are giving not only of their material means—this they have always done generously—but of their talents, business abilities, civic and social contacts to spread the Church's influence and increase its prestige. It is *this* laity, intellectual and enthusiastic, prudent and prosperous, eager for its own sanctification, that asks more of Sisters, indicates new avenues of service in which they would be welcome, and calls on them to make themselves more accessible to society.

Two Conclusions Evident

From this practically universal situation, two conclusions are evident. The first is that Sisters in the past and in the present have done their work so well as to win for themselves the esteem and confidence of the laity, and to have left an indelible impress upon them. The second is that Sisters, by reason of their *being Sisters,* with all that the title implies, have something to give to the laity that they want and need, and which they cannot find elsewhere. This is the challenge that, at this moment, is laid down. This is the challenge that the Church wishes religious women to take up.

The thought is sobering. Far from contributing to complacency among Sisters, it could be profoundly disturbing—and to some it is. The platitude, the cliché, "The world is changing" becomes a startling reality when Sisters see on every hand that religious Communities, too, are changing. Conformity to what was done in the past, even in the days of the holy founders and foundresses, no longer serves as a lodestone; traditions long deemed sacrosanct are now being questioned. That this questioning attitude is accepted by the majority of Sisters intelligently and in a spirit of faith is due to the wise foresight of the Church. Rome has its finger on the pulse of time, past and present. Foreseeing the present situation a full ten years ago, Rome has taken large and sweeping measures. In some instances only radical measures will prepare the Sisters for the new and fuller role they are to play in society. This new role will have to be played by the Sister of today, for there is no other. New recruits must come from the society of *now,* since the "now" is all we have. A flood of new recruits to the religious life is needed if the calls of society are to be answered. This flood is not in evidence. Why?

Vocation Shortage

If a business is to succeed, it must attract more and more customers. If a product is to sell consistently, it must have more and more satisfied buyers who find that its advertising claims have real merit. Just at the moment, the business of being a religious is not attracting enough customers, and it is losing too many that it does attract. Let us face it. Truth is often embarrassing to confront, but it is lethal if ignored. The giving of one's self to Christ, a life of dedication to God by vows, the goal of which is so deep a love of God and so wide a fraternal charity as to make a religious life, according to St. Vincent de Paul, "a veritable paradise on earth," does not appear to be backing up its advertising claims. Yet it has the best sales slogan ever invented, not only because of its attractive, generous promises, but because of the reliability and unquestionable integrity of its inventor: "Everyone that hath left house or brethren or sisters or father or mother or wife or children or lands, for My name's sake, shall receive an hundredfold and shall possess life everlasting." (Matt. 19:29) There is no question but that this is an attractive offer. Why, then, are there so few takers?

Why are the words "vocation crisis," "Sister shortage," and similar terms, on all lips, while Catholic journalists, religious and lay, write a score of books and hundreds of articles on the subject? The explanation most commonly put forward is the state of today's society. Detailed, the surface explanation sets forth as obstacles to a girl's following Christ's call to the religious life (for no one denies that He *does* give the call) these factors: the instability of family life, the debasing effects of mass media entertainment, the attractions of financial independence, the deplorable practice of steady dating begun in the too early teens, and the softness of American youth.

Catholic Lay Action

On a higher plane we hear, and this often from religious themselves, that Catholic Action, in its many fertile and laudable forms, satisfies the desire of fervent Catholic youth to serve the

Church, and that for those young women who desire to go further, but who do not wish to enter any of the well-known active Orders, there are secular institutes. Then there are girls who stifle the call to a religious life by a self-reassuring "I can do more good in the world." This, of course, shows an ignorance of the very nature of a religious vocation, which is a call to perfection; a call to *be* something, not only to *do* something. For this ignorance who is to blame? Religious themselves. The retailer must not depend entirely upon the sales slogan to sell his goods.

Peace Corps and Papal Volunteers

In answer to the first classification of obstacles to following the call to a religious life—all of which are indictments of American youth as lacking in moral fibre and wanting in the spirit of sacrifice—the success of the Peace Corps, Papal Volunteers, and similar associations disproves this assessment. In reference to the Peace Corps, our government laid on the line the conditions for acceptance: "He must dedicate himself to the service of others, and he must have the conviction, perseverance and stamina to perform the services in the face of hardship and frustration." This is quite different from the "Well, give it a try, anyway, you can always leave," which is proffered, sometimes by priests, to many not-quite-decided aspirants to the religious life. Poverty? In answer to the question, "What will the volunteers be paid while abroad?" The one-word answer is, "Nothing." It is explained that they will receive allowances to pay for food, clothing, and incidental expenses, according to the standard of living in the country to which a member of the Peace Corps is assigned.

This remuneration is identical with that which a Sister receives from her Community, "in kind" rather than in money. On his severance from the Peace Corps, a young man will receive seventy-five dollars for each month of service.[1] The amount is the equivalent of the average school Sister's "salary." Any qualified American citizen, male or female, over eighteen years of age is eligible for the Peace Corps. The thousands of applicants prove that the

---

[1] *U.S. Peace Corps Fact Book*, April 1, 1961, Washington, D.C., p. 9.

spirit of self-sacrifice is alive and burning today in the hearts of American boys and girls. Their response shows how seriously they took the challenge of the late President Kennedy's words in his inaugural address: "Ask not what your country can do for you—ask what you can do for your country."

It is only fair to add, however, that the Peace Corps and Papal Volunteers ask only two years of one's life. Christ, in giving a religious vocation, asks a total giving—one's *whole* life. Therein may lie a partial answer. It is also true that the Peace Corps offers in the field of service an element of novelty which has been termed the "fifth need of man." Consequently, the answering of such a call is far from being an exact parallel to answering the call to a religious vocation. The latter calls for a total and timeless dedication.

But the recruitment methods used by those seeking to fill the ranks of the Peace Corps *et al* might profitably be pondered by religious Communities in their efforts to increase vocations. Those patriotic agencies do not minimize or play down the amount of sacrifice involved, nor do they persistently present the advantages offered by the agency. Personal growth through voluntarily assumed hardships, the satisfaction of having used one's time and talents for the betterment of one's fellow man, and the ennobling sense of having served one's country—these are the only rewards promised. Those who respond do so with the conviction that they are taking up the challenge of President Kennedy's words: "Ask not what your country can do for you; ask what you can do for your country."

It is not impossible that the idea of Peace Corps service might seem more attractive to a young girl today than would the more austere invitation of total dedication in the religious life. Even older Sisters may come to say to themselves—and perhaps many more do than we would like to believe—"Maybe I could serve God, souls and society better in the world. There I could bring Christ to the market place (a favorite expression without an accompanying geographical or local explanation) in many areas— political, social, economic—from which not only my religious habit, but also my rules bar me. Or I could work among the cultured classes; I could bring Christ to tea tables, literary gatherings, social clubs, and associations for charitable purposes."

Such temptations—let us not balk nor hedge at the honest medieval word, emasculated to the libido-ego-id of modern terminology—are markedly like to the specious proposition made to Christ to throw Himself down from a height and, by remaining unharmed, prove His divinity. The ability to do clear, straight, intellectual thinking will lead a Sister to the source of grace and enlightenment more surely than will a dozen frantically made novenas to "put the thought out of my mind." Here will be proved the value of a sound, pre-service foundational formation, which forewarns and forearms against such temptations. A formation which consistently integrates the religious and the intellectual will serve a Sister well in reasoning such temptations through to a proper conclusion.

Teen-Age of Community Life

Such thoughts do not usually trouble a Sister in the early years of her vocation but come rather in what we may term the "teen-age" of the religious life; that is between twelve and twenty years after entering the convent. Dedication does not exempt one from discouragement, doubts, restlessness, for "weariness, too, is a law, the ebb tide of the spirit's flow." This state of mind is accentuated if the Sister has heard of "a temporary vocation," as some very few members of the clergy hold.

Then, too, change is usually a painful ordeal, and there is scarcely a Community left unchanged by Pope Pius XII's doctrine of *aggiornamento*. *Aggiornamento* should be interpreted for what it is, the Church's desire to make active Orders more and more truly relevant to today's needs, which require modern means for understanding and answering them. Frequent papal pronouncements of Pius XII, John XXIII, and Paul VI, as quoted in a previous chapter, have emphasized that the Church's works of mercy and charity are inconceivable without the strong right arm of the active Orders. *Aggiornamento,* as proposed by the Church, should convince a Sister that she *is* both a servant of society and a constant witness to Christ in whatever market place her Community apostolate puts her. If *aggiornamento* will make Sisters more relevant, more necessary, more essential to the Church and society, why fear it? Why seek to delay it?

Then there is the question of semantics: "leaving the world" is the most unfortunate terminology that could be conceived for designating the entrance of a girl into a Community. It is as if one said, of a young man entering West Point for its very rigid officer-training, that he had renounced his country. It has an almost tragic connotation. Many a girl who wavers in agony, chewing her finger nails to the quick, asking herself the question: "Can I leave the world?" would have her hands folded in happy, affirmative surrender did she ask herself: "Can I follow Christ? Can I, at His call, love and serve the world and teach my fellow men to love and serve as He loved and served them?" But "You're leaving the world" has been dolefully dinned into her ears for the weeks or months preceding her entrance into religious life.

From her postulancy on, the young candidate's meditations, readings, and instructions deal frequently with "the snares of the world," "the dangers that lie in wait in the world," "the illusions of the world," "the cruel serpents hiding beneath its flowers of flattery" on *ad infinitum,* so that she finds it difficult and upsetting to square her own experience of the world with that which is presented to her now. Is there much doubt that many of the meditations and ascetical readings of the 19th century and the retreat instructions and conferences even in our own day should be brought into line with sound, modern theology, truth, and good sense? Here is an area in which few Communities will not find plenty of room for *aggiornamento*.

Rather than using the word "world" with its heavy implicit connotations of evil and wickedness, let us call it society. With our rapid modes of transit we have now truly one world, but our apostolate is in its many societies. Within twenty-four hours one can travel from the sophisticated society of a cosmopolitan city in America to a primitive tribe in an African jungle. True, the term "the world" is used metaphorically in ascetical treatises, but the examples and illustrations used are taken from persons and

situations in society, so that the writer or speaker identifies with
them.

Secular Society of Today

The girl who comes to a Community today comes from the
society of today. She does not come from Mars or from the moon.
She does not come from a society of twenty-five years ago. This
is a vital fact to which those who have charge of her guidance and
formation must give more than lip-service. Communities do look
closely into an applicant's familial background, health, education,
and other matters deemed necessary. But the girl is not only a
product of her family, she is a product of her environment. She
is a product not only of her family, school, and church, but of
the social, economic, industrial, political atmosphere in which she
has been an observing and participating member up to the time
of her entrance into religious life. She brings with her the God-
given talent of vocation, which the Community is solemnly obligated to God, to the Church, to the girl, to itself and to society, to
develop to its greatest potential. Possibly it is the last-mentioned
area of responsibility to which Superiors are apt to give the minimum of their time and attention.

When Bishop Wright of Pittsburgh was asked the number of
persons in his diocese, he unhesitatingly replied: "Two million."
His questioner, in astonishment, replied: "Surely, Your Excellency,
there are not two million Catholics in the Diocese of Pittsburgh!"
Earnestly the Bishop replied: "Not two million Catholics, but two
million persons, every one of whom is my concern." We cannot be
concerned about that which we do not know; it behooves Superiors
to take a look at today's society whence today's Sister comes. To
know it will be to concern ourselves about it.

It is a dynamic, hugely automated, restless, and secular society.
So quick are the changes evolving from advanced technology, as
one invention renders obsolete another before the ink is dry on
its patent, that no one can evaluate its total effects on those now
living, nor what its impact on posterity will be. Many attempt
a partial evaluation. Walk into any library and ask for a book on

"Society" and you will be directed to files containing hundreds of cards; sub-titling and cross-indexing, if followed through, will bring the number well into the thousands. Of the vast majority of these, the ones on contemporary society are written in a vein of fear engendered by the genie-out-of-the-bottle viewpoint. It is difficult to find one that does not sound a note of pessimism, if not downright panic. John Kenneth Galbraith's *The Affluent Society,* William H. Whyte, Jr.'s *The Organization Man,* Walter Kerr's *The Decline of Pleasure,* Solon Kimball and James McClellan's *Education and the New America,* David Riesman's *The Lonely Crowd* are but a sampling of the books which take an apprehensive and uncertain view of our industrialized civilization and our social life. When one peruses these hard-written and not easily read books, one is moved to give an accolade to their authors. Each in his way is trying to be a savior; each, out of concern for his fellow man—en masse at least—is crying out to him: "Face reality!" The fault is that even those who make the plea are themselves standing with their backs to the essential view.

An Age of Fear

It is with no Marxian mote nor Cartesian cataract that Major Superiors view society. The Great Reality—accepted by Christians but applicable to all—is that God, Infinite Power, Infinite Wisdom, Infinite Goodness guides the destiny of all men individually and collectively. Within His province and providence the falling of a nuclear bomb and the falling of a hair fit with equal ease. With this as a premise, it might be profitable to take a summary view of today's society of which religious are themselves a part, in which they serve, and on which they depend for continued existence through additions to their ranks.

It has been debated whether our age will go down in history as "The Age of the Atom," "The Age of Automation," or "The Age of Anxiety." There is a clear relation—almost identification—in the three terms, and they all imply fear. From that fear springs an avid desire for more and more knowledge motivated by the Cape Kennedy complex that grimly grips our country. Rightfully grips

it, for the certainty that a thing *can* happen—the thing in this
case being nuclear war—makes us live under the shadow of dread
that it *will* happen. "I do wear his chains if he but nod his head
to have me wear them." Horace Mann's extravagant certainty of
what universal education would do for mankind is but a vague
hypothesis in comparison with the desperate confidence our society
places in more and more knowledge, which must be acquired with
more and more rapidity. For it is not a question of the betterment of social conditions, but actually a question of survival.

Preoccupation with Education

Since knowledge is intrinsically bound up with education, we
may logically trace the stormy barrage of criticism aimed at education, now and during the past decade, to society's fear for its very
life. The authors of *Education and the New America* state: "However ludicrous such charges (against education) may be, they are
a clear, albeit backhanded, tribute to the belief that the educational process is a significant and even central aspect of contemporary society."[2] That society gives such a prominent place to
education is good even though it be motivated by the fear of seeing
realized the paraphrase of an old proverb: "From cave man to
cave man in three million eons."

Point one, then, for Communities to keep in mind is that the
girl of today comes from a society largely preoccupied with education. In her own home and in her social circle, she has heard of
the war of ideologies between Christianity and Communism and
how every Christian must be not only prepared to defend his belief with clear and cold logic, but to show also its bearing on man's
schema of life, materially and socially as well as spiritually. Consequently, she comes expecting to find in the religious life a large-
ness of view and a depth of comprehension which will make her,
in her role of apostle, an effective adjunct to the Church's forces.

It is notable that among applicants to religious Communities,
college graduates, or girls with some college background, as well

---

[2] Solon Toothaker Kimball and J. E. McClellan, *Education and the New
America* (New York: Random House, 1963), p. 19.

as young women from the professional ranks, are steadily increasing in number. Their formation is not so simple as is that of girls who come immediately after being graduated from high school; but they seem to strike deep roots more promptly and bear fruit more quickly. "Fruit" here has no reference to the professional services they will render the Community, but rather to their quicker grasp of spiritual values and their appreciation of the intrinsic dignity of a dedicated life. Communities are warned against the danger of utilizing the so-called "prepared" subjects in the apostolates too soon. They may indeed be "prepared" as teachers, nurses, accountants, pharmacists, dietitians, etc., but they are not prepared to perform these same works with the interior spirit that a religious should bring to them.

An Age of Automation

The girl from today's society comes from a world wherein the fears of a Frankenstein monster threaten to prevail. The rapid strides of automation have their repercussions in every area of man's activities. In his contribution to the seminar on *The Ethical Aftermath of Automation* held at Woodstock College, August 5–11, 1961, the Right Reverend Monsignor Higgins said: "Let me emphasize . . . that it would be a serious mistake to imagine that all of the moral and spiritual problems connected with automation are in the socio-economic order. On the contrary, automation is likely to have its greatest impact, either for weal or for woe, in the broad field of culture, including education and religion."[3]

In the same seminar, an industrial executive, John O'Neil, of the General Tire and Rubber Company, spoke even more definitely: "Since the prime figure in automation, or in any other economic problem, is not a simple machine, but man, a child of God and brother of Christ, destined by God for an eternal share in His own life, it is his character, destiny and dignity that are the controlling factors in this problem."[4] In the formation of young religious,

[3] Quoted by Francis X. Quinn, S.J. (ed.), *The Ethical Aftermath of Automation* (Westminster: The Newman Press, 1962), p. 239.
[4] *Ibid.*, p. 131.

these same factors of character, dignity and destiny are of prime importance to Superiors.

Consider how automation has been with a young religious since, as a five-year-old, she first put a nickel into a vending machine and received three brightly colored balls of bubble gum in return. No exchange of communication between her and a clerk took place. No shy proffering of her nickel, no lisped request, no friendly pat on the head from the one who served her. A little later a dial phone eliminated the need of an "operator" for her hour-long chat with her girl or boy friend. At school, automation served her from examination entrance tests to machine-scored exams and term report cards.

The very definition of automation alerts us to the inherent dangers in it, which are far from being as obvious as are its immediate good effects. It has been defined as "mass production applied to the point where the substitution of human labor and human control by mechanical labor and mechanical control is made complete or nearly complete."[5]

The definition in its cool objectivity calls for penetrating thought. When men and women, no matter what the nature of their work, spend one third of their lives where "mechanical control is nearly complete," what subconscious repercussions will it have on their personalities? Where responsibility to a machine replaces responsibility to another human being, must not new sources of inner power be strengthened to the end that individuality be preserved intact?

Depersonalization of Man

The most familiar and most frequently repeated surrenders to automation are the signal lights and signs in traffic. The girl driving a car watches for the signal lights, red, yellow, green. She stops at the red light, "tunes up" at the yellow, and goes at the green. Neither she nor one other driver in a hundred thousand ever thinks of all of the legislation, local, state, and national, involved

[5] Samuel Eugene Rusinoff, *Automation in Practice* (Chicago: American Technical Society, 1957), p. 1.

in the lights that she obeys. For the driver, all of this is reduced to two words "Stop" and "Go."

Communities have been held up to scorn for exacting "blind obedience," and certainly the practice is not one to be enforced today, but automation requires more blind obedience from human beings—and gets it, as a matter of course—than did ever any medieval religious Community. Out of today's society comes the girl accustomed to blind obedience to machines. Superiors must be on the alert that she does not transfer this same blind, automatic obedience to the Constitution, Rules, and Customs of the Order. Here could be an inner spirit of the world carried into the religious life under the mask of virtue.

Automation, gaining every day through technological advances towards greater and greater control, contributes to man's depersonalization. He becomes a cog in a wheel, a decimal point in statistics. This depersonalization is the antithesis of the Christian ideal, to the obligation every Community has to develop to the full the natural and supernatural potential of each member. There are no vending machines for virtue, there is no push-button production of sanctity, and the final examination is scored individually—strictly. Religious are not made by pouring them into a mold, as plaster images of saints are made and then turned off an assembly line, each identical with the other.

The two outstanding saints of the Carmelite Order are Saint Teresa of Avila and Saint Thérèse of Lisieux. Within the framework of Carmelite spirituality, to whose Rule they both adhered with the highest degree of fidelity, they remain startlingly different, startlingly individual. Even today as we read of them, one after the lapse of five centuries, the other almost of our own day, they challenge our admiration; not because they were Carmelites, but because, being Carmelites, each attained to a different and distinct sort of sanctity strictly her own.

While the entrance of a girl into a Community will not automatically make a saint of her, she will find plenty of automation in the Motherhouse even as she did in her home. Automatic heating plants, dishwashers, laundries, floor scrubbers and polishers, intercommunication systems, and many other forms of labor-saving machines, which will enable the girl, from postulancy on, to spend her time more profitably. (May this forever lay to rest the hoary fables of novices scrubbing and re-scrubbing spotless floors and scouring already shining pots and pans at the whim of a fictional Novice Mistress.)

Mechanized Manipulation

But labor-saving devices do not, according to some, come properly under the classification of automation; though some claim that it began with the making of the first stone implement. The main difference is that labor-saving devices save man's brawn, while claims are made that automation substitutes for man's brain. Automation in the form of electronic teaching, mechanized book-keeping, and the highly technical diagnostic machines used in hospitals are all part of a Sister's daily life when she is engaged in the works of the Community. What the Sister must be formed to perfect as far as is humanly possible is her person-to-person responsibility to student, employee and patient. Johnny is still her responsibility whether or not he responds to the latest "programmed learning." The employee is still her responsibility even when mechanized data show him to be failing in the production of optimum man-hours; the patient is still her responsibility far beyond what X-rays, laboratory tests, and electrocardiograms show.

S. P. R. Charter warns us of this weakness, quite dramatically, when he says: "Conclusions drawn from mechanized manipulations with almost lecherous abandon are considered to be objective and profound. The fallacy here is not that man designs and uses amazingly complex equipment, but that his dependence upon his mechanized extensions has become so deeply rooted that he, himself, is becoming increasingly an extension of his own mechanics and is increasingly becoming incapable of functioning as a total human being."[6] We grant that in its totality this warning, as directed to a Sister, is extravagant. But that she should need to be

6 *Man on Earth* (Sausalito, California: Angel Island Publications, 1962), pp. 121–22.

so warned in any degree is deplorable. Let us remember that it is something by which she may have been affected unconsciously in her background of experience; not an attitude, not a belief of her deliberate choosing. Responsibility is a burden as well as a dignity, easier to shift onto a machine than onto a fellow man.

Secularism Banishes God from Man

Secularism banished God from man and his activities, using statistics as one of its most powerful depersonalizing agents. Napoleon spoke of his "faceless" army, but we now have lengthy categories of faceless classes of society. "Lower-income bracket" does not paint a picture of men, women and children inadequately fed, housed and clothed. "School drop-outs" in terms of percentage does not tell of the blighted lives of boys and girls. The expression "minority groups" scarcely hints of racial strife, of prejudice, of inhumanity or violence. "Migrant workers" have a suave sound, utterly at variance with the conditions under which labor, imported seasonally, works and lives. "Polio rate" does not conjure up the pain and agony of a child, nor the despair of a mother. For purposes of government allotments, larger and better school facilities, legislation, and medical research, each human being concerned is reduced to a decimal place.

From any shade of this extremely un-Christian viewpoint Sisters must be freed. Christ identified Himself with every person individually, and they must see in one they serve not only another human being, but Christ Himself. A "school drop-out" will be the Sister's personal concern, with every effort made to remedy its cause; "two and three-tenth per cent increase in polio" will arouse her sympathy, her prayers, her efforts to make its symptoms and means of communication more easily known. "Lower-income bracket" will cause her to detect the school child who is listless because of insufficient nourishing food, or who feels humiliated because of his shabby clothes.

Practically all religious Communities have a screening process for applicants, and many a girl ruefully discovers that it is easier to get out of a Community than to get into it. Yet there are factors and forces in society forming its members which no tests will reveal. Familial conditions have vastly changed with the adding to the labor forces of millions of women, many of them married, who now constitute no small percentage of that force.

With Mommy leaving an hour earlier for her work than do Dick and Susie for school, and returning two hours later than they (having made such provision for them during her absence as she thinks best), there is not so much a break in family ties as there is the creation of an entirely new pattern. If this type of family living begins for Susie at the age of six, and continues until she has been graduated from high school, and Susie then enters a Community, she will find the regular way of religious life either amazingly comfortable or frighteningly strange. Certainly those responsible for her spiritual guidance and formation should not use as their norm the familial conditions of a quarter of a century ago.

It is significant that most modern homes, in the suburbs and outlying portions of a city, feature "areas" rather than rooms: the dining area, usually a snack bar; the recreational area, the TV area; the social area, the reading area. The occupants shift easily from one area to another; from TV to books, from books to billiards, or get away from it all at the honk of a horn.

As a contrast, there is the city apartment-type home, where space is at a premium, and every room is multi-purpose. The living room is transformed into a sleeping room at night by a couch that opens up into a bed; the closing of a cupboard door hides a complete kitchen, Hoover style. Dining tables fold into the wall. Complete baths take up no more space than three-by-six feet. Clothes closets have accordion doors. A rather attractive bit of furniture of chrome and enamel is actually a washing-drying machine. The apartment faces a busy street, with a row of other apartment houses on each side. This is the home; this is the environment the new postulant lives in until the day she says good-by to her family to begin her religious life.

House Sickness Versus Homesickness

In contrast to such living conditions, the Motherhouse to which the postulant goes is well calculated to serve up an abysmal feeling of "house sickness" masquerading as homesickness. For the most part, Motherhouses are situated away from city sights and sounds, with extensive, well-landscaped grounds, and a (deceptive) air of otherworldliness and leisure. When a girl, after the second day in the postulate, presents herself, weeping, to the Mistress of Postulants, declaring she must go home—"The life of a Sister is not for me; I didn't think it would be like this"—she cannot mean the religious life because, after the lapse of twenty-four hours, she has learned nothing of it more than she knew the day before. Yet the response to the Mistress' question: "How long did you think of being a Sister?" is often "Since I was in seventh grade."

The understanding Mistress will recognize that the postulant is overwhelmed with the contrast between the home environment to which she is accustomed and that to which she is now introduced: the Community refectory, large, spotless, tables in orderly rows, and an air of silence permeating the large bright room; the dormitory—happily most Communities now provide private rooms, but these are still what the name means, "a place in which to sleep"—with its exquisitely neat beds, plain night table, straight chair and clothes cupboard. No knickknacks, no stuffed animals, no photographs. Even the Chapel, into which she walks with the group, taking the place assigned to postulants, seems strange and the tabernacle remote. Even the Mistress' office has an air of austerity about it—she never saw such a bare desk!

The wise Postulant Mistress will be able to discern "house sickness" from homesickness, and not only allow but encourage the girl to "spill out" how strange, stuffy, and unreal she finds it all. With a sense of humor, she will tide the girl over this first battle with herself, knowing that strain, like all else, in moderate amounts serves its good purposes. The Motherhouse environment (vastly different from that which, in the Community's active works, the Sister will later encounter) needfully and wisely designed, serves an excellent purpose. It personally, quietly, and consistently infuses discipline, restraint and self-control, much more effectively and without the possibility of resentment than would individual warning or admonition. This atmosphere, once the girl becomes familiar with it, is a strong contributing factor to that interior life which, even as a postulant, she must begin to live.

Organization Versus Isolation

Society today presents two seemingly antipodal characteristics: organization and isolation. Citizens of the United States are known as "joiners." This would seem to render less difficult the adjustment of a girl to "joining a Community." It is not the case. The term organization has little to do with fraternal, civic, or social groups, but rather with great national forces organized for defense of their rights—as they see them—and armed with antagonism against other groups which infringe or curtail them. The daily papers headline strikes, lock-outs, sit-downs.

Management and labor are almost daily locked in a struggle somewhere. More and more large producers combine and absorb smaller producers, and more and more find themselves at loggerheads with the government—a tremendous organization in itself —over the legality of such combines. Consumers organize themselves nationally to fight, or to obtain fair prices—according to their view. Professional associations are highly organized, constituting powerful pressure groups to keep their members strictly in line with the association's policies. Information on these situations and struggles is fed to the public through daily papers, weekly periodicals, professional journals, radio and TV.

It is almost inescapable that the postulant's parents, or she herself, in a position of business employee, nurse or teacher, should have had at least some fringe involvement in these organizations. She may well bring with her an inclination to judgmental attitudes foreign to her predecessors of twenty-five years ago. The exercise of judgment is, in itself, a good thing, since, free of bias, prejudice or ignorance, it can contribute to prudence. The tendency to judge calls for understanding, careful handling of the young religious to inhibit this habit without destroying it. She will be in no position to pass judgment on the Community's way of life until she is well-grounded in its spirit, its ideals, its practices. On the other hand, her Superiors should be slow, very slow, to designate her as forward, insubordinate or aggressive. One must beware of rooting up the wheat with the cockle.

The 1963 encyclical of Pope John XXIII emphasizes that socialization is one of the major results of the evolution of the modern world:

Since God made men social by nature, and since no society can hold together unless some one be over all, directing all to strive earnestly for the common good, every civilized Community must have a ruling authority, and this authority, no less than society itself, has its source in nature, and has, consequently, God for its author[7]

Reverend François Houtart, in speaking of "the Sociology of Vocation," states:

Because man lives in society and shares a certain culture, the personal and ecclesiastical aspects of vocation will be conditioned by social factors. Indeed, the perception of values which every vocation supposes (for although a vocation is a call of God, it is also man's response) can be very difficult according as a person belongs to one social milieu rather than another; e.g., a rural environment rather than an urban one.[8]

But from whatever stratum of society the girl comes, she must be continuously impressed with the truth that a religious Community is not a commercial, industrial or professional organization based on self-interest, but a "state of perfection," founded on the desire of each member to seek personal sanctity and to cooperate with Christ in the sanctification and salvation of souls.

The reaction against an organizational structure on which a man or a woman depends for financial and social security stems from a desire to be recognized as an individual. For men are not like so many ingots of iron, dropped into a crucible and fused, but rather like the many strands of steel that are united in a cable for some purpose, with each remaining what it was before it was so united. It is ingrained in man's nature to be known for his *whole self,* and not as a part of a whole, save in those circumstances when his good and that of society require it.

---

7 *Pacem in Terris* (Washington, D.C.: National Catholic Welfare Conference, 1963), p. 13.

8 *Today's Vocation Crisis,* A Summary of the Studies and Discussions at the First International Congress on Vocations to the States of Perfection, Dec. 10–16, 1961. Trans. and ed. by Godfrey Poage, C.P., and Germain Lievin, C.SS.R. (Westminster: The Newman Press, 1962), p. 23.

Again, the rapid pace of living in our free-wheeling and fast-moving contemporary society, aided and abetted by the high degree of technology which affects our lives at every turn, insidiously makes millions of citizens find peace and smooth running in isolation. Consider, for instance, a person making a coast-to-coast flight, as hundreds do daily. The previous day, reservations are made by phone, the cost and time of flight ascertained. The traveler is carried to his destination by one word to the cabman, "Airport." Enroute he listens to the news on his transistor radio. Watching the meter which automatically registers the cost of the trip, he has the money ready to drop into the driver's hand. Automatic doors open into the airport waiting room. He walks to a desk, gives his name and flight reservation—a matter of some seven or eight words at the most—and is handed his ticket in silence. Or, if the man at the desk (who even now seems something of an anachronism and will, doubtless, soon be replaced by a machine) is a chatterbox, he will say "On time."

It is wholly unnecessary that he say that, since bulletin boards furnish the information. On his way to the designated gate, the traveler buys cigarettes from one vending machine, a paper from another, and pauses at a third mechanized board where he punches a button to ascertain what the weather is on the eastern coast. Aboard ship he gives his name to the stewardess; replies "Yes" to the question as to whether he wishes to have dinner; "coffee" indicates his choice of beverage, and that is the extent of his conversation with his fellow men for a three-thousand-mile flight. All done in a dozen words. Contrast this with the geniality and cordiality that was part of a cross-continent journey by rail twenty-five or thirty years ago.

It is not only that people are in a hurry, that time must be saved; our manner of life has cost us a large share of neighborliness. How much truth is there in the warning that is almost a plea: "Man needs a new idea of himself for himself; a new perspective to meet a challenge and a new threat; a new faith, a faith in himself as a warming assurance against the loneliness of the cosmic cold encroaching upon him with each impressive step of the computerized intellectuals of our time."[9]

9 Charter, *op. cit.*, p. 121.

Time Needed to Relish the Ecce Quam Bonum

It may well be, then, that the Sister-to-be coming from a laconic-living home, from a society where electronic machines give all the answers, may take some time to understand and to relish the *ecce quam bonum* of the religious life. The beginning postulant or novice is frequently told: "You left the world" (the sooner we get rid of that phrase the better), "but you brought yourself with you." How necessary for those who have her formation in hand to remember it also; remember that she brought more than her physical self, that she brought views and attitudes, ways and manners, which are the impress of the society she left. The label of "anti-social" should not be pinned on the new Sister-to-be, at least not until she has been given much time and many opportunities to acquire the Community social spirit which is part of the charity of Christ.

Turning to view the Catholic lay world from which the girl will come to a Community, we find that it is one where the layman plays a far larger role than ever before. His love for his religion leads him to desire a deeper knowledge of it and a more intelligent approach to its practices. Thousands of parishes have study clubs in which the papal encyclicals are read and concrete application of principles made to daily living both in the home and in business affairs; Church-State relationships are discussed; the liturgy, studied under the tutelage of priest or well-versed layman, becomes a living thing to be loved. The Bible, with all the enrichment of new scholarly translations and recent archeological discoveries, is studied with eager reverence.

Laymen now do much more than usher in church and take up collections; laywomen have more than an Altar Society. Where there is a matter of parish financial investments, a building program, organization of youth groups, expanding school facilities, harmonious racial relationships, inter-faith dialogues and other such matters, the pastor looks to laymen for information and advice. Particularly are many bishops and pastors on the alert for laymen and laywomen gifted with leadership, and the ability to make their position known in clear, cogent fashion at political rallies, civic meetings, industrial conferences, and public gatherings.

For the Church exists in society as leaven in dough, and more and more dependence is placed upon laymen to make the leaven permeate all areas of society. From the homes of capable, devout, intelligent parents will come candidates for Communities. These have frequently taken an active part in the Church's social and charitable activities. They have developed leadership which, when firmly established in the following of Christ, will be invaluable to the religious Order they have entered.

This quality must be disciplined and directed, but never destroyed and never belittled. Christ's first invitation to His apostles was "Come." His later direction was "Go." It is after the same fashion that a Community should plan for its recruits. Between the "come" and the "go" should be a period of sound, solid, unhurried formation. The "go" should not be given until the Sisters are fully prepared to face the arduous apostolate awaiting their courage and zeal. In his *Letter to Women Religious,* speaking directly to members of the active Orders, His Holiness John XXIII says:

May those who are dedicated to the active life realize that not only prayers but also works can bring about a new course of society . . . since the areas of education, charity and social service require personnel who are prepared for the increased demands imposed by the present-day order of things, you must strive, in obedience, to study and obtain the degrees which will allow you to surmount every difficulty.[10]

The founding, growth and phenomenal expansion of missionary Societies within the United States in less than half a century points up a lesson profitable to all Communities. Whether founded for health, catechetics, education, or for any of these purposes combined, they have as a fixed goal the Christianizing of a society other than their own. The rate of perseverance among their members contradicts the sometimes heard statement that girls are attracted to a missionary life because of its glamor. (How wryly will the experienced missionary smile at that word—glamor!) The rapid growth of missionary Communities, while most Congregations are

10 Pp. 12–13.

deploring the fewness of vocations, is undoubtedly due in large measure to the preparation Superiors give their subjects for the foreign society they are to serve.

Preparation for Foreign and Home Missions

Not only are the future missionaries reasonably fluent in the language of a country before they are sent there, but they are instructed in its social customs, economic conditions, religious beliefs, system of education, local mores, vital statistics, form of government, and the various problems they will face. The number of years that this preparation requires is amply justified by the results of their labors. From the postulate to final profession, service to society is integrated with their personal sanctification. Thus prepared, when sent as a representative of the Church to serve in foreign lands, their constant exertions are neither a distraction to the interior life nor a detriment to spiritual development. Their work is an integral part of their striving for sanctity.

Factually and actually, is it not necessary to take the same attitude towards preparing Sisters for the apostolate in their native country as is taken to prepare them for foreign missions? Except for those Orders founded for missionary work alone, the vast majority of the members of any religious-apostolic Community will work at home. Our pluralistic society must necessarily be also secularistic. Karl Rahner's frequent reference to the Church and to individual Christians as living in a diaspora may be disturbing to those of us who look upon our own country as basically Christian. "That there are no longer any Christian countries (with the *possible* exception of the Iberian peninsula) is a fact. Christianity, though in varying proportions, exists *everywhere* as a diaspora . . . nowhere does it fill such a role of effective leadership as would permit it to set upon the age, with any force or clarity, the stamp of a Christian ideal. We are undoubtedly in an era which is going to see an increase in this diaspora character, no matter what causes we may assign to it."[11] This being true, a Sister should

11 Karl Rahner, S.J., *The Christian Commitment* (New York: Sheed and Ward, 1963), p. 17.

be well prepared to work in this diaspora situation, and be hampered by no illusions concerning it.

Depending upon its geographical territory, a Community may have schools in different strata of society. A Sister's first assignment may be a newly established school in suburbia, with parents of the pupils educated and in the better-than-average income group. Her next assignment may be to a school in a blight area, with pupils exclusively from minority groups, a high truancy rate, incipient delinquency, and the majority of parents illiterate. Yet she has the same curriculum to teach, the same number of hours for each subject, and the same examinations to administer as she had in her former assignment. The Sister may easily become either disheartened or indifferent.

Should she not have been prepared, during her formation period, to meet such situations? Does not a Sister's responsibility as a teacher demand that she make every effort to lessen the number of drop-outs, that she become acquainted with her pupils' living conditions and with their parents? It may mean changing the horarium in her local Community, lessening her non-teaching duties, or working in collaboration with social agencies in order to find time for these new duties. A great advance in teaching was made when the admonitory maxim was coined: "We teach pupils, not subjects." In the hospital world, this was represented by "We nurse patients, not diseases," and in the social field by "We aid clients, not cases." But "pupil," "patient," "client," still have a depersonalizing ring. Now we must go further and have as our goal to serve each person according to the unique needs engendered by the society of which he is a part.

How eloquently does His Excellency, Most Reverend John J. Wright, Bishop of Pittsburgh, put it:

Persons are terribly important at the moment because of the trend of the times. The mechanistic, highly organized, impersonal ties make all our institutions and commissions, despite their necessity in organized society, less important than organic, dedicated, individual persons. These are always the strength of the Church.[12]

12 Conference at Sister Formation Institute for Formation Personnel: "Persons in Religious Life," *Sister Formation Bulletin*, IX (Spring, 1963), 11.

Child of a Changing World

To sum up: the girl who comes from today's society is, by and large, the finest type of girl. She is a more intelligent Catholic, is better educated, has greater stamina, and a more precise sense of values than had her predecessor of twenty-five years ago. She is capable, fervent, self-reliant and generous. These are splendid qualities which Superiors note with deep satisfaction in older religious. Finding them in a young religious, they should most truly rejoice. The girl has an apostolic perspective which she looks forward to broadening, having already identified her concern for her neighbor with her love for Christ.

She is a child of a changing world in which no wonder, such as the circling of the earth in seventy-eight minutes (as has been done), or the landing of a man on the moon (which may be done before the end of this decade), is considered the ultimate wonder. Exactly because she *is* a child of a changing world, she looks for unchanging values. These are not found in Community trivia. These are not found in adherence to external forms, practices, customs, and modes of dress which had meaning for earlier times but have no meaning for our own. "Oh, what a loss is there!" if the early enthusiasm, the eager desire for sanctification which a postulant brings, is blunted by archaic incidentals.

It is for the girl from today's society that the Church cries out to Major Superiors to remove from their Communities those things which are now meaningless—not only meaningless but harmful, inasmuch as they could divert a girl from acquiring a true interior spirit, and perhaps discourage her, out of sheer bewilderment, from persevering in the religious life.

This is the finest hour—or it can be—for active religious Orders. The Church, through its Sovereign Pontiffs and the Sacred Congregation of Religious, is crying out for adaptations and renovations which will free all Communities from practices inherited from monasticism, but which are now a detriment to the piety, zeal and manner of life to which Sisters are called today. Forward-looking Communities will not hesitate to make the changes indicated as desirable by the Church. Hence it is that the next decade could be the most critical, yet the most rewarding, in contemporary history. Our late Holy Father, Pope John XXIII, said that after every Ecumenical Council there is an upsurge in religious vocations. Faith dictates the belief that each Community will receive of that upsurge in proportion as it has, in the spirit of Vatican II, prepared a soil where the precious gift of a religious vocation will bear fruit in abundance. Above all, each Community may well hope for an increase of vocations in proportion to its obedience to the Church's directives concerning the pre-service formation and education of its young Sisters.

10

The Essence of the Religious Vocation

In this era of fear and frustration, of decreasing security and devastating doubts, the religious life stands out like "a city set on a mountain." (Matt. 5:14, Conf.) Founded on the gospels and, in its essence, found in the gospels, the purpose of religious life is to extend to the time, place and circumstances amid which religious live, the life of Christ Himself. Now, perhaps more than in the age of martyrdom, Sisters are called to bear witness by the example of their lives that Christ still walks among men and loves them; still compassionates their needs, ministers to their wants and understands their weaknesses. Never, as this book continually points out, were Sisters more relevant to the Church and to society. Never were they more appreciated by the laity.

Yet because of the strange and conflicting times in which we live, and by reason of the almost universal opportunities for education—opportunities which generate intellectual curiosity— the religious life is called into question as never before. Not in an unfriendly way nor in a bigoted way, like that which in the past caused widespread calumny and persecution. It is rather in an intellectual desire that the world seeks to know more about, and understand better, what a religious vocation is; why some young women are called to be Sisters and why others are not. What motivates withdrawal from a world that is—in spite of its miseries—a good, an interesting, a fascinating place in which to live? Asked such questions, a candidate for the religious life replies truthfully: "I am leaving home became I honestly believe I have a call. God wants me to be a Sister. He has given me a religious vocation." Pushed by further questions: "What is a religious vocation? How do you *know* you have it? What does it *mean?* The candidate may answer: "It's something I've wanted since I was in sixth grade. Why *me?* I don't know exactly. It's something I can't explain, and even if I tried, *you* wouldn't understand."

The Mystery of Christ's Call

A religious vocation is a mystery. It will always remain a mystery, and perhaps to no one will it remain so deep a mystery as to the one favored with it. Of the millions of young women down the centuries who have heard the call of Christ, "Come, follow Me" (Luke 18:22), and have answered it, not one could honestly attribute the call to any merit of her own. Christ, in extending an invitation to follow Him in a way of special perfection, a strict observance of the evangelical counsels of poverty, chastity and obedience, has exercised His divine prerogative to do as He wills. "You have not chosen Me," He reminds the one to whom a religious vocation is given, "but I have chosen you." (John 15:16)

Herein lies the deep mystery causing the one so honored to ask herself again and again, "Why has Christ chosen me among so many who would have loved Him more, and have appreciated the honor more? Why?" The question remains unanswered, for mystery demands faith, that is, a response of the entire person, intellect, will, personality. On the bedrock of faith in a Divine Call a Sister's vocation is founded. Mystery yields no easy answers. It is faith that hears the call of Abraham echoing down the ages: "Go forth out of thy country, and from thy kindred, and out of thy father's house, and come into the land which I shall show thee." (Gen. 12:1) It is faith that hears the promises and makes possible the sacrifices attendant upon the affirmative answer Abraham made to his call.

It is this total response to Christ's invitation exercised to an heroic degree that enables a young woman to answer Christ's invitation to leave father and mother and sisters and brothers, home and possessions, to come into a strange land to find and possess Him. It is a willingness to prove her love by making the sacrifices that love always entails. For love is the very essence of a religious vocation: a greater, deeper, more responsive love of God; an outgoing, practical, fraternal love of the neighbor; and flowing from this love, an active zeal for the works of the Community to which she has been called.

Stating the matter so simply seems to clarify the mystery, and one is tempted to say: "Now I understand: Vocation is a call to love God and one's fellow man and, through love, to serve according to the rule of a particular Order." This is true, but the call to love is a call to holiness, and the concept of holiness adds to the sense of mystery. When Christ said, "If you will be perfect . . . come follow Me" (Matt. 19:21), the invitation was extended to all the people of God. Why, then, does it seem to be reserved to a comparative few to accept the call literally and withdraw, as did Abraham, to a strange land? Herein lies the mystery which can never be fully understood.

The Church, through the centuries, has recognized the mystery of this special call to sanctity, and has designated it as entering "a state of perfection." This "state of perfection" is so called because it requires a withdrawal from those things which, of their very nature, would militate against acquiring the habit of virtue. It facilitates the practice of poverty, chastity and obedience, which remove the main obstacles to the acquisition of holiness of life. Abbé Gaston Courtois warns:

The literal translation of *status perfectionis* as a "state of perfection" is liable to lead to various misunderstandings: it might give the impression that those who live in these states have personally reached perfection, or that these states represent a sort of monopoly outside of which one could not attain perfection. It might be better to speak of the *juridical* or *canonical state of striving towards perfection*.[1]

Certainly all religious would prefer to have their state in life defined as a state of *striving for perfection,* since they are quite aware (and it is quite obvious) that they have not as yet attained

[1] "Introduction," *The States of Perfection*, ed. Gaston Courtois (Westminster, Md.: The Newman Press, 1961), p. xiv.

to their goal of holiness. However, the Church does employ the term to designate all those who have embraced a way of life that puts love of God and the neighbor first among their goals. Perhaps "the religious life" is the simplest term of reference.

To realize that the religious life is an integral part of the Church is to give a Sister an appreciation of her dignity and a more complete understanding of her obligations. Pius XII gave expression to the Church's esteem and to the *raison d'être* of the religious life when he said:

The reason for the existence of the religious state and the explanation of its value lie in the fact that it is intimately connected with the special purpose of the Church, namely to lead all men to the acquisition of holiness. Though every Christian is bound to attempt to reach that sacred pinnacle . . . the religious proceeds on a path which is entirely her own, and relies upon helps of a higher nature.[2]

The "helps of a higher nature" spoken of by the Holy Father are primarily the grace of God, and through this grace the vows of religion: poverty, chastity and obedience. These vows, far from depriving a Sister of liberty, free her to fulfill in an extraordinary degree the two great commandments essential to perfection: "Thou shalt love the Lord, thy God, with thy whole heart, and with thy whole soul, and with thy whole mind . . . and thou shalt love thy neighbor as thyself." (Matt. 22:37–39) The keeping of these commandments in their full perfection is the basis of all sanctity.

The Essence of Sanctity

The evangelical counsels of poverty, chastity and obedience, motivated by charity, represent the ideal of Christian perfection. Through her love of God and her fellow man a Sister projects to the world the image of a loving Christ, poor, chaste, obedient. It is by striving for personal holiness that she renders her greatest service to the Church and to her fellow men. Pius XII insisted upon this as the chief reason for the existence of religious Orders:

2 "Allocution to the International Congress of Religious," *The States of Perfection*, p. 174.

The Church, the Bride of Christ, would not indeed be fully in accord with the desire of Christ the Lord, nor would the eyes of men, bright with hope, look to her as to a *standard unto the nations,* were there not to be found within her fold those who, by the example of their lives even more than by words, shine with added grace from the splendor of the Gospel.[3]

It might well be said, then, that each Sister has a mandate from the Church to be holy as her Heavenly Father is holy. The Church *needs* her holiness, since the successor of Peter assures us that the Church would be incomplete, and men's hopes unfulfilled, if Sisters should fail them in the sanctity promised by the gospel. For a Sister vows to become holy, and her state in life makes it possible. Father Schleck points it up this way:

A "state" of perfection is an external arrangement of life which gives not only the opportunity but the *obligation* and the *means* to practice certain actions, those which are of perfection, that is, those which lead one more firmly and easily and quickly to the higher perfections of the virtue of charity.[4]

In the end, a perfect love of God and complete conformity to His Will are sought. The vows are a most potent means to this end by partially removing the chief obstacles to union with God.

The Vow of Poverty

Before a young woman enters the religious life her sense of values often centers on possessions—the possession of things over and above what is conceded to be necessary to her well-being. By the vow of poverty she renounces not only the "goods" of this world but all opportunities to acquire them, and all yearning for them. It is not unusual to hear a postulant or novice say: "I find I hardly know myself any more; my whole scale of values has undergone a complete change. I am ashamed to admit it, but I used to choose my friends from among those who could afford to

---

[3] "Exhortation to Superiors General of Religious Orders and Institutes," *The States of Perfection,* p. 317.
[4] Charles E. Schleck, C.S.C., *The Theology of Vocations* (Milwaukee: The Bruce Publishing Company, 1963), p. 99.

wear the best clothes; attend the best theatres, the best concerts. In a way, my whole world seems to have turned upside down."

As a Sister passes through successive stages of the religious life, she notes that she may still use the "goods" of the world. She may live in a reasonably comfortable environment, drive a car, travel, work in a well-appointed office, or have the latest equipment in a laboratory, or other furnishings in the area where she carries on her work. But she does not own any of these conveniences; they are placed at her disposal strictly for her use *there*. When she is changed from one house to another, as Sisters frequently are, she takes none of these conveniences with her. In this sense they cannot be considered possessions. This is the viewpoint she must cultivate in using them. When transferred to another house, she may find none of the conveniences she "enjoyed"—or at least made use of—on the former mission. If her attitude has been formed by a spirit of detachment, she will perhaps humanly miss them, but she will not make an issue of it. Her vow of poverty exacts a very real detachment from the use of conveniences, and at times even of what seem to be necessities.

A curious contrast may be seen here which the candidate to the religious life is quick to notice. Once she attached value to possessions, and even, by her own admission, chose her friends on the basis of purchasable values. She now comes to see that where, as a lay person, she attained a certain status by the amount, variety and value of her possessions, as a Sister, she loses prestige and status in the eyes of others when she shows a tendency to accumulate possessions such as books, baggage, material comforts and conveniences of a personal nature. When she encourages lay people to give her personal gifts, even though they respond generously, they are disillusioned. In proportion as she practices poverty "above and beyond the call of detachment" she is admired and emulated.

Nor should she practice poverty and detachment from any human viewpoint, such as to win admiration or emulation. She discounts status-seeking as unworthy of one called to love God in the highest degree possible. The vows engender freedom from desire, giving her the liberty to love God, and to take no thought for the morrow so far as she herself is concerned. Thus she is able to devote herself whole-heartedly to the work assigned her. If, however, this spirit of detachment from the goods of this world does not find its corollary in a deep attachment to God and a desire to imitate Him in the strict poverty He practiced on earth, it fails of its purpose. Detachment could indeed be practiced from a pagan or a philosophical motive, as witness Diogenes.

But Christ has, by His teachings and example, raised voluntary poverty to the dignity of a virtue which enables those who practice it to resemble Him. The gospels present Him as the Exemplar of poverty from the cradle of Bethlehem to the Cross of Calvary. Renunciation of earthly possessions is one of the first sacrifices Christ asks of those whom He calls to share His mission. A Sister loves poverty because Christ loved it; she embraces poverty because Christ embraced it. She sees in poverty a key to genuine freedom, and she sees in it a way to become Christlike.

The Vow of Chastity

Virginity goes back to the Incarnation, and its value, dignity, and place in the plan of redemption can be understood only in light of this momentous event in the history of mankind. That the long-looked-for Messiah would be born of a virgin was prophesied in the Old Law: "Behold a virgin shall conceive and bear a son; and his name shall be called Emmanuel." (Is. 7:14) St. Luke gives us in reverent detail the story of the Incarnation; an angel appeared to Mary and told her she was to be the Mother of God, reassuring her that she would become a mother without violating virginity. Mary's "Behold the handmaid of the Lord" (Luke 1:38) closed the first act in the great drama of the redemption. Through the example of Mary, virginity dedicated to God became identified with Christian practice. "Virginity refuses one form of love only to assume a higher or total form directed immediately to Christ Himself."[5]

The love a Sister renounces forever by her vow of chastity is conjugal love. This is a love which in its fullness is limited, after

---

[5] R. W. Gleason, S.J. *To Live Is Christ* (New York: Sheed and Ward, 1961), p. 128.

the love of God, to one person, to one family, though it is, of course, accompanied by love, in a lesser role, of the neighbor. In other words, a married man is required by his vocation, to love God above all things, and then to concentrate his love on his wife and family. Fraternal charity is subordinated to the demands of conjugal love.

By the vow of chastity, a Sister consecrates herself, not only to the love of God above all else, but to an unlimited love of the neighbor. It is a love in imitation of, and in union with Christ, which requires her to cleave to no one human individual, but frees her to love and serve the whole human race. This liberation is not a negation of love, but rather it is its unlimited fulfillment. Far from abdicating the right and role of maternity, it permits the Sister to become a spiritual mother to thousands. Pope Pius XII calls the vow of virginity "a liberation which places the one who makes it entirely at God's disposal for the good of the neighbor."[6] He further says:

We feel the greatest joy at the army of innumerable virgins who, from the first centuries of the Church up to our own day, have given up marriage to devote themselves more easily and fully to the salvation of their neighbor for the love of Christ, and have thus been enabled to undertake and carry through many admirable works of religion and charity.[7]

When, through love of God, a Sister shares vicariously in the sorrows and trials, the fears and anxieties, the deprivations—material and spiritual—of those whom she serves, rich and poor, her very love renders these miseries her own personal burden and sorrow. This is but a reflection of Christ's solicitude: His weeping over Jerusalem, His compassion for the sick, the afflicted and the outcast. It is a Sister's vows of poverty and chastity that make these services possible, enabling her to serve the whole human race according to its needs. Her strength derives from the certain knowledge that she is doing what Christ did while He was on earth, and this gives purpose and direction to her whole life.

[6] Encyclical on *Holy Virginity*, p. 7.
[7] *Ibid.*, p. 9.

The Vow of Obedience

By the vow of obedience a religious renounces the natural right to self-determination, or self-direction. By this renunciation she places her entire life in the hands of others. In this she imitates Christ, who "became obedient even to death, the death of the cross." (Phil. 2:8) His motto, if one may so speak, was "I do always the will of Him who sent me." (John 6:39) From this derives the dignity of the Sister who vows obedience for life— obedience to the Church, to her Community, to her Superiors for the love of God and in imitation of His divine Son. It is an expression of her theological response; were it practiced through natural reasons, it would degrade her human dignity.

The ordinary layman is apt to consider obedience as a sort of bondage, a servile subjection to the mood and whim, perhaps, of Superiors who do not understand the art of governing, because they do not know how to use authority. This misunderstanding of obedience is seen, sometimes, even in candidates for the religious life who say, "Well, I expect to find obedience very hard. I like to do things my way." Yet, as will be enlarged upon in later chapters, this young person was perhaps quite submissive to some erratic, perhaps autocratic, employer. For a bi-monthly check of a specified number of dollars she was willing to subordinate "her way of doing for his way"—even when his way was rigidly authoritarian. Indeed, the writer has had girls tell her: "My boss even curses and swears at me if I don't do my work just the way he wants it done." Questioned as to why they remain in the employ of such persons, the response is, "The pay is awfully good."

That no religious would ever be subjected to such indignities in order to satisfy the most exacting of religious Superiors goes without saying. That a prospective candidate should fail to see the total difference between obeying for the love of God and obeying for the love of dollars not only proves the materialistic values of today, but it indicates the need for a complete and proper understanding of what is required by the virtue of obedience. The requirements of the vow of obedience seldom enter into the daily life of a Sister; it is rather the virtue of obedience flowing from the vow that she deals with daily, and this she must thoroughly understand.

To this end, as we have noted, all religious Communities have as an entrance requirement that every candidate possess at least average intelligence. It is not snobbery or utilitarianism or self-serving that places emphasis on this requirement. Actually, it is the opposite, for the requirement is born of a deep-seated respect and concern for the girl who wishes to dedicate herself to God by the vows of religion. These vows are important; they are the *sine qua non* of the religious life and must be kept as perfectly as human limitations make possible. Hence an understanding of obedience must be guaranteed; one can take no chances of an imperfect understanding of the obligations that the vows place on every member of a religious Community.

At least a good, average intelligence is essential to the full understanding of the vow of obedience. It cannot be rightfully understood as a passive conformity to doing what one is told. It implies intelligence and discernment, neither of which can be abrogated without injuring the integrity of the person. Neither the vow nor the virtue of obedience is honored by a mindless: "Just tell me what you want me to do and I'll do it." When there are honest questions in the mind of the one to obey, there should be honest answers given from the person expecting obedience.

Obedience must rest on the solid foundation of faith. "I do this because I believe it to be the will of God" is the only intelligent answer to "Why should I obey?" Since obedience has always an apostolic dimension, there is always need for remembering that it is God who gives the religious vocation, but it is through the Church that one is permitted to do the works of the Community. Therefore obedience extends downward from God, to the Church, to the Community. Unless obedience, intelligent and cordial, is accorded to the Church, and the apostolate is seen as leading souls not to ourselves but to the Church, then one cannot consider oneself as *sent,* which St. Paul declares essential to an understanding of obedience. This obedience is always given to the Community directly, but ultimately to the Church.

On the Community level, obedience is given to the General or Provincial Superior, and then to the local Superior. It is most frequently when obedience reaches the provincial or local level that faith is needed to combat vigorously the mutual weaknesses and foibles of human nature. It is here that a Sister is liable to lose sight of the dignity and holiness connected with obedience by separating it from the divine source whence it emanates.

A Sister Is "Sent" by the Church

The words of St. Paul to the Romans are applicable to this situation, or to any other in which a Sister finds herself through obedience: *"How are they to believe him whom they have not heard? And how are they to hear if no one preaches? And how are men to preach unless they be sent?"* (Rom. 10:14–15, Conf.) A Sister is *sent* immediately by the Community and mediately by the Church to any duty assigned her. She is *sent* by the Church, for example, to teach fourth grade in a parish school, as definitely as is her companion who has been selected for a mission in Uganda. To the students in a classroom, the patients in a hospital, the clients in a welfare agency, a Sister has been *sent* by God, by the Church which has given a mandate through her Superiors, that she may bear witness to Christ *where she is*. Very Reverend Elio Gambari, S.M.M., of the Sacred Congregation of Religious states:

It may be said that Sisters are invested with a canonical mandate. This apostolate is specialized: it is an apostolate of conquest, of penetration, of irradiation, and of protection. . . . The apostolate of religious pertains to the universal Church, even when it actually takes place within a determined diocese or parish.[8]

With the safeguard of canonical mandate, accepted in a spirit of faith, the Sister finds no horizons too narrow or too vast, no work too old, too new or unexpected, for her to attempt.

The happiness of Sisters on foreign missions has often been remarked; they have a gay disregard for material things which in the home missions are deemed essential. Fraternal charity is practiced in a high degree, and neither failure nor hostility from those they serve can dampen their enthusiasm. They have a high *sense of mission* which sustains them. It is precisely this same *sense of mission* that should sustain every Sister on the home missions in all circumstances. A home mission is, in every sense,

[8] *Religious Life in the Church Today*, p. 81.

as holy and as meritorious as a foreign mission. Emphasis is on the word *sent*. A Sister is as truly *sent* by the Church, through her Community, to work in an annex of the Motherhouse, a nearby city, or to the far-away Congo.

It is obedience to the word *sent* that is the essence. The need of her Community for a person with her ability in a certain work was but a secondary factor in her assignment. God willed from all eternity that she, and only she, should exercise a certain apostolate in a certain place at a time ordained by Him. He foresaw the difficulties she would meet, the obstacles which would prevent her from succeeding. Nevertheless, because she has placed her whole life in His keeping through her vow of obedience, He *sent* her to this hospital, this school, this institution of charity. She would be failing Providence and the Church by refusing to cooperate with God's plan for her, were she to allow any natural element, either in herself or in any human circumstances, to interfere with her bearing witness to Christ by imitating His obedience.

"How can a man preach unless he be sent?" A Sister in accepting an assignment made by obedience cannot always foresee the kind of "sermon" she is to preach, but she can always be unshakably confident that she has been *sent* by God, by the Church, through her Community. It is in fostering this conviction in a spirit of faith that Sisters will find that peace which surpasses all understanding.

Trying to Penetrate the Mystery of Vocation

It is impossible to understand a religious vocation apart from the vows of poverty, chastity and obedience. They are an integral part of a Sister's deep and abiding love of God, the manifestation of that love, and part of the other virtues which derive from her efforts to achieve a perfect charity—a love of God so great that it includes all men of all races in its boundless devotion. The mystery each Sister tries to plumb is why God chose *her*, why He who searches all hearts and knows all the answers called *her*, allowing her to make the promise of loving Him forever. It is in the *foreverness* of the vows of poverty, chastity and obedience—a call accompanied by His grace for her entire life—that mystery overwhelms.

His Excellency, Gabriel Marie Garrone, Archbishop of Toulouse, in a book as remarkable for its insights as for its solid doctrine on the religious life, has some penetrating observations to make on the difficulty many laymen have in understanding the religious vocation. In *La Religieuse Signe de Dieu Dans le Monde* ("Religious, Sign of God in the World")[9] he remarks that when one tries to explain the religious vocation to people who cannot understand either the life itself or those who embrace it, one is tempted to explain the too natural side of it. Thus, one points to the work religious do in the Church: the care of abandoned children, the nursing of the sick, the comforting of the miserable. He says this view is really false, because if science were some day to eliminate all suffering from the world, religious would still be necessary to the Church, because they represent holiness, a call from God to a life of love of God which will never end in time. Their response to God's call is based on the certitude that God exists and that His love for all men is infinite, as He proved by dying on the Cross. His love is made more concrete by the choice He makes from all eternity of individual men, of particular women, who are to belong to Him in a special manner, entirely and totally, and who love Him in return and are willing to make great sacrifices to prove their love.

This is why the religious life can never be divorced from the vow of poverty which detaches from earthly goods; or from the vow of chastity which enlarges the power to love and expands it to limitless boundaries so that no one is excluded. Nor can the religious life ever be divorced from the vow of obedience which causes Sisters to renounce their own will so that the Church may "send" them as witnesses of Christ at home and abroad. Such people are indispensable to the Church because they are irreplaceable.

Archbishop Garrone urges Sisters constantly to revivify their certainty: "God's love sought me out in order that I might live exclusively for Him. I can always count on Him, for He knows that I have preferred Him to all others, and to all that is not God.

9 2nd ed., Paris: Editions Fleurus, 1963, p. 243.

By my vows I am forever His."[10] Frankly, and to the point, Archbishop Garrone asks some pertinent questions, and his answers follow with relentless logic. "From the viewpoint of the casual observer is the religious truly poor? If the poverty she practices simply gives her a right to ask for alms, this is not the true spirit of poverty or what God asks of her by the vow." He continues:

If chastity is merely living without a spouse and results in a lack of sentiment; if it begets a certain hardness, then chastity has lost its true essence. To live in chastity does not mean to live without a heart; on the contrary it should make room for more love—love for all peoples of all nations and races. Above all, it makes room for fraternal love of Sister companions, whatever their faults or short-comings. This is the real meaning of chastity.[11]

Again:

If obedience is merely a disposition towards passive conformism, it is no longer obedience. On the contrary, obedience is an effort of the will, an effort which overcomes inner tensions and blossoms, in-dividually and collectively, into all manner of initiatives which give expression to the love of God . . . In the interest of the Church, the most daring works of charity are always born of obedience, never outside of it. Obedience is not a willed paralysis.[12]

If Archbishop Garrone's book had been translated into English, and read side by side with Cardinal Suenens' *Nun in the World,* a more accurate understanding of the latter would have been achieved. There would have been a richer, more inspiring grasp of the essence of the religious vocation which would bring peace and a quiet inner joy to many Sisters now disturbed by certain passages of Cardinal Suenens' book read out of context.

The Gospels Can Serve to Explain Mysteries

In seeking to define for the Sister herself and the public at large the reality of the religious vocation, and the answer to a puzzled but sincere question on the part of some lay people: *"Why do*

10 *Ibid.,* p. 244.
11 *Ibid.,* p. 245.
12 *Ibid.*

young girls of eighteen, twenty, twenty-two give up the world so full of *good* things, just when life is full of fun, and enter a stuffy convent? They can save their own souls and do so much good for others right here in their own parish. What *makes* them do it?" And these people often add: "And the worst of it is they really seem to *like* it; they honest-to-goodness even look *happy!* Why?"

Perhaps the gospel holds the secret; perhaps a study of our Lord's words will reveal the mystery, since He alone is the object sought in a religious vocation. What are these words? He has spoken them for all men and for all time; and from the days He walked the hills and vales of Galilee, men and women have been answering His call, and finding in the acceptance of His invitation a happiness and, in proportion to saying "yes" to the conditions laid down, a strange and lasting peace.

Elements of Vocation

Four elements seem to stand out in the invitation Christ extended to all: (1) "If you *will* be perfect, (2) sell what you have and give to the poor, (3) take up your cross, and (4) follow me."

1. *The Search for Perfection.* This invitation was not reserved for a special few, it was a gift to all men of good will, predicated upon the first element, that is, *the desire for perfection.* To this state, many are called, but in the end few are chosen, because few can take the other three elements that follow as a result of the first choice.

Analyzing the invitation, then, one can at least in part solve the riddle of vocation by studying the factors that comprise the whole statement. Perfection is the love of God to an unusual degree, including not only love as an expression of feeling, but a union with the will of the Beloved. Conformity to God's will is the summit of perfection. Since God wills a true and abiding love for the neighbor, fraternal charity is no small part of the love of God. St. Paul went into great detail on the subject of charity because he knew it was the fulfillment of the law. "Charity is patient, is kind: charity envieth not, dealeth not perversely, is not puffed up, is not ambitious, seeketh not her own, is not provoked to anger, thinketh no evil." *And of faith, hope and charity, these three, there is no choice as to which is best:* "the greatest of these is charity." (I Cor. 13:4–5, 13)

The invitation could well have begun with the words, "If you will practice charity perfectly. . . ." The rules of all Communities ask for as near perfect a practice of charity as is possible for poor human nature; a charity towards God that makes one love Him in preference to all others; a love of neighbor not less than that which we have for ourselves, wishing him all the good we hope for ourselves; shunning all that could hurt him as we shun being hurt ourselves. Our neighbor is more directly the member of the Community with whom we live; these first, then all others.

Charity seeks those things for which Christ promised eternal life when He said: "I was hungry and you gave Me to eat." (Matt. 25:35) (It might be that a Sister companion is hungry for a word of praise justly earned; a word or gesture of affectionate recognition. Sometimes these things take precedence over hunger for food, or a need for shelter or clothing.) "I was naked and you covered Me." (Matt. 25:36) (Sometimes a companion is wounded, bereft of happiness because of an unthinking word, a hurt; sometimes she is—mayhap because of a crotchety disposition—without friends, without consolation in a trial.) How is she clothed? With kindness? A Sister companion could sometimes be far more needy than the "glamorous poor"—those who kiss one's hand in eager gratitude; who make one feel like Lady Bountiful. Examples could be multiplied as to what does *not* call for Christ's grateful "As long as you did it to one of these My least brethren, you did it to Me." (Matt. 25:40) It takes discernment to know what constitutes real charity or perfection in the all-seeing eye of Christ.

In any case, the first element of a religious vocation is to really *want* to attain to holiness; a perfection that has none of the itemized piety that the Pharisees sought (and counted) so assiduously. The charity of Christ was full of forgiveness. It demanded the love of enemies as well as of friends; it was content with no selfish love based on an expected return of love. As St. Paul put it, *love seeketh not her own, never acts perversely, and is foreign to the word revenge.* Love, then, the willingness to strive for holiness, is the first element of a religious vocation.

2. *Renunciation.* Renunciation is the second essential element in a religious vocation. It frees a Sister from lesser loves and lesser concerns in order that God may be more perfectly loved. Christ willed during His time on earth to give the virtue of detachment a predominant place in His life both by precept and example. From Bethlehem to Calvary, self-denial marked His path. Placing Himself in even greater need than that of the animals He had created, He said of Himself: "The foxes have holes, and the birds of the air nests: but the Son of Man hath not where to lay His head." (Matt. 8:20) This was Christ's answer to a man who expressed a wish to follow Him. So consistently did He require the renunciation of all material things as a prerequisite to discipleship, that Peter, when asking, in the name of all the apostles, what reward was to be theirs, was careful to remind our Lord, "Behold, *we have left all things, and have followed Thee.*" (Matt. 19:27)

The rich young man spoken of in the gospel could easily accept the call to perfection as loving God and the neighbor. He found no difficulty in the entire decalogue: To keep holy the Sabbath; to covet no man's goods; to bear no false witness against his neighbor. "All these," he said, "have I kept from my youth." (Matt. 19:20) Knowing the truth of what he said, Christ looked upon him and loved him. His reply, tremendous in its implications, was: "If thou wilt be perfect, *go sell what thou hast, and give to the poor. . . .*" (Matt. 19:21) It is here the young man faltered; he could not accept renunciation as a way of life, although Christ made it indispensable to discipleship. "He went away sad," the gospel reports, "for he had great possessions." (Matt. 19:22)

Not everyone can renounce the attractive things of life; above all, few can renounce *themselves,* and that is why, although many are given the invitation to holiness, few can follow the call to its logical end—Christ. That is one of the imperative reasons that a candidate to the religious life should have sufficient intelligence to understand the obligations such a life places on her. It calls upon her to determine not only what she can *do* but what she can do *without;* not only what she can *give,* but what she can *give up.*

A Sister's giving up is but a preliminary step towards giving *all*. An athlete frees himself from all encumbrances—all that could in any way deter him from success—for a definite purpose: That he may win the contest in which he is engaged. The contest which engages a Sister is that of attaining to perfection, which is total love of God. The renunciation of possessions and of all desire to attain them is an outward sign that a religious has adopted a set of values diametrically different from those of people in the every-day world of secular values.

Persons of the world use—not reprehensibly—a monetary measure by which they judge of material things as "good" or "bad": A man's salary, his home, car, clothes, education, living standards, are judged *prima facie* on what these things cost. By contrast, a Sister judges her way of living "good" insofar as she is absolutely freed from all status symbols, all solicitude for personal and financial needs, in order that Christ may be the center of her thoughts and of her life.

Having renounced material possessions, a Sister begins in earnest to *give*. She gives herself to complete and loving confidence in Divine Providence. At one time this Providence may (as was suggested earlier in this chapter) place her in a convent where resources are adequate, providing all that she needs for the work in which she is engaged. This may mean a quite comfortable standard of living. Within forty-eight hours the same Sister may be transferred to a house wherein poverty is visibly present. Since detachment from possessions should mean a greater attachment to Christ, this change in her material surroundings should not in any way affect her interior peace. To be thus independent of circumstances is no small reward; it gives to a Sister that security which persons relying on human means and agencies seek in vain. This is a point not readily understood by all laymen—or even by candidates to the religious life.

A Sister can live in well-appointed convents, schools, or "rich-looking" modern hospitals, where nothing seems lacking in human comfort or scientific conveniences—yet be very poor and humble in spirit. Under these opulent conditions a Sister can remain detached, practicing in private an austere poverty. On the other hand a Sister could live and work in a slum area where dirt and squalor surround her, and within her heart desires could grow into a yearning for conveniences and even luxuries. It is not where one is placed by circumstances and obedience that counts. It is one's *attitude* that makes all the difference.

By her renunciation of possessions, a Sister finds herself, like the poor everywhere, under the obligation of working. This is for her another source of union with Christ, since He Himself was engaged during a large part of His life in the humble trade of carpenter. It is the consciousness that, whatever and wherever be her apostolate, she can, with Christ, say, "I do the will of Him Who sent Me." (John 4:34) This conviction gives her a steadfastness and a determination to put into her vocation everything that God has given her.

Thus does this second element—renunciation of possessions—fit a Sister to serve the Church through the works of her Community, and to realize that a religious vocation is much more than a personal matter of an individual's response to Christ's call. The entire Church is involved in that response, since a Sister becomes its representative and holds a mandate from it. By her close association with the Church the Sister assumes the obligation of becoming a "specialist" in holiness. All things in her life are ordered towards that end: Prayer, ascetical practices, spiritual direction, the common life, and the works of her Community's apostolate. As Father Gambari expresses it: "The love of God for His Church is forcibly expressed by a gift to the Church of a state of life and institutions and persons totally and exclusively obligated to manifest sanctity."[13]

It is precisely because a religious vocation is a giving of self to God through the Church that no one is allowed to make that gift impulsively and without a thorough knowledge of all that it asks—and of all that it offers. Ample allowance is made for a "margin of error"; error on the part of a Community in admitting a candidate, and error on the part of the candidate in thinking that she has a religious vocation. This "margin of error" extends over the periods of postulancy, novitiate, and of temporary vows, totaling, in many Communities, more than five years. Every precaution is thus taken to insure a Sister's stability in her vocation.

[13] *Religious-Apostolic Formation of Sisters*, p. 8.

The sacredness and the *foreverness* of the religious vows may well be re-stressed in these days when from some clerical sources one hears of "temporary vocations"—a notion repugnant to sincere and *thinking* persons—to justify defections from the religious life. Father Herbert F. Smith, in discussing this matter, wisely points out that the question can be answered only by resorting to divine revelation, which, in its essentials, is the source of the religious life. He brings out that this source gives no support to the claim of two types of vocation—temporary and permanent—that the purpose of the evangelical counsels is an unlimited, unflagging following of Christ. His concluding words are an inspirational summary of his thinking:

Like Abraham, the religious was led to the promised land through his acceptance in faith of the Lord's special call to him. His surest defense of that faith in Christ's special love for him is to make Christ a return of love so ardent that it will shatter doubt.[14]

There should never be any serious credence given to an idea that implies a temporary call to holiness. Vocation is a two-way response: a response to a Sister's love of Christ, and the response of Christ's love to her in return. Could anyone seriously entertain the idea that Christ's love could ever be temporary? No matter how often a Sister might fail Christ in the perfection she once promised Him, He will never fail her.

3. *The Cross*. Christ's often repeated words: "If any man wishes to come after Me, let him deny himself, take up his cross daily, and follow Me" (Matt. 16:24, Mark 8:34, Luke 9:23) are recorded in three of the gospels. He makes the cross a condition for even ordinary discipleship. But for those who are to belong to Him in a total way He constitutes it an essential element of the religious vocation. No one can seriously think of holiness as existing without the cross.

Not uncommonly, spiritual writers, when treating of the religious life, imply that the initial sacrifices called for: the leaving of parents, friends, and family; the renunciation of material posses-

---

14 Herbert F. Smith, S.J., "Temporary Religious Vocation," *Review for Religious*, XXIII, No. 4 (July, 1964), 444.

sions; the surrender of one's life to the ordering of religious Superiors—strangers to her at first—are the truly great sacrifices she makes. They are indeed sacrifices. Without the help of powerful actual grace, she would be unable to make them.

But the sufferings attached to these sacrifices are foreseen. They are, in themselves, thoroughly understandable, and pre-entrance counseling helps her to appreciate and bear them joyfully. Moreover, the candidate is usually young. The buoyancy of youth loves a challenge—and often the more difficult the challenge, the greater is her will and desire for conquest. Then, too, the candidate is getting what she wants; usually a vocation is something she has dreamed of and longed for since her elementary-school days.

But bearing the cross, in one form or another, is the lot of all men, regardless of their state of life, of their belief or unbelief. It would be strange and even contradictory if the religious life, which is a public profession of following Christ, should alone be exempt from trials and suffering, since wherever Christ is, there too, is His cross. True, the cross has its compensations, for Christ promised those who renounced all things to follow Him a hundredfold of happiness in this life, and joy eternal in the next. The joy, the happiness which most Sisters evidence, is almost as much of a mystery as is the religious vocation itself. They ponder it; they wonder about it; but they never fully understand it.

Large, formidable crosses are for the saints; the ordinary Sister experiences the small crosses common to all men by the very fact of living, of just being human. But even small crosses can become weighty by the very reason of having to be taken up daily. Sooner or later, in Community or out of it, life itself makes it abundantly clear that our everyday crosses usually arise from the ought-nots of human nature. A Sister ought not be envious of a companion; a Sister ought not to be fond of her own ease (often the beginning of boredom and unhappiness); a Sister ought not to be uncharitable in her conversations, lacking in generosity, irritable when things fail to go her way. Above all, a Sister ought not to lose her sense of humor, her ability to laugh at herself, even on occasion to laugh out loud.

Christ does not specify what crosses must be endured. He does not say what size they will be or how hard to bear. But those who have lived the religious life (and loved it) know that it is the ought-nots that constitute the petty trials of Community life. They are not more numerous than in any other walk of life. Actually, they are less numerous; for although one might rightly expect to find more ought-nots where there are more people, still among the people found in convents are those who are striving hardest to become holy. And it can be said with truth that, there too, is found a sense of humor and a capacity to enjoy the simple things of life which, most of the time, make Community living what St. Vincent called a veritable paradise on earth.

But the cross—suffering—is a very real thing; and it has tremendous intrinsic value. One who has never suffered, who has never known the purification that derives from painful uncertainty, self-doubt, anguish born of one's failure to measure up to one's own ideals, remains in a sense immature—these are the stuff of which understanding hearts are made. Observe a Sister who has, in a sense, lived only on the surface of life: she has conformed, taken an almost natural delight in routine. Perfection for her has been bounded by the horarium, the strict observance of external rules and customs. Her quick answer to any implied charge of imperfection is usually: "I've done the best I could." No doubt; no questioning. None of the tormenting: "But *have* I done my best? *Have* I made the most of life's opportunities for bearing witness to a suffering Christ?"

Surface-living has never yet produced a truly empathic person whose influence is boundless in bringing others closer to Christ. Suffering, borne for the love of Christ, which in the end makes one Christlike, is the pearl of great price. It is a talent which should be prized, and the capacity for it redoubled, and even tripled. For such is the life of the gospel, made attractive by the example of our Lord's life on earth—a life full of human suffering. For any Sister whose life is truly a "taking up of the cross daily" the gospel is like a road map, on which is clearly traced the sufferings of Christ. He was misunderstood. When He professed Himself Christ, the Son of God, He was called a liar; when He moved the people with His wonderful words of wisdom, He was a seducer, one who "stirreth up the crowds"; when He worked miracles, it was said He did so by the power of the devil; when He went into the house of Simon, "they watched Him" ever on the alert to trap Him in His actions or in His speech. Suspicion dogged His steps; calumny was His daily bread. This was the life of the great Model on whom a Sister builds her life.

Suffering, like the religious vocation itself, will always be a mystery to the uninitiated. Suffering does not make one self-satisfied. The habit of bearing it well will prevent one from being "thrown" when conflict, misunderstanding, or other trials make themselves felt. One who truly loves Christ will never wish the disciple to be "above the Master"; she will be "at home" with the cross. Such a one will have words for others when words are needed to quench bitterness, or resentment; words for one tempted to lose faith, either in others or in herself. Suffering brings the richest dimensions to life. What a pity that even the bravest cannot seek it, desire it for its inherent good, its strong remedial therapy —but at least they can accept it when it comes. And that is what Christ asks of those who would follow Him.

A comprehensive, analytical appreciation of this third element in a religious vocation is vital to the Sister herself. It would be unrealistic to deny that she can lose sight of this. It would be less than honest to ignore the fact that some do lose sight of it. This loss does not necessarily lead to the abandonment of one's vocation, but it can result in restlessness, in discontent and dissatisfaction with the religious life. This has been clearly evident in the last two or three years, and the reason is not too difficult to trace. Since *aggiornamento* was first talked about, changes and rumors of changes have filled the very air that Sisters breathe. The Church is engrossed in self-appraisal. Whatever affects the Church is bound to affect religious Communities, because they are an intrinsic part one of the other. Amid the talk, the considerable and unconsidered talk, that abounds where freedom of expression is uninhibited, all ideas from the petty to the preposterous are aired. Charges are made that the Church has lost contact with a society grown too secular and sophisticated for an institution two thousand years old. It is hardly surprising, then, that similar notions would be bruited about, suggesting that religious Orders are no longer relevant or effective instruments of the Church. Nothing could be farther from the truth.

It is Christ who instituted the religious life through the principles from which the Church developed and organized it by approving the Constitutions and Rules of various founders. Is it correct to say that a desire for holiness, a detachment from material possessions, and an endeavor to understand suffering as a means of personal purification, are incompatible with the world as we know it today? Far from any need to question the relevancy of the religious life to contemporary society, it is a time to appreciate today's opportunities: for it is the golden age of the religious life, the best of all times to live the gospel to its fullest splendor. But some few Sisters have not awakened to this fact—and a few discordant voices can disturb the harmony of the ensemble. These are the voices that echo the pseudo-philosophical claim, "One cannot reconcile the religious life with today's needs."

Studying this situation of anxiety and unease among Sisters, Reverend Mothers have tried to analyze occasions, sources and causes. Two groups stand out as worried: Sisters who have set themselves adamantly against change and will resolutely try to prevent it as a threat to the very existence of their Community; and Sisters, impulsive Sisters, who want to see changes made overnight—and above all, want a hand in making these changes, and in making them drastic. They do not see that customs were, in some Orders, centuries a-building. These cannot be ruthlessly overthrown without an analysis of what brought them into being.

Always, in time of trial and uncertainty, Communities have turned to experienced, well-balanced priests who, by their wisdom and grace of office, have been able to counsel Superiors and enlighten them in ways that have brought solace as well as prudence and foresight in handling problems. But some Reverend Mothers, having studied carefully what their Sisters have discussed with them, have come reluctantly to fear that not a little of this unease is due to a few young, inexperienced—and some not so young but certainly unwise—priests with an unfortunate sense of humor, who delight in heckling Sisters about convent life. They hold up to ridicule certain archaic rules and customs, the importance of which in the over-all picture of Community life they exaggerate. A few such priests seem to be found in each section of the country.

Knowing that the Church is engaged in studying the need to change or update certain Community practices, these priests seek to hasten the process by attempting to get Sisters "ready for change." To achieve this they imprudently, and no doubt unintentionally, downgrade the respect and reverence Sisters have for authority, for their rules and for long-honored customs. They fail to realize that time and patience are necessary to bring about renewal and adaptation.

Sisters have been reared from infancy, in the Catholic atmosphere of family life at home, to have a tremendous respect for priests as "other Christs." This attitude has been strengthened in Community life, where constitution and rule decree that the respect accorded to a priest—even in informal social situations—be always in line with the reverence due him when he is performing sacred functions at the altar. One can readily see, then, that even the most informal remarks of a priest are, for some Sisters, invested with a certain authority and respect that derive from his character of *alter Christus*.

For these Sisters (too credulous perhaps) a profound unease results from an over-jocular reference to rules and customs or respect for authority, or gratuitous assertions that religious life is passé, démodé, and destined for dissolution. These priests are visibly appalled when they hear of defections quite possibly attributable to their imprudence. They would be more than appalled by what they do not hear. A vocation is a sacred call. It should never be dealt with jocosely.

How much more rewarding it would be if these young priests (and some older ones) would use their grace of office to encourage Sisters; to urge them to bear the crosses God sends in peaceful conformity to His holy will; to help them see that crosses are the lot of all Christians, no matter what state of life one chooses. To lead a Sister to see that a loving Providence watches over her and that she will always have the grace to measure up to whatever God, through her Community, expects of her, is to inspire her to the practice of hope and fortitude. To encourage her to confide in her Superiors is to give her new confidence and a stronger spirit of faith. Sisters want to be encouraged along these lines and are disappointed when less than the ideal is presented as a line of conduct to follow.

Years ago it was quite common to hear some priests say, even from the pulpit, but more commonly in personal interviews with young women thinking of a possible religious vocation, that a girl could do more good in her parish at home than she could as a Sister in any given apostolate. Vocations declined rapidly; so much so, that Pius XII issued the following monitum:

> To all of these beloved sons and daughters who in any way have consecrated their bodies and souls to God, we address ourselves, and exhort them earnestly to strengthen their holy resolution and be faithful to it.
>
> However, since there are some who, straying from the right path in this matter, so exalt marriage as to rank it ahead of virginity and thus depreciate chastity consecrated to God and clerical celibacy, our appostolic duty demands that we now in a particular manner declare and uphold the Church's teaching on the sublime state of virginity, and so defend Catholic truth against these errors.[15]

The effect of the papal declaration was profound. Once again the religious life was extolled from the pulpit and priests counseled girls to follow their attraction to God's call. Vocations increased almost immediately. It is a noticeable fact that the vast majority of priests have a remarkable influence on vocations to the Sisterhoods. Where they are interested there is no shortage. What power in human hands! What a loss to God, to the Church and to society when this power is not used to the advantage of all three.

4. *Come, Follow Me.* "Follow Me" is the fourth and culminating element of a religious vocation. This, with the other three elements: the desire for perfection, the renunciation of possessions, and the taking up of the cross, leads to living the life of the gospel, the true imitation of Christ. It is a way that calls for total oblation. Where a Sister has made a total oblation as far as the limitations of human nature permit, she will find in the religious life an almost perfect happiness. Restlessness and discontent are rooted, not in what she is asked to give but in what she refuses to give.

15 Encyclical on *Holy Virginity*, p. 3.

The price of not giving is very high. When a Sister finds herself restless in the religious life, she may find enlightenment in meditating on two words, *oblation* and *total*. In the proportion that her dedication is total, in that measure she is happy; for she has penetrated, as far as is humanly possible, the mystery and the meaning of a religious vocation.

Archbishop Garrone reassures all Sisters today in these words:

Pre-eminently, you are signs in the world—signs of the reality of God. In the Church, it is the hour of the religious. It is your hour because it is the hour of poverty . . . of chastity . . . of obedience. . . . It is the Church's hour because it cannot define itself without defining you. Do you ask, "How shall we survive?" Ask only, "How shall I best live the religious life?"[16]

16 *Op. cit.,* pp. 12–13.

11

Sisters and Their Lay Colleagues

A thorough understanding and deep appreciation, not only of her own vocation, but of that of her lay colleague to a life in the secular world, is essential to the fulfillment of a Sister's apostolate today. A new interrelationship of Sisters and laity is no small part of the Church's general *aggiornamento*. Possibly the changed role of the laity is more dramatic at the moment than that of the Sister, but both are very much in the spotlight. Inevitably—and desirably—the dynamic forces at work within the Church are bringing new religious-laity contacts and effecting in many areas a merging of their respective apostolates. Each partner to this merger should have a vast respect for the other's contribution, knowing that each is truly his brother's keeper and that inherent in each apostolate is the endeavor to fulfill God's holy will. In this, perhaps, the religious has more to learn than the layman, since the place of religious in the Church and in society has been well-established for centuries—though definitely not always clearly understood—while a new era of lay renaissance is just dawning.

There is a particular and unique call to the layman today to serve in the front ranks of the Church. It is of paramount concern for every Sister to recognize this, since it has far-reaching implications for her own apostolate. A lack of knowledge of the lay movement, and a want of understanding of its nature and extent, will delimit her apostolic opportunities and deprive her of the distinctive privilege of our epoch: working side by side with the laity in the mission of the Church to bring Christ to the world.

Pius XI—Pope of the Laity

This has been called the Age of the Laity, and so it is. Books, well-written, theologically sound and ably documented come off the press by the dozens, telling of the new, dynamic position of the laity in the Church. Scores of articles treat of the same subject, describing the changing attitude of the laity, of their awakening to a consciousness of their responsibility to make their faith both relevant and vital to the society in which they live. It is the Catholic laity, in their millions, who come into direct and daily contact with persons of other faiths or of no faith. It is to them the Church looks, not only to exemplify her teachings in their own lives, but by their mental alertness and intellectual ability to spread her social and religious doctrine. Dialogue is not a matter only of words. The Catholic businessman by his fairness, the Catholic employee by his integrity, the Catholic physician by his ethics, the Catholic housewife by her devotedness, the Catholic student by his honesty, the Catholic woman by her uncompromising moral code are hourly engaged in the most effective of all dialogues. Because their faith is relevant to their lives, they make it relevant to the world in which those lives are lived.

Ever since the modern impetus to a recognition of the place of the laity in the Church was given by Pius XI, deservedly designated as "The Pope of Catholic Action," his successors have furthered and fostered it. Pius XII declared that the aid rendered by the laity to the apostolate is an indispensable necessity. Two World Congresses of the Lay Apostolate held in Rome, the first in 1951, the second in 1957, emphasized the growth and importance of the movement as well as the Church's interest and encouragement. The late Pope John XXIII, speaking of the enormous development of the apostolate of the laity in modern times, promised that it would be given detailed consideration, and prove "an object of vital concern and special study" of the hierarchy at the Ecumenical Council. He included the Apostolate of the Laity in the ten Council Commissions of Vatican II.[1]

What is a matter of vital concern and special study to the

---

[1] Motu Proprio on *Appropinquante Concilio*, trans. National Catholic Welfare Conference News Service, 1962, p. 7.

Conciliar Fathers cannot but hold great import for Sisters who, as representatives of the Church, work continuously and in such close and varied contact with the laity. Church-laity relationships and clergy-laity relationships are topics of three-dimensional discussion. Religious-laity relationships have, perhaps, been too long overlooked. How often we see in print references to "the Bishop and the laity," "Church-laity," "clergy-laity" and, less frequently, "Church-religious-laity relationship," but rarely is there a reference, even in passing, to "Sister-laity relationship." Their mutual interests and those of the Church would profit by a little airing. But this airing or this analysis must be done within the context of the characteristics of the times.

Social Changes in the Church

An all-inclusive view indicates that, in providential conjunction with the Age of the Laity, it is also the age of many astounding social changes in the Church. It is the golden age of active Orders, in which a great ferment of *aggiornamento* is stirring as constitutions, rules and customs are revised so that the members of these Orders may, in the words of Pope Pius XII, "Serve the world of today as it needs to be served today." It is the age of the strictest contemplative Orders, whose increase in numbers and expansion of monasteries immediately after the close of World War II caught the attention of the entire nation. It is the age of newly founded Communities, dedicated to medical work in foreign lands; to social work in our own country; to catechetical teaching at home and abroad. It is the age of secular institutes, a relatively new form of religious life. It is the age when the Church, awesomely manifesting her latent power, is working as leaven in the world. In a word, we see realized the words of the late Pontiff John XXIII, that a new Pentecostal time has come in which a pristine freshness will be restored to the Church.

Paraphrasing Dickens' words, we might say "It is the worst of times and it is the best of times." It is the worst of times because in the world, already secular and materialistic, Christianity is losing ground. The world would turn the advances of science and technology, not only to de-Christianizing human society, but to depersonalizing and dehumanizing it. It is the best of times because the wave of ecumenism, initiated by Pope John XXIII and fostered by his successor, Paul VI, and Vatican Council II, bids fair to break down barriers that have separated Christians for too many years, substituting for them strong bonds of union and charity. This spirit, engendered in the highest possible ecclesiastical source, depends in a large measure on the laity, Catholic and non-Catholic, for its spread, preservation and ultimate triumph. Under what obligations are religious to foster the lay movement, and how can they best contribute to inspiring the laity to the fullest use of the grace of their day? Where will their contacts be made?

Meeting Ground of Religious and Laity

The obvious is frequently so completely overlooked. The apostolates of religious and laity have an extensive and long-established meeting ground, of which all too little notice is taken: The meeting ground of employer and employee. In the many commendable efforts now being made to have Sisters work with adults, no focus has been placed on the employer-employee economic situation, in which Sisters have worked almost wholly with adults for years. Would it not be logical and profitable for Sisters to strengthen their religious-lay apostolate where they work side by side, in a contemporary setting, in conventional surroundings, subject to all the pressures and variations, gratifications and annoyances, successes and failures of American life? If there is something lacking here, is not a re-examination and reappraisal of the situation in order?

At present, the majority of Sisters exercise their apostolate in an institutional setting. No one is suggesting (save for current controversial questioning of modifications in the parochial school system) that Sisters close their institutions and find other outlets for their zeal. Obviously, then, it will be, for the most part, Sisters serving in Catholic institutions who will answer the call for closer contact with adults and the serving of society in new ways. That they may be successful in new and untried areas of working with the laity, Sisters would do well to assess the relationship to which they are wholly accustomed, that of employer-employee.

It seems strange, and it even grates on the ear, to hear religious spoken of as employers, but such they are, and in no small way. No definite statistics are available as to the actual number of lay persons in the employ of religious in the United States, but it is safe to say that it runs into the millions. In many—in fact, in most—institutions and agencies, Sisters are vastly outnumbered by their lay colleagues. In a survey recently made by a multi-service Community, it was found that in one hospital alone the Sisters were outnumbered by 80 per cent. In one social agency there were 28 lay persons for each Sister. In schools, a ratio of 3 Sisters to 1 lay teacher is considered a desirable norm, but one which the fewness of Sisters frequently makes impossible to maintain. In colleges and universities and in certain social works a much higher percentage of lay personnel exists. Here is a field "ripe for the harvest," where Sisters can extend their apostolate and the laity intensify theirs.

Not only is it a permanent field, but it is daily expanding as religious seek for lay persons in ever-increasing numbers to associate themselves as employees with the Church in its organized, institutional works of mercy and charity. Sisters should view the situation realistically—and gratefully, instead of regarding it, as some do, as a "temporary" situation. We not infrequently hear a Sister say, "We have a lay teacher in seventh grade this year, but we hope the Motherhouse will send a Sister for it next year." Or, "My, I am so sorry we have a lay supervisor in pediatrics; but several Sisters are being prepared in that field, and perhaps we will get one of them when they have received their degrees." And again, "Miss X is a very satisfactory group mother for our junior girls, but I do wish we had a Sister instead."

The examples cited are just frequent enough to result, unfortunately, in two things: (1) Job insecurity is created in the mind of the lay person; (2) The Sister is rendered oblivious to the opportunity within her grasp to promote fine apostolic teamwork. In this, all Communities might profit immensely by taking a leaf from the book of Congregations devoted wholly to missionary work. Recognizing that the cooperation of lay people is vital to the success of their works, they indoctrinate their young members from the beginning of their religious life with this viewpoint. Junior Mistresses could well make note of this and give some time to preparing young Sisters to work hopefully and helpfully with the laity who will later constitute a large part of their professional world. As was noted in Chapter 7, it is essential to integrate a sound philosophy of apostolic service with concrete experiences in both the academic curriculum and co-curriculum activities.

Sisters Outnumbered by Laity in All Apostolates

The outnumbering of Sisters (and other religious) by lay persons in hospitals, schools and other Church-affiliated agencies is not a circumstance to be deplored or regretted, but one to be seized upon and explored hopefully. With a firm and final good-by to the mind-set "We will employ a lay person until we can get a Sister," Sisters should look squarely at the picture. In the field of education, which claims by far the largest number of Sisters, half the Catholic children of grade-school age and almost two-thirds of Catholic high-school students are in public schools. Ask the Mother General or Provincial of any multiple-works Community how many requests for Sisters to work in both new and old fields she has had to refuse in any one year, and the number will often run as high as fifty. In fact, the acceptance of any work, of whatsoever nature, sets off a sort of chain reaction of requests from other sources to take on similar works.

As vocations increase—and, thanks be to God, there was in the United States in 1963 a modest increase of 2,098 vocations in the teaching field alone—the most urgent of the pleas for Sisters are answered. But Communities of the United States are becoming more and more missionary- and ecumenical-minded; they show a growing interest in the needs of other countries. This interest is not only a strictly missionary one but extends to countries which have a long Christian and decidedly Catholic heritage of faith. Educationally, socially and economically these countries are disadvantaged. It was for them that the Mothers General and Provincials of the United States were asked in 1961 by Right Reverend Agostino Caseroli, representative of the Holy See, to make a Ten-Year Plan to extend health, welfare and educational aid to South American nations. Part of the plan, the key concept, eloquently set out by His Excellency, was that each Community pledge a tithe—that is, ten per cent of its present number would be assigned

to Latin America within the next ten years.[2] The response of
Major Superiors is already most gratifying. But this sending of
Sisters to serve abroad emphasizes the need of their working in a
more apostolic manner with their lay colleagues at home. It may
well be that the lamented "Sister shortage" will prove to be a real
blessing, as Sisters come, not only to a greater understanding and
appreciation of the vocation of the layman, but also to provide for
its implementation in his place of employment.

In their own religious vocation, it is common for Sisters to
experience a haunting sense of unease lest their work detract from
their prayer life, or lest they fail to carry their prayer life into their
work. Will it not come as a new thought to many Sisters that the
layman's vocation makes the same demand on him that he be
faithful to his vocation wherever he is and whatever he is doing?
A strong statement is made to this effect in a recently published
book:

> The authentic layman must embrace the world as his monastery. If
> he attempts to withdraw, he is playing false to his lay vocation, which
> is to bring Christ to the world, indeed to be Christ to the world. And
> this world is not just an extension of personal relationships; it is a
> vast complex of social systems and cultures, to which the layman
> must bring the Saviour.[3]

Recognition that the lay person has a *holy* vocation should make
Sisters eager to aid him in fulfilling this call, realizing that they
work together in the common cause of bearing witness to Christ
which can be done *only* when the spirit of charity is the motivating
power.

The Layman as "Christ in the World"

If the layman is to "be Christ in the world," his place of employment must necessarily be largely the place where that role is
played. A great number of laymen, possibly the majority in the

---

2 "The Urgent Needs of the Church in Latin America," *Religious Life in the Church Today*, pp. 37–39.

3 Donald G. Thorman, *The Emerging Layman* (Garden City, New York: Doubleday and Co., Inc., 1962), p. 57.

average- or lower-income bracket, cannot, because of obligatory family and social claims, give either time or money to apostolic works *per se*. It is imperative that a Sister have a deep, practical consciousness of the reality of her lay colleague's "call" to lead a Christ-oriented life, so that she will act towards him consistently with a knowledge and consciousness of the obstacles that beset his path in the apostolic life.

It seems almost superfluous to say that this attitude is to be maintained toward all lay co-workers, Catholic and non-Catholic. In those sections of the country where non-Catholic employees predominate, Sisters should give conscientious adherence to the words of the late Pope John XXIII: "Every being has a right to honor God according to the dictates of his conscience, and therefore the right to practice his religion privately and publicly."[4] Sisters have long counted on—and rightly so—the example of their own wholly committed lives to win others to Christ. But have they sufficiently recognized and honored the dedication and commitment of the laity? To do this will require more than casual thought. It will require, in many instances, a purifying, painful re-thinking, not unlike that which a convert to the faith goes through.

When we say "Sister-teacher," "Sister-nurse" or "Sister-social-worker," we mean that a profession is being practiced by one who will exercise it *differently* by reason of the higher obligations arising from her total commitment to Christ. Sister-employer should carry the same connotation. Sisters' responsibility as representatives of the Church must be evident in the business and economic field, even as it is in the professional. Lay persons have been partners with Sisters for years in every Church-oriented activity—teaching, nursing, social work—and every subsidiary avenue opened up by these major fields of endeavor. So far as the direct object of the Sister-lay apostolate is concerned, whether it is centered on the patient, the pupil, or the needy person in whatever category, the recognition that each complements the other works admirably, and to the best interests of the third person who is the object of their combined services. But there seems to be a tendency to "short-circuit" the religious-apostolic aim when (pre-

[4] *Pacem in Terris*, p. 6.

scinding from pupil, patient or client) the immediate employer-
employee relationship is considered in itself.

Every employee, whether president of a bank, city street-
sweeper, department-store clerk or a university professor, has a
commitment to the place of his employment. What affects the
place where he spends one-third of his life affects him. His family
and social life are colored by the environment of his employment.
The interests of his employers are his interests. He *wishes* to be
part of it. He *wants* to be proud of it. This psychological factor—
lower in the scale of values than the religious-apostolic, but still
strong and valid—can be capitalized on by the Sisters to create a
strong, personal bond between themselves and those they employ.

Knowing how eager and zealous Sisters are to spread the Kingdom of God on earth, and how willingly they sacrifice themselves
for this end, it is regretful to note that all too often there seems to
be a "blind spot" which partially prevents Sisters from seeing the
possibilities for apostolic action among their colleagues and other
employees. Today, when there is a veritable and laudable ferment
among Sisters to work with lay adults, it is of paramount importance to raise the question: "What relationships exist (or should
exist) between Sisters and their lay colleagues in the spiritual and
corporal works of mercy?" Once raised, the inescapable answer is:
"They are complementary one to the other, each needing the
others to perfect their respective apostolates."

Lay Apostolic Climate Necessary

For Sisters not to recognize that gainful employment in a Catholic institution can constitute a fruitful form of lay apostolic action
is deplorable. Working for a livelihood, whether in a white-collar,
blue-collar or no-collar job, is a fulfillment of God's command
after the fall of Adam: "Thou shalt earn thy bread in the sweat of
thy brow." Monthly or semi-monthly pay checks do not rule out
dedication. Here it would be nothing less than unjust for a Sister
to project her personal scale of values into the world and life of
the layman.

In working for the best possible salary that his talents and skills
can command, and in being ambitious for higher positions, the

layman is being absolutely faithful to what his vocation demands of him. A religious should recognize this fidelity to his vocation as a virtue, just as he recognizes and pays tribute to the virtue she exercises in being faithful to her calling. The freedom of a Sister to take no thought for the morrow is countered by the obligation of the lay person to do that very thing. Blessings that are with us continuously tend to be taken for granted and so lose their impact. The freedom of Sisters from the monthly struggle with bills for rent, food, electricity, education, payments on furniture and/or home, insurance, clothing, etc., can make Sisters overlook, in dealing with lay employees, the fact that the latter are subject to that constant economic anxiety.

The first step, then, towards creating a lay apostolic atmosphere in an institution owned by religious is the payment of adequate salaries. Unity and charity can never be built upon a foundation of injustice. Not only should the salaries be in line with those paid by other institutions in the area for the same kind of work, but all so-called "fringe" benefits should be included: vacations, sick leave, overtime pay, pension plans, hospital insurance and in-service education. Who, if not religious, should be the first to put into effect that aspect of the Church's social teachings? That an adequate wage is a part of the Church's teachings, is clearly spelled out in *Mater et Magistra*.[5]

But salaries, "fringe benefits" and wholesome working conditions are only indirectly pertinent to the blending of the apostolates of Sisters and laity. Trade unions could bring about the first, but only the charity of Christ can bring about the latter. The "We pay them" has, in the minds of some religious, set up a block to this union. Receiving a salary has become a line of demarcation which should be effaced; it is, once and for all, no deterrent to a layman's apostolate, nor to his sense of dedication.

What More Can Sisters Do?

Assuming, then, that salaries, working conditions, job security, tenure and other material aspects of a lay person's position are in accord with justice, what *more* can Sisters do to make working

5 P. 23.

under Catholic auspices a genuine aspect of Catholic Action and a source of spiritual satisfaction to lay people? What *more* can Sisters do to make it different from, and more attractive than, working under secular authorities? This is something entirely beyond the range of personnel policies, job analysis and department regulations. It is a person-to-person matter wherein the religious honors in her lay colleague the vocation which every child of God has to strive to sanctify himself by the pursuit of perfection according to his state in life. This implies that every Sister needs to recognize fully the part Divine Providence plays in guiding a person to seek employment in a Catholic environment. The Sister needs to accept, too, her responsibility as the chief instrument for carrying out the designs of Providence in bringing them together. With this attitude, she will greet with real interest, rather than active annoyance, normal changes in personnel that will put her in touch with new and different employees. After all, the turn-over in employees that frequently occurs in large institutions can be looked upon as providing new opportunities to meet and influence people which Providence from all eternity intended her to meet. But, as a matter of fact, if Sisters really look upon the laymen and laywomen with whom they work as "apostles" who are true comrade-in-arms, will not the turn-over become less frequent?

Depersonalization is a sort of creeping paralysis in our time. Sisters should combat this as they would combat any pernicious disease. How far are religious involved in the depersonalization of their lay co-workers? When the chemistry teacher fails to appear for duty, the principal of the school is understandably disturbed because a teacher must—somehow—be supplied for the class. But is she equally concerned with what it means to the chemistry teacher to forfeit a day's pay? Does the principal know the home conditions of the teacher? Is she concerned lest the teacher be ill and alone with no one to give her personal attention? Or, if the teacher is married and must remain at home because of the illness of her husband or one of her children, does the principal *really* share in the wife's or mother's concern? Which weighs the heavier —the absence of the teacher or the cause of her absence?

There is much more involved here than a matter of sympathy,

understanding and kindness. There is the deeper and more basic need, on the part of the Sister, to see the situation from the value judgments of the lay person's vocation. By her very state, conjugal love and all that emanates from it *must* come first, because God has so ordained it. If fulfilling her duties towards husband and family means a sacrifice of her employment, the laywoman must make that sacrifice, and her Sister colleague should help her to make the sacrifice with courage, and even joy. This attitude towards a sacrifice on the part of her lay colleagues is something a Sister should appreciate, encourage and applaud. She should never in any degree lessen it by manifesting irritation at the inconvenience which the lay person's conflicting interests occasion her. The subordinate-superior situation should not enter into the Sister's thinking, but only the situation where one person, dedicated to her vocation, honors another person's dedication to hers. This is a contribution a Sister can make to her lay colleague's sense of mission and conformity to God's will made known to all of us through human occasions and events that call for sacrifice.

In hospitals and social agencies, even more frequent occasions arise which require that the Sister have a deep-rooted belief in the vocation of her lay colleagues, and an understanding of their commitment to its values. A supervisor of a hospital division, for instance, is asked, on short notice, to give a week's leave of absence to a nurse who wishes to attend her brother's wedding. Does the Sister judge of the request in terms of her own or in terms of her lay colleague's vocation? The Sister retains a deep love for her family, but she is not closely associated with its social activities nor with its daily events. A wedding in the family means, for her, a congratulatory letter, the offering of a Mass for the happiness of the new couple, and a small gift. The wedding has no bearing on her own life, personal or professional.

But for her lay colleague it is quite different. Not only will her attendance at the marriage ceremony be a festive affair, but it will deepen family ties, enable her to live more intensely, for a brief time, in an atmosphere that is essential to her own well-being, and provide a lifetime memory that will be dearly cherished. A Sister who gives only a grudging or half-hearted permission to the nurse for the requested leave is guilty of more than a selfish act. This she will later recognize and regret. But, more profoundly, she has missed an opportunity to foster her lay colleague's vocation to Christian family living: she has forfeited an occasion to show respect for the strengthening of family ties. She has failed the nurse in her apostolate, as much as the nurse would fail a Sister in *her* apostolate did she look grudgingly upon a Sister-supervisor's absence from the division necessitated by her religious exercises, recreation, or some other aspect of Community living.

To extend these practical examples for further clarification of the Sister-laity relations, it can be noted that Catholic institutions share with others the lament that the percentage of turnover in employees is so high as to impair efficiency. To quote an irritating and all too frequent instance, the director of a social agency receives word from the office of Catholic Charities that a new social worker is being assigned to the institution. The Sister-director is perturbed, saying to herself: "This is the third social worker assigned to us within a year and a half. How can they get to know the children and give them the help they so sorely need unless they are with us over a prolonged period?" The Sister's concern for the children is to be admired and commended. Her concern is based upon sound principles of child care. But would it not be helpful— and also, perhaps remedial—if she gave some thought to the "why" of the rapid change-over of social workers?

She might well ask herself whether she and the other Sisters had manifested a sharing spirit with the social workers. Had they made directed efforts that the social worker might come to know *them* as well as the children? Had they been quick with an encouraging word, pointing out how this or that child had improved under the social worker's guidance and counseling? Had there been sincere warmth and acceptance of her as a person as well as a comrade-in-arms? How much had the Sisters really known of the social worker's family life and personal obligations? Had they looked upon her merely as an employee, or as a co-laborer, called to a specific work, who should "catch" from them the spirit of apostolic zeal?—a quality caught, never taught.

The combined apostolate of religious and laity requires that personal interest, unfeigned and unfailing, be extended by the Sisters to every employee, from the highest paid professional to those in the lowest rank of unskilled labor. True, the Sisters are pressed for time, and the very nature of their vocation causes them to center their attention on those who are the immediate object of their apostolate: pupils, the sick, dependent children, the aged, the handicapped and all others upon whom they expend, with the unstinting prodigality of Magdalen, the precious ointment of their loving care. But how far these loving services could be expanded, were every employee to become also an apostle, captivates the imagination. If, motivated by working with Sisters, they were to extend their own apostolate into those areas beyond both the reach and the competency of the Sisters, what hope there would be for a truly better world!

The extension of the lay apostolate beyond the place and time of their regular occupation; their active participation in Catholic Action, organized or unorganized, will require a generous, fervent and self-sacrificing spirit. Where will the lay person better acquire this spirit than in daily contacts with persons who, as employers, exemplify in their principles and practices the virtues of justice and charity? Religious are seldom lacking in outward manifestations of respect and fraternal charity towards their fellow religious. But it must be frankly admitted that the same admirable line of conduct is not always present in their dealings with lay colleagues. A sharp reproof, or an explanation brushed aside, however infrequent, lessens morale and introduces a discordant element into the working environment. This can lead to resentments that are later aired among co-workers, to the great detriment of fraternal charity, and possibly to a diminished esteem for the Church.

One Weight and One Measure

If there is to be a mutual furthering of apostolates, in the matter of respect and cordiality Sisters should not have two weights and two measures: one for their fellow religious and one for their lay colleagues. The same loyalty and charity which causes them to refrain from mentioning a Sister companion's faults should be exercised habitually towards their lay associates. Many Sisters lament the fact that lack of time and absence of opportunity prevent them from bearing witness to Christ in the various ways to which the Church and modern society invite them. These Sisters have but to explore the opportunities in their daily environment. True, such daily efforts may lack the appeal of the unusual, and the stimulus inherent in novelty, but it will have a more immediate impact on the interpersonal relationships of their everyday life. By creating a climate of cordial cooperation, first in her particular office or duty, and then in the institution or agency in which she exercises her apostolate, the Sister is preparing herself for leadership. A leader has been defined as "A person who makes you *want* to follow him." The one word "want" makes all the difference.

It is wholly commendable that Sisters should strive to fit themselves to be leaders, eager to assume the responsibilities that leadership carries with it. It is even more commendable when they seek to develop leadership in the lay people with whom they work. Lay persons, both Catholic and non-Catholic, freely accord a Sister status. It is the individual responsibility of each Sister to accord status in return to every lay person with whom she works. Where she finds ability she should strive to develop it so that lay persons under her guidance attain to the fullest stature of which they are capable. It is a measure of the Sister's own status and stature that every lay man or woman coming under her influence becomes a better person and a more zealous apostle by reason of this contact. It is a further measure of her stature when she can as readily and fully applaud professional recognition given to a lay co-worker as when the same recognition is accorded to herself or to a member of her Community.

Sister-Laity Apostolate and Obedience

The religious-laity apostolate as carried on within an institutional setting can raise certain questions of an interesting, though perhaps delicate, nature. For one example, how far can self-determination, indispensable to a layman's state of life, find its fulfillment in an employee in a religious Community? For another, how far can he exercise a legitimate ambition to "get ahead"—to seek top positions with attendant increments in salary and prestige? Experience shows him every day that key positions of authority have always been held, as a matter of course, by members of the religious Congregation with whom he is associated. Sisters have always been principals of the schools where they taught, whether these were owned by the diocese or by the religious Community itself.

Sisters have almost always been the chief administrators of Community-owned colleges, hospitals and social agencies; but he now sees that these institutions have expanded beyond the dreams of their founders and have also become exceedingly complex. The number of lay employees is constantly increasing. Many of them, because of their educational background, professional experience, and the possession of many other skills, occupy positions of authority in their civic community. Now the question arises: Should there be a limit, inherent in the situation of working in a Catholic institution, which would prevent a lay person from rising to the highest position in a Catholic agency?

In many Catholic secondary schools today priests have been appointed principals. May not a lay man or woman teacher in a Catholic school aspire to the same position? Recently a laywoman was selected as principal of a Catholic grade school. This sets a precedent. Many Catholic hospitals frequently have lay assistant administrators. Is the top position always to be closed to them? Even to raise such a question a few years ago would have seemed preposterous. But there is scarcely any question dealing with things as "they have always been" that is preposterous today, for change is in the very air we breathe. It is safe to predict that within a decade we will have multiple examples of lay people in top roles of authority in our Catholic institutions.

As we have just said, the joint religious-lay apostolate raises interesting but delicate questions. Two parallel viewpoints must be considered, both of them of first importance. The viewpoint of the layman (and whatever is said of laymen includes what needs being said of laywomen) is that he has a right and a duty, within the framework of his state in life, to seek the highest position he is capable of filling. If such a possibility be denied him because he works under Catholic auspices, it would appear that he should seek employment elsewhere. Obviously, such a situation would not occur frequently for the simple reason that persons of high calibre and competency, personally and professionally, are not easily found. Catholic institutions need gifted co-workers and are anxious to retain their services. Also, the roles of Sisters in administrative functions require the use of their talents in special duties that lay-women or laymen cannot fulfill: for example, her role of spiritual leader to the Sisters as Sisters. This means that, in many instances, laymen will have to be hired in order to free certain Sisters for executive services within the framework of religious Community life. This new role of the layman and the new role of the Sisters seems to call for study, revision, and adaptation. Studies are in progress in this area and statements that have a startling sound are being made:

Traditionally, the institutions of the Church, owned and operated by religious Communities, have been carrying on their work with the aid of laymen; today's apostolic facts are such, however, that these same institutions now need to be owned by the religious Communities, but operated by and through lay people, with the religious helping.[6]

This brings us to a question within the framework of parallel viewpoints. The problem can be better analyzed if put on a frequently occurring level, such as has been cited by way of example, where a local Superior of a large institution is required of necessity to delegate her authority not only to other Sisters but also to lay persons. A personnel manager, or assistant administrator, say of a hospital or college, would offer an example. For the sake of good order, smooth running, harmony and efficiency, Sisters as well as lay colleagues would obey that person within his or her jurisdictional province. For the Sister a question arises: Does she exercise the virtue of religious obedience? Far from being an academic question, this is one that must be resolved to avoid a seeming dichotomy between a Sister's religious and her professional obligations.

So far as her *vow* of obedience is concerned, the obligations arising from this situation are exclusively in relation to her religious Superiors, each within the competency given her by the constitution of the Community. There can be no question of any Superior's

[6] Trafford P. Maher, S.J., *Lest We Build on Sand* (St. Louis: The Catholic Hospital Association of the United States and Canada, 1962), p. 10.

delegating authority deriving from the vow, for the Superior herself seldom has occasion to use this special type of authority. It is true that the vow enhances the merit of a Sister's works since it makes of them acts of religion, but it is the *virtue* of obedience and not the vow that a Sister habitually practices in her daily life.

Since obedience has as its sanctifying end the fulfilling of God's will, it would seem that when the exigencies of a situation and the judgment of a Major Superior require that another Sister or a lay person be appointed as the immediate professional superior, the cooperation a Sister gives to this person is truly accorded to properly constituted authority. It arises from the circumstances in which she is placed and from the fact of being in full accord with her Superior's desires. Any lack of cooperation with such a Sister or lay person holding delegated authority by reason of her executive position would be seen as a distinct act of disobedience and a lack of cooperation with the professional superior. Conversely, then, it follows that cooperation under these circumstances is an act of obedience to the professional superior, whether a lay person or another Sister. And such obedience would be as fully meritorious and as intelligently edifying as if her obedience were directed to a religious Superior. Our Lord gave the entire world an example of His regard for the concept of subsidiarity when He required the people of God to recognize the apostles with the same respect accorded to Him personally: "He who hears you," He said to His apostles, "hears Me."

The acceptance of this view will open to Sisters a whole new segment of their apostolate in which they can bear witness to Christ. Since all authority comes from God, all who exercise it do so as His delegates. Christ made this clear for all time when He said to Pilate: "Thou shouldst not have any power against Me, unless it were given thee from above." (John 19:11) With the life—and death—of Christ constantly before them, to be imitated and emulated, obedience is the *élan vital* of the religious life. Daily, Sisters practice heroic obedience. Occasionally this is apparent to all, as when a Sister, in response to the call of obedience, leaves a dearly loved work and appreciative companions, to report, sometimes on very short notice, to another agency in a distant part of the country. But for the most part, the obedience of Sisters is a beautiful hourly sacrifice they offer to God in taken-for-granted ways. It is the source of unshakeable serenity, at once a matter of admiration and wonder to those not blessed with a religious vocation. How greatly would the vocation of her lay associates be enriched, if this same spirit of cooperation should be extended to them, when the respective positions of lay persons and Sisters called for it.

New and Vital Roles in the Sister-Laity Apostolate

Both the laity and Sisters have new and vital roles in the Church's functioning. Neither is yet wholly clear as to the nature of their role nor where it will lead them. Speaking of the layman and of his uncertain, questioning attitude, Daniel Callahan writes:

The self-image which emerges here is, broadly speaking, one of some degree of repression, frustration, disenchantment, mild cynicism and thwarted zeal and intelligence. The layman cannot speak when he wants to, cannot be sure anyone will listen when he does speak, is not consulted even when his thinking and experience could be of profit to the Church.[7]

Now would seem to be the time for Sisters, who are daily in contact with millions of the laity, to relieve them of this frustration, to make full use of their zeal and intelligence in their places of employment, that is, in their apostolates. It is indeed the time for Sisters and laity to speak to each other in "new tongues."

But it takes two to create a dialogue. It takes a willingness and a *wanting to* on both sides, a meeting of each other halfway, for the Sister and her lay colleague to reach full understanding. For the lay person can be unreasonable at times too. Daniel Callahan is big enough and fair enough to see both sides. If we substitute the word "Sisters" for the word "clergy," what he says may be paraphrased to portray rather typical situations that arise in Sister-laity relationships by reason of the uncertainty both feel concerning their joint roles in the apostolate:

[7] Daniel Callahan, *The Mind of the Catholic Layman* (New York: Charles Scribner's Sons, 1963), pp. 117–118.

First, it is by no means clear that the contemporary layman knows exactly what he wants. Most commonly, he will speak of the need for more communication between laity and (Sisters); for greater freedom to exercise personal judgment and responsibility; for freedom from (Sisters' maternalism); for a (Sister's) recognition that the temporal order cannot be scorned or degraded or the world denied; for the layman to be free to speak in the market place and bring the Church to that secular world in which he lives. Yet at the same time he may complain that the (Sisters) do not tell him what to do in the world; that (they) do not provide him with sufficient guidance and directions to enable him to cope with the modern age. This ambivalence—between a desire to be free and a desire to be led—is rarely absent from even the most sophisticated writing and speaking by laymen.[8]

This ambivalence should be easy to understand (although it is not) by every Sister whose vocation places her in immediate Sister-laity contact. It is something she should learn to understand and take in stride—a loving, generous stride—for how many of us have said with more feeling than our lay people ever dream: "What would we ever do without the laity! They are the perfect complement we need to carry on our work in and for the Church."

Nothing that man has invented acts so thoroughly, so deeply, as the grace of God. No orbital flights, no metallurgical miracles, no wizardry of automation can change man. But grace can change him. This is the eternal verity on which all men can lay hold as proof of their worth and dignity in this onrushing, changing world. With laity and religious working in close harmony and real understanding, the Church will be better recognized for the beneficent power that is hers; and Christianity will be helped to attain a widening, more vital and saving power of leadership.

[8] *Ibid.*, p. 142.

12

Aggiornamento of the Sister-Teacher

"Readiness" for a number of years was a key word in primary grades. Reading readiness, number readiness, writing readiness were, theoretically, to be determined by observation of a child's interests and abilities, and he was not to be introduced into the mazes of reading, arithmetic and writing until he was ready for it. The readiness theory has its protagonists and antagonists. But another kind of readiness, transferred from pupil's desk to teacher's rostrum. is here and now: readiness for change. Change, drastic change, not only in methods, technique, teaching aids and materials, but in the intangibles of objective, climate, approach and attitude admits of neither dispute nor delay. Not to be ready to change is to cease to be useful as a teacher. For the Sister who teaches, the readiness to change which she manifests may well be an index to her sanctity, as it is an index to her obedience to the Church.

The Mandate to Teach

The Church in its sweeping *aggiornamento* has placed special emphasis on her Divinely-given mandate to teach. Consequently, she is taking both a broad look and a hard look at her education system. She has decided that what she sees calls for study, analysis and change. This is nothing new. The foundations for the *aggiornamento* now being implemented were laid in the pontificates of Paul VI's three immediate predecessors. Nothing that modern educators are now demanding expresses so well the commitment of education to the whole person as do the words of Pius XI:

Christian education takes in the whole aggregate of human life, physical and spiritual, intellectual and moral, individual, social and domestic; not with a view to reducing it in any way, but in order to elevate, regulate and perfect it.[1]

If the Church's interest in education is not new, what *is* new is its focus, intense and unremitting, on those who are her representatives in the teaching field. Not only does she desire that religious have a professional education superior to that of their lay colleagues; she insists further that the spiritual and the intellectual development never be separated, for they are complementary. This requires a formation of which the professional is only one part. This focus has spotlighted every facet of preparation for the teaching apostolate: time, place, faculty, facilities, curriculum. All must be in accord with what is required of teaching today. "The school before the church" was a slogan which served splendidly in the early, struggling days of Catholics in the United States. This has now been changed to "Sisters before the school," as plans for new school buildings remain on drawing boards until pastors have a signed agreement from a Community to provide Sisters to staff their schools in a certain ratio to lay teachers. Many bishops look with approval on those Communities whose Superiors take a firm stand against accepting any works for which their Sisters have not been adequately prepared. Among the hierarchy, the attitude is growing that a Sister not prepared spiritually, mentally and professionally for her duty can be more detrimental than no Sister at all.

This attitude of the Church is of vital importance to more than the 104,000 teaching Sisters in the Catholic school system of the United States and to their Superiors. That a school is only as good as its teachers is axiomatic. Therefore, while the Church has heartily urged the *aggiornamento* of religious in every field of service, special stress is now laid on the updated preparation of the teaching Sisters. A Sister's efforts to attain to excellence in her

[1] *Christian Education of Youth*, p. 36.

professional work, according to the talents given her, are an integral part of her striving for sanctity. Pius XII pointed this out explicitly:

The first consequence of the deepening of your spiritual life will be a more elevated notion of your educational mission and a greater professional consciousness. We mean a more ardent will to achieve the greatest possible competency in your own field, or in anything pertaining to either theory or practice.[2]

An ardent will to achieve the greatest possible competency spells out a rejection of mediocrity and a striving for quality. That this will be the natural result of a deepened spiritual life puts things in their proper perspective; it should forever lay to rest the spectre of pride of intellect which for years has stalked the path of Sisters in the realm of the intellectual. Nothing less than an inquiring, informed, disciplined and scholarly mind can measure up to the excellence which the Church expects of religious teachers today.

Today. Always the Church's directives take into account the conditions of the world *today,* and the imperative necessity of adapting to today's intellectual resources, to today's methods of teaching, to today's inventions and to today's discoveries in order to give a Christian orientation to the lives of people in today's world. That the Church's views on changes in education coincide with those of secular authorities in the professional field gives to Sister-teachers a spiritual motivation which associates professional improvement with spiritual progress. Given this motivation and the excellent programs of pre-service formation Major Superiors are providing for their Sisters, the future is bright with promise. In less than two decades the Sister-teachers in America may well be among the best educated women in the world, occupying positions of leadership recognized alike by national and international professional organizations. Of course, this happy prediction depends for its fulfillment on the collaboration of all Superiors, making universal the effort that is, as yet, only a partial endeavor to correct

2 In an Allocution to the Executives of the Italian Catholic Union of Secondary Education, January 4, 1954, *Education: Papal Teachings,* p. 478.

what sorely needs correction in providing full formation for all Sisters at the pre-service level.

Parents Well-Educated Today

A very important factor which today's teaching Sister has to take into account is the higher educational level attained to by the parents of their pupils. Almost universally men and women are better educated than were those of even a decade ago. Many are college graduates, and there is an increasingly manifest desire for cultural improvement for themselves and for their children. A college degree has become a status symbol; just as the high-school diploma replaced the eighth-grade certificate for average parents some thirty years ago, so now a college degree has replaced the high-school diploma. This has a twofold effect relating to the teacher. The parents take an eager, intelligent interest in the school program and their children's progress. The pupils, even quite young ones, come to school from an atmosphere which reflects the wider literary and liturgical horizons of their parents. With knowledge gleaned from many sources of information other than the school, the child now comes with many questions. In informal class discussion the "Sister, please tell us . . ." is frequently replaced by "Sister, did you hear that . . .?" as an average pupil mentions the latest press release on archeologists' findings in Antioch; the civil rights bill; a predicted pronouncement of the Ecumenical Council, or news of the latest attempt at conquering space. To remain a trusted leader and effective teacher in this atmosphere calls for sound preparation and continuing education. Many Communities recognize their obligation so to prepare their Sisters, and their number is constantly increasing. But there are still too many who, while recognizing the soundness of the Church's directives, do not catch their urgency. They still let expedience rather than excellence decide the professional pre-service preparation of their young Sisters.

Some Congregations have adopted a compromise policy. While recognizing the need of some pre-service preparation, they send Sisters to teach before they have obtained their degree. Their reasoning is that this will contribute to the Sisters' maturity and will enable the Congregation to know and judge them better before admitting them to even temporary vows. The validity of this reasoning can be questioned on the following grounds:

(1) It interrupts the planned, well-integrated Sister Formation program before its goal of forming the holy and effective religious has been accomplished. It means a change in midstream for a Sister in her formative years before she is ready for it.

(2) It necessitates that she take her practicum in directed teaching, with its so necessary follow-up conferences and teaching seminars too early in her studies before she has completed her major, and the necessary sequence in education courses which will prepare her step by step for her classroom role. Or—and this is more likely and deplorable—it means forfeiting them altogether or taking the chance of "making it up" at a much later date which never arrives.

(3) This means the young Sister goes into the classroom without the necessary experience. Surely such a program rather inhibits maturity and provides a fertile medium for the growth of feelings of inferiority and anxiety complexes. Such a Sister is fearful of her inability to manage a classroom; of working side by side with better-prepared lay teachers, and dealing with parents. Such a Sister seldom matures as she should. She remains a prey to insecurity and a strong sense of inadequacy. It may lead to defections.

Further, she is subject to scruples as to the justice of appearing as a full-fledged teacher before pastor, people and pupils; or of the need to defend herself by self-deprecatory remarks such as "I'm not fully prepared yet"; "This is my first teaching assignment." These and similar statements may engender in parents a tolerant sympathy for her, but they will neither lessen the discontent of parents nor solve the problems of her own classroom discipline, both arising from poor organization and presentation of class work.

On the other hand, there may be the even more undesirable result of a false maturity, as evidenced by a blustering show of efficiency and self-confidence. This could well be the beginning of "bluffing one's way through" professionally, an attitude which can hardly be kept from spreading to other areas of a Sister's life.

What does this aggressive ability to bluff do to the Sister as a *person,* her character, her sense of wholeness as a religious?

Examples of Insufficient Formation in Sister-Teachers

One instance of recent origin will illustrate the harm done to Sisters, pupils, parents, and to Catholic education by such a policy. At the opening of the school term, four Sisters were newly assigned to a modern, suburban school. They taught from second to seventh grade. The pupils reported, "Those new Sisters are young and pretty." But in a few weeks a restlessness developed when many pupils began commenting, "Sister says we mustn't ask questions." The subject came up informally at a P.T.A. meeting when one mother, laughing nervously, remarked, "It all began with Job"; the explanation being that when Sister in a fourth-grade Bible History class described Job, his pains and his patience, one of the pupils said, "But, Sister, Job was not a real man. He is just a lesson to show us how to bear bad things." Sister was shocked. "Why, Cecile, the story of Job is in the Bible and we have to believe it because it is the Word of God. Job was a *real* man and don't say he wasn't!"

This started off a "that-reminds-me" session. Another mother said, "Peter's in the seventh grade and terribly interested in Andrew Jackson. When he asked Sister if people were changing their minds about him, she just said, 'That's not in your lesson today, Peter; no questions, please!' " Another contributed, "My Mabel was put out of the sixth-grade Christmas play because she said the Magi did not go to the stable but came weeks later to a house where the Holy Family lived, and maybe they were not kings at all." Yet another mother, a former schoolteacher, said with a puzzled shake of her head, "When Susie and her second-grade Canadian classmate asked Sister to settle the dispute as to which was bigger, Canada or the United States, Sister just said she wouldn't take sides." Finally, it was issued as a school policy that no questions were to be asked in any classroom.

The parents were distressed. They really loved the Sisters, but interest in their children's education sharpened their perceptions as to the Sisters' poor cultural background. This led them to pro-

pose several remedies, none of which proved acceptable to either
the pastor or to the Sisters. An unhappy year was ridden out; more
competent Sisters were appointed to the school the next year, but
the experience was scarring to all concerned.

This unfortunate affair—for what has been related is actual
fact—has its parallel in many parts of the country. It downgrades
Catholic education in the eyes of the public; stirs doubts in the
minds of some Catholic parents as to whether they are doing
educational justice to their children; and has a deleterious effect
upon the Sisters themselves. They become anxious, tense, insecure,
fearful that they cannot keep the class periods within the limit of
the material they have prepared. They know that their pupils,
exposed to informed adult conversation in their homes, will ask
questions whose relevancy to the subject the Sisters can neither
deny nor handle.

In conferences with the parents the Sisters experience the same
insecurity, which may mask itself under a cold and even hostile
manner. Wanting with all their hearts to be both good Sisters and
good teachers, they are troubled in their consciences (unduly, for
they are not responsible for the position in which they find themselves), and there is the temptation to relate failure as a teacher
to failure as a religious. From this point it is but a step to the deep
harassment and doubt as to whether or not they have a religious
vocation. Sisters can be helped over this hurdle; but how much
better it would be for them, for the Church, for the Community,
and for Catholic education had this failure been prevented by a
sound pre-service formation.

Education Formational Rather Than Informational

Spiritually, mentally, and physically, Sisters are benefited by
entering their classrooms not only sure of their ability to master
each situation, but aglow with the possibilities of making education a formational rather than an informational process. It is truly
a shortsighted policy that sends Sisters into the teaching field
before they have received the professional and spiritual preparation the Church wishes them to have, "because demands are so
pressing and Sisters are so few." Such a policy aggravates the

problem of "Sister shortage," since tense, insecure, irritable Sisters, far from attracting others to the religious life, are more apt to repel them.

The all too inadequate number of Sisters is real; but the problem will never be solved by fostering a sense of inadequacy in the Sisters themselves, or inadequacy in their number. The problem of too few vocations, which is felt most heavily in the teaching field, is patently a real one. But it is disastrous to base the solution of a long-term problem on expediency. The solution needs to be based on principle; here the principle involved is the moral obligation of every Community to educate its Sisters properly for the duties to which they will be later assigned. There is the further matter of justice to parents and children alike.

As a corollary to this, there is a moral obligation for the Sisters, both pre- and in-service, to make the most of the educational opportunities provided by their Communities. Unless a Sister recognizes her moral responsibility to perfect herself constantly in the art and science of teaching, neither advanced courses, modern equipment, functional classrooms, nor a lessening of the teacher-load will bring about a change in the Sister. That change must come from within, based upon an alertness to society's needs today, and an awareness of her obligations to meet them, within the framework of her Community's apostolate. This supposes a Sister well-grounded in self-sacrifice, for change is always a painful ordeal. To many, it seems a reflection on what has hitherto been satisfactorily accomplished; also, it requires conformity to new views and new values which, in turn, calls for serious thinking— a process painful to any but the most conscientious Sister determined to make the most of every opportunity provided.

"Change" and "New" Not To Be Equated

Here a word of warning should be sounded. "Change" and "new" should not be equated. What is new is often inherently attractive, while change evokes a defensive reaction. For instance, a Sister who taught a foreign language for years may ostensibly oppose the installation of a language laboratory for many plausible reasons. But her opposition really stems from a resentment against changing her mode of teaching. Conversely, a Sister may apparently welcome the new and step cheerfully into a modern classroom equipped with the latest in teaching aids. But she has not changed her goals or widened her educational horizons. She still has as her objective to cover the content matter of her course as quickly, comfortably, and competently as she can, and maintain discipline rather than provoke a spirit of inquiry in her classroom.

Such a teacher may well be likened to a man who turns in his old automobile for the latest model. His fundamental objective in securing a new car is identical with that which he had for the old; that is, to transport him quickly, safely and conveniently from one place to another for business or social purposes. He has not been touched with zeal for discovery, nor has he caught the zest of exploration.

This change in the Sister-teacher's approach to her work means extending the scope of the classroom to include the entire community with its population, Catholic and non-Catholic; its job opportunities and recreational facilities; its housing problems and minority group grievances; its pressure personalities and its civic leaders. A symbol of this changing aspect of education—spelled out by Pius XI in his Encyclical on *Christian Education of Youth* —is found in the architecture of contemporary schools with their glass walls and one-story construction.

Neither ivory towers nor ivied walls serve the purpose of education today. The Church, equally with the State, recognizes this and is deeply concerned, but the Church is in a far better position than is the State to bring about the changes so urgently needed. The dedicated lives of those whose will is one with hers tip the scales in favor of the Church.

But the Church will do no detailed thinking for religious Orders. She makes known her wishes, some phases of which are incorporated in Canon Law. She provides guidelines and sets goals, then leaves to Major Superiors the finding of the ways and means for their implementation. How well and promptly Major Superiors of women's institutes in the United States have complied with the wishes of the Holy See has been told in a preceding chapter. But the effectiveness of the response of Major Superiors is in the hands of the individual Sister with whom it lies both to implement and supplement the wishes of Rome and those of her

Superiors. Here is where the local Superior can play a vitally effective role.

The responsibility of the individual Sister was never better put than by Bishop Fulton Sheen when, addressing a group of Sisters, he said: "What is the difference between France and the United States in their political, economic, and national life? *You* are the difference, Sisters. Think of the great wisdom of the early bishops of the United States, who insisted on religious schools."[3] But note that it is not the difference in citizens practicing their religious faith that the Bishop points out, but rather the difference a Catholic education makes in the political and economic and national life.

Influence of Individual Sister

The individual Sister's power for influence and her obligation to be prepared to exercise it fully are almost staggering. From kindergarten through university, there are more than six million young citizens of the United States enrolled in the Catholic school system. Checked against a total population of two hundred million, this could mean that one-thirty-fourth of the youth population of the United States may come immediately under the influence of the Church during their formative years. Priests, Brothers and countless competent and dedicated lay persons share with the Sisters the responsibility for staffing Catholic schools, but it is with Sisters, save on the college level, that Catholic education is most identified. The Sister then should approach with dedicated intelligence and steady courage the duty of her own *aggiornamento*. Obedience to her Superiors, the honor of the Church, justice to the students she teaches and civil authorities demand it.

In the majority of our fifty states, and in many dioceses, a baccalaureate degree is the minimum requirement for entering the teaching field. Where the diocese does not ask it, the requirement must still be fulfilled through the system of State certification. (True, James Conant in *The Education of American Teachers* vigorously attacks the validity of the system, but it *is* what we have to deal with now and probably will be for quite a few years to come.) The larger number of teaching Communities sees to it that every beginning teacher has a bachelor's degree, obtained in

3 "Invocation," *The Mind of the Church in the Formation of Sisters*, p. 4.

full-time study, which has also provided for her spiritual growth and guided induction into Community life. Indeed, to comply with the Church's wishes, this degree should have a wide and deep foundation (such as is presented in Chapter 7) which will insure a broad culture, making the Sister truly poised and at home in the company of other cultured individuals and groups. Such persons will be found in increasing numbers among the parents of parochial-school pupils and high-school students.

This meeting with parents on some basis other than a conference on a report card, a class-play costume, or refreshments for the next P.T.A. meeting, is distinctly part of the Sister-teacher's apostolate. Parents have a huge stake in the parochial school system. The educational future of their children will be largely determined by the quality of their early intellectual formation. Consequently, they are taking an increasingly critical interest in it. Then, too, they contribute half a billion dollars annually to its maintenance and, with American practicality, they want to get a fair return on their investment. Their judgment of the school will almost universally be based on the performance of the individual Sister as a teacher, and on her personality as evidenced by her alertness, knowledge, culture and self-control.

This contact is even more important in inner-city schools where disadvantaged parents may have absolutely no contact with culture of any sort save through Sisters in the parish school who are willing to take an interest in them. What a new world of warm-hearted love and opportunity could be opened up to such parents by adult classes in English, elementary reading, writing, and religion. What a world of difference it would make in the drab lives of disadvantaged parents! What a rich reward for their teachers! And what immediate rewards would accrue to the children in their family life, in the neighborhood, the parish and the entire civic community.

Intercommunication with Parents

Further, the Sister needs this intercommunication with parents for her own full development as a person. A Sister's life is made up, socially, of opposite elements. In her classroom, she is *the* authority; and however widely and wisely she encourages discussion and individual research, however flexible she makes her class schedule, to allow for unanticipated interests and events, her pupils and/or students tacitly recognize that Sister must be deferred to as having the last word. Passing from classroom to convent she is in an entirely different atmosphere. Rules and customs of her Community govern her actions; the horarium dictates how her time shall be apportioned; she is a dutiful subject to the local Superior. To become fully mature, to achieve fulfillment as a woman, a religious and a citizen, the Sister needs an in-between area. She needs contact and conversation with her Sister companions, her lay colleagues and other adults who will meet her on an intellectual level, and converse with her on other than "shop" interests. She needs contact with persons who exercise no authority over her but who communicate with her on terms of equality. Finally, she needs cordial and unconstrained relationships with her Major Superiors as persons who have the greatest interest in her as an individual in her own right as well as a member of the Order.

But what about the danger to a Sister's religious spirit, perhaps even to her vocation, which this association with lay persons may bring about? This question will be raised. This question must be answered. It will be raised by some in honest fear, by some in automatic adherence to tradition, by some in hope of reassurance. The answer will be found where most answers to questions concerning Sisters will be found: in a carefully planned preliminary preparation for the apostolate. This preparation should be of sufficient length to enable a Sister to understand and establish herself in those values which constitute the intrinsic difference between the religious and the lay state. These values create a proper psychological distance between a Sister and a lay person which is a safeguard that both instinctively wish to maintain. When and where this barrier is breached, the Sister loses influence and the lay person loses confidence.

Cardinal Suenens says a Sister has not performed her full apostolate until she has initiated ten laywomen disciples in bearing the same witness to God that she does; ten lay disciples to help her expand her teaching duties, perhaps by way of adult education or study clubs. Danger? Yes, there is danger, but the danger of doing a thing must always be weighed against the danger of *not* doing it. Cowardice can mask itself as prudence. Laziness can mask itself as caution or religious reserve, as is evidenced by "pious reasons" given by a Sister who dislikes attending P.T.A. meetings.

The danger of limiting a Sister's association with persons to the strictly professional, and to children or to the poor and illiterate, is twofold: First, to the Sister herself, who is liable to live in an unreal world where such things as bills for rent, food, clothing and taxes do not exist, or it may lead her to take a magnified view of the most trivial trials, and to develop a dependent pattern of behavior. This view may, among other things, cause her to make a fetish of exactitude to routine for routine's sake, from which no burgeoning spiritual life emerges and no growth in holiness is ever likely to emerge. In a word, there is danger of personality damage summed up thus: "Religious characterized by sensitivity and immaturity are liable to be living in a self-contained world, having refused to walk through the doors swinging outward where the self can be extended and actualized."[4]

Second, there is the danger for Superiors of having to deal with a warped, self-centered, critical subject who, far from contributing to the peace and happiness of the convent in which she lives, engenders constraint, coolness and sometimes conflict.

These dangers are set forth, not as certainties, but as possibilities, which the experience of some Superiors bears out. It is certain that an excessively restrictive policy of association of Sisters and parishioners will prevent much good.

Sisters and Parishioners

Such contacts by a Sister can, most conveniently and fruitfully but by no means exclusively, be made with parents in adult education classes. In many instances the parents will be college graduates or of college calibre, as shown by their successful use of adult study clubs or seminars. They will be happy (and perhaps at first surprised) to find the young Sister *au courant* with national and international events, familiar with controversial legislation,

---

4 Sister Jean de Milan (s.g.c.), "Towards Greater Maturity," *Review for Religious,* XXII (September, 1963), 519.

and concerned with such matters as consumer's rights, air pollution, sales taxes, civil and racial rights, equity of job opportunities, and the government's concern with inner-city poverty and disadvantaged neighborhoods. For the most part they will know more about these matters than will the Sister (a good thing in every way for her), but it is necessary that she know something of them and show an interest in knowing more. Confidence and respect for the Sister will be notably increased when she shows a realistic attitude toward the issues and problems of daily life, from a rise in the price of bread to the pros and cons of building bomb shelters. It is significant that in a questionnaire filled in recently by seniors from a number of high schools to ascertain what about the religious life attracted and/or repelled, a fairly high percentage listed under the "repel" column, "The Sisters know nothing of what is going on in the world."

How is the Sister to keep up on such things? By realizing that it is a part of her apostolate of teaching—to keep up with the literature of the times—and by willing it. Time? The Sister-teacher should avoid that state of mind that leads her to believe that in some unique way she has been deprived of the twenty-four hours a day that have been apportioned to all men by their impartial Creator. Unlike money, time is equally apportioned, every person having the same number of seconds to the minute, minutes to the hour and hours to the day. When Sisters look upon the spending of time with the same conscientious eye which their Vow of Poverty makes them cast upon the spending of money, they will just as carefully avoid waste in one as in the other and be agreeably surprised to find how "rich" they are in time accumulated through thrifty vigilance.

Time to keep up with current events can begin with a quick glance at the daily paper and selective use of radio and television, which practically all Communities now make available to their Sisters with some restrictions required by communal living. Excellent news weeklies, Catholic and non-Catholic, furnish not only facts but different viewpoints. These and other journals of fact and opinion should be read critically, weighing statement against statement, opinion against opinion. Through this process Sisters can and should develop their own judgment. From this practice there will be a carry-over into their spiritual lives, buttressing them against prejudice, instilling prudence, and sowing deep a sense of realistic justice based on solid facts rather than sentimental hearsay evidence which often closely relates to idle gossip.

While current events are an excellent introduction on the social plane to helpful interpersonal relationships between Sisters and parishioners, parents and lay colleagues, and other adults who come—or should come—within the sphere of a Sister's influence, they are only a breakthrough, a bridgehead, as it were. Theology and philosophy are now subjects in which the ordinary layman— *not* the extraordinary one—is interested and informed. Journals of opinion feature articles on these subjects for the consumption of the layman, and monthly books on the same subjects roll off the press. Books authored by laymen inform laymen even on ecclesiastical matters, as befits their changing role in the Church. The Sister's background studies in these fields should have whetted her appetite for more, and her close contact with adults will convince her of the necessity of further, continuous study and reading in these fields.

She will need the resources that a knowledge of theology and philosophy gained in the Juniorate now gives her. When a young woman, or an older one for that matter, because of her confidence in a Sister, appeals to her for help and advice, she must have something more to offer than "We'll make a novena to St. Jude for this," or "Just keep up your prayers and everything will be all right." She should be able to give more substantial spiritual counsel, and she will, if she uses the daily experience that life in Community provides to those who make full use of its rich opportunities.

Sisters as Counselors to the Laity

The words "spiritual advisors" applied to Sisters may sound an unpleasant note in some ears and an alarming one in others; but what else have they been through the years, without benefit of special preparation for the responsible and delicate task and without official recognition of their right to perform it? Now is the time for them to fulfill this role more competently, in conformity with Catholic dogma and doctrine and in line with the Church's social thinking. This view is stoutly upheld by Cardinal Suenens who, while urging Major Superiors to take appropriate action to attain this end, says:

It could be respectfully but insistently demanded of the Conciliar Fathers that they:

Affirm the principle of the new role of the nun as the one to inspire and direct the feminine laity both young and grown up.

Express the wish that adequate theoretical and practical training for this role be given to young nuns.

Express the wish that nothing in the Constitutions should be a hindrance to the needs of the apostolate in the world of today and that Constitutions be revised in this sense.

Express the wish to see the religious life so organized that this new function becomes an integral part of the community life and has by right its recognized place therein through the organization of special meetings to control and foster specific activities.[5]

Cardinal Suenens' views on the most effective use of religious women and of a more specific official recognition of their stature is shared by an increasing number of the hierarchy and clergy. This is facing the fact that Sisters are adult women, well-educated and competent counselors of their own sex. Too long have they been regarded as "innocent minors," cute little nuns, some of them sheltered from the world and its wounds, ignorant of its urgent needs. Msgr. George W. Casey, after commenting with apparent relish and admiration on the presence of a thousand Sisters at a baseball game in Boston; and on others, with the permission of their Ordinary, of course, enjoying rides on merry-go-rounds and roller coasters at Palisades, New York (shudders!) does a right-about-face and asks soberly:

[5] *The Nun in the World*, p. 168. The appointment of Cardinal Suenens by Pope Paul VI as one of the four moderators of the Second Vatican Council gives great weight to the opinions expressed in his internationally read book. Following up these opinions, press releases during the second session of the Ecumenical Council tell that the Cardinal asks for women representatives at the Council; and that he specifically requests "That representatives of religious orders, both men and women, who teach the gospel throughout the world, be invited to the Council sessions." (*Chicago Sun-Times*, October 23, 1963.) We now know that this request, seconded by other bishops, has been granted.

Can there by anything wrong with this joyful picture? Only this: It is all kid stuff. It is the sort of thing you do for altar boys and Sunday school children, and it reveals the present position of the Sisters in a poignant way. They are minors . . . it is not mostly in the realm of recreation that the Sisters need or want an *aggiornamento* of their own. It is in the realm of status and policy making. . . . There were observers at the Second Vatican Council from every Church in Christendom, and representatives from every male Community in the Church; but no Sisters in the Council chamber. . . . The position of women religious in the Church seems woefully dated and calls for a new day. The dynamic virtues, responsibility, leadership, initiative, imagination, enterprise and the quest of knowledge must be upgraded to go along with those that make for discipline.[6]

But where are these dynamic virtues to be cultivated if not within the Order itself? Is it not possible that if an indulgent prelate treats the Sisters as minors, he is but reflecting the Order's mental and social atmosphere? The fact that Pius XII felt impelled to defend religious against the charge of "infantilism" in itself shows that the notion is rather widely held—to the distress of mature religious. And while His Holiness asserted that the majority of religious were not suffering from infantilism in either their intellectual or their emotional life or even in their actions, he conceded: "Some Communities and Superiors constrain them [the Sisters] . . . to adopt modes of thought and action which give color to this reproach."[7]

In this day and age which calls for the widening and deepening of Sisters' spheres of influence, it is required that both Superiors and subjects make sustained efforts towards attaining to the "mature measure of the fullness of Christ." (Ephes. 4:13 Conf.) This they can do by consistently acting in accord with maturity and refusing—even at the risk of offending—those pastors, priests and parishioners who, from misguided but well-intentioned kindness, seek to treat them as children. Sisters may profitably examine themselves rigorously as to their contribution to the idea that they are cute (ugh!) "little nuns" instead of mature religious women with a serious role to fill in Church and society.

---

[6] "Now for the Grown-up Stuff," *Oklahoma Courier*, August 9, 1963.

[7] Pope Pius XII, "Discourse to the Members of the Second General Congress of the States of Perfection," *The States of Perfection*, December 9, 1957, p. 312.

Dependence on Prayer and Fraternal Charity

To attain to this maturity, dependence must be placed first on prayer, the grace of God and directed efforts at total formation. There are, however, psychological principles which cannot be ignored. Every local Superior, and those who hold delegated authority, such as principals, supervisors, consultants and others, should bear in mind how important self-realization is to each individual. How important it is for Sisters to know that the work she gives her life to is purposeful and of value, and that it has the sympathetic support and approval—indeed, even the admiration—of her Sister companions. The more of this kind of appreciation a Sister receives from within, the less likely will she be to seek it without. If she receives it from both sources, the inner will far outweigh the outer.

Even Christ complained that "A prophet is not without honor but in his own country." (Mark 6:4) One wonders what strides would be made in fraternal charity if every Sister were encouraged in her own Community to use her talents to the fullest—whether these lay in the mechanical, domestic, managerial, artistic or intellectual field—as a true bearing witness to Christ, and applauded by her Congregation when she succeeded. Blessed is that Community where the capacity for leadership is looked upon as a God-given gift, and not regarded suspiciously as a mark of ambition or worldliness. Blessed is that Community wherein a mature Sister, whose common sense has kept pace with her spiritual growth and professional development, is accorded the loyal support and unfeigned charity of her Sisters; where using her gifts is hailed as "bearing witness to Christ," and in which witness both lay and religious share. Then will leadership of the laity be achieved without painful internecine strife, but rather with marked profit to the Church by the establishment of helpful, harmonious lay-religious relationships.

Authority and Leadership Distinguished

It may be helpful here to distinguish between authority and leadership. Authority is bestowed from without, leadership develops from within, through cultivation and manifest growth of

certain inherent qualities. It would be out of character for a Sister
to seek authority in or outside of her Community; much less
should she seek power. But if she possesses leadership ability, she
should seek, not shun, opportunities to use it. One of the basic
techniques of Communists—one of which they boast—is to get
prospective followers involved with people and their problems,
with the design of drawing them to "the Cause" and of finding
there the answers. If Sisters give the impression that their life is
a quiet stream, running parallel to the active and often turbulent
river of life, to which it is a tributary at fixed times but never a
part, their influence so greatly needed *now* will not reach beyond
their specific work. Persons pressed daily to the point of anguish
will readily ask for the Sisters' prayers but seldom for their
opinion; they will maintain vigil lights in convent chapels, but
end an interview in the parlor at the "convent curfew."

To exercise this influence effectively, to acquire leadership, the
Sister needs to build assiduously upon the solid, preliminary
foundation given her in the Juniorate. With the dynamic changes
in the educational world, she will need to take courses during the
summer that will enrich both her knowledge of subject matter
and her techniques of teaching. If these can count towards a
Master of Arts or Science degree—which her Superiors will
certainly wish her to get—she will be fortunate, but she should
shun pursuing studies with the amassing of credits that will "count"
as her only objective. She should have an eagerness for them to
count towards her personal development and professional efficiency. A summer given to courses in liturgy or biblical studies
will be richly rewarding whether or not they count towards the
particular master's degree she will eventually need. Nor are these
studies to be considered as something extra and apart from a
Sister's whole life.

Properly motivated by her undergraduate formation, the Sister
will always place equal emphasis on spiritual and social growth
with professional and apostolic development. She sees no necessary
dichotomy between being an excellent religious and an outstanding
teacher esteemed by students, parents, and her colleagues in the
profession itself. Continuous growth is necessary for a Sister's
self-confidence; and in proportion to her progress will she reach

out to her colleagues, both lay and religious, to share with them the fruits of her efforts. Her example of virile but modest self-confidence, her sureness in offering aid to others, will be a source of admiration and emulation. Thus will she shun the Master's censure reserved for those who, through laziness or human respect, or both, bury their talents because it is a "safer" way to live.

Lay colleagues look to a Sister for leadership and a strengthening of the *esprit de corps* (frequently badly lacking in their school) by someone who will help *them* to realize their best potential. They look to her as a real comrade-in-arms who will take satisfaction in seeing them become more spiritual, more zealous for professional excellence, knowing that she will rejoice when they are recognized for their accomplishments. This is to be a true leader; one whose followers are purpose-directed, not person-directed.

Cultivating Leadership Qualities

Essential to leadership is the ability to express one's views, both in writing and speaking, in clear, logical, forceful terms, while tactfully avoiding polemics. The Sister-teacher should, therefore, continue the practice of smooth, interesting, exact and, if she is so gifted, creative writing, begun in her pre-service preparation. Writing will not only clarify her thinking but oblige her to present her thoughts and views in logical sequence and with substantiating proofs. This will facilitate speaking in a convincing manner on formal or informal occasions. The ability to speak clearly, briefly and to the point is not given in the same measure to all, but it can be cultivated. Let us remember Demosthenes with his mouthful of pebbles beside the roaring sea.

A leader, whether it be in a convention hall of five thousand or in a Committee room of seven participants, can be recognized by the facility with which she can make pertinent comments in a spontaneous, attention-catching manner within the limits of thirty seconds. It is regrettable that so many Sisters, qualified to do this, let slip golden opportunities. Rather paradoxically, it is Sisters in the academic field who, on public, professional occasions, are less vocal than Sisters in other fields. These latter, particularly those in hospital and social work, are frequently applauded contributors to discussions, or ringing challengers of views with which they do not agree. In convention "breaks" they are sought out by lay persons for an elaboration of their remarks—a valuable service to their profession and to the Church. Perhaps a clue to this difference in ready speaking—"a hint of an explanation," so to speak—may be found in the very nature of a teaching Sister's environment and work. These do not often provide for contact with adults. Too often her teaching is restricted entirely to children and adolescents. Nurses and social workers are constantly dealing on terms of equality with adults. Teachers should initiate other apostolic contacts for their own growth and development, without losing sight of unselfish and other-directed goals.

A growing number of the clergy are coming to look upon the teaching Sister's apostolate with adults in a new and favorable manner. This change may be a valuable by-product of having so many priests assigned by their bishops to teach in our secondary schools; and also to serve as superintendents of elementary schools. This policy, begun some years ago and constantly growing, gives priests a colleague's view of a Sister's work and activities and shows the extent to which dealing with adults can be an intrinsic part of the teaching apostolate. These priests, having in time assumed other duties, are quick to see that Sisters' talents can be put to better use than counting collections, managing the school cafeteria, planning an altar boys' picnic or remaining "back stage" during parish events, ready to answer emergency calls for their domestic skills. Some diocesan superintendents of schools have experienced the benefits to both sides of having the Sisters interest themselves in the young parents of elementary-school children.

One diocese centers on visits of the Sisters to the home of high-school freshman students; visits which involve not only the parents but all members of the family—if the parents so desire. All superintendents see what services Sisters in their diocesan offices can render on all levels of school services and in contact with all ages of people connected with the office as educators or as clientele in search of help, personal or professional.

One superintendent feels so keenly about this need for the adult apostolate that he made giving a highly prized secondary school (highly prized because of its vocation possibilities) to a certain Order contingent upon this agreement: *For every girl registered in the school at least one of her parents should be invited to register for an evening adult-education class once a week in the school.* He recommended that the classes for adults be varied so as to allow for a choice of courses: Poetry, the short story, a critical period in history, literature, liturgy, Scripture, sociology, current events, etc. A stipulation was that several Sisters, in addition to their daily classes with high-school students, should take on the extra apostolic evening assignment. A *quid pro quo* was that the Sisters be responsible for no parish "chores" of any kind, and that extra-curricular activities of the students, which take up so much of the Sisters' time, be held to a minimum.

Surely the Holy See, calling so persistently for the *aggiornamento* for Sisters, had in mind extending their sphere of influence in just such a way for greater and broader services to a troubled and a threatened world.

Talents Differ from Sister to Sister

True—and we must recognize it—not every Sister, by nature or endowment, is gifted with a talent for teaching adults; just as not every Sister is the artist or "artisan" required to teach first grade, for certainly the first-grade teacher has need of a special array of talents. It is not necessary that *every* Sister teach adult classes or engage in adult discussion or study clubs. This can be reserved for the several Sisters who *can* do this type of teaching very well. For those not gifted for adult education, there is, as St. Paul points out in his First Epistle to the Corinthians, Chapter 12, a "more excellent way." One such way that parents would appreciate immensely would be some coaching in the modern mathematics appropriate to the grades their children are in—just the same simple instructions the Sisters give their pupils in helping them appreciate the understanding of concepts and skills involved in the "new math"—which really isn't new after all, but which mystifies parents by its terminology of "sets," "open-and-closed curves" and plurality of number systems.

"If the trumpet give forth an uncertain sound, who will prepare

himself for battle?" (1 Cor. 14:8, Conf.) No one will deny that
the parochial school system is in an embattled position, more
threatened by doubt and division from within than from suspicion
and enmity without. Who is so capable of sounding the ringing
blast of certainty as the Sisters themselves with whom the system
is identified? Convinced that the answer to the question whether
Catholic schools are worth the cost should be an unqualified
"Yes," they must be able to imbue others with their convictions. To
give a sure, convincing answer to the query as to how good the
Catholic schools are, they must be ready to demonstrate how good
Catholic schools can be when based on four-dimensional pre-
service preparation of Sister-teachers, and a continuing in-service
education in the same manner. To all of their Sisters, all Communities must be prepared to give this type of formation as a
measure and means of survival.

Much has been written of the fresh winds blowing through the
Church. These same winds are blowing through school halls,
college campuses and convent corridors, and working up to gale
velocity. If faint hearts there be in some circles, if there be centers
of doubt radiating to circumferences of compromise, these should
not be found in the ranks of Sisters. For the Sisters, so close to
the parochial school system, so much one with it, gather courage
and wisdom from what that system has done to place the Catholic
Church in the United States in the enviable position it enjoys today.
They realize proudly, not fearfully, that the problems our schools
are facing arise from their very success, not any failure.[8]

Take the tomes that have been written about the difficulties of
maintaining Catholic schools; add to them the articles that appear
on the same subject with almost hysterical regularity in both
Catholic and non-Catholic presses; and what do they all boil down
to? To put it boldly, even crudely: Not enough dollars, not
enough teachers, not enough buildings—and in that order. All
three factors are inextricably bound together. Why bound together?
If Federal or State aid is to come, if shared time with public
schools is to be part of the answer to "Sister shortage," if foundation grants in large amounts are to be secured for building, all or

---

[8] William H. Conley, "Editorial," *Catholic School Journal*, LXIII (September, 1963), 4.

each will be contingent upon the competency and qualifications of teachers in Catholic schools.

To some this may seem an absurdly naïve solution, but put it this way and then think it over: If overnight the number of highly qualified and fully formed teaching Sisters were quadrupled, how many of the other problems of parochial schools would remain?

As an increasing number of Sisters, thoroughly grounded spiritually and with an excellent professional preparation, alert to the needs of contemporary society, go into the classroom, a desire to imitate and follow them stirs in the hearts of those whom they teach and with whom they associate. It is generally conceded that only a small percentage of those to whom a religious vocation is given follow that call. The Sisters, both Superiors and subjects, realize that not all of the obstacles to answering that call come from the attractions another type of life offers, nor from opposition in the home.

They see, and they are working unremittingly to remove, the stumbling blocks which the life of a religious as seen from the outside might offer to aspiring candidates. Rules have been changed, antiquated customs dropped, horaria altered and Constitutions amended—all with a view to enabling religious to be better Sisters and more wholesome persons. Professional preparation has been stepped up. One university alone reports a seven hundred per cent increase in the enrollment of Sisters in graduate study in ten years. Free the Sisters from the accretions of noneducational work which have slowed their professional progress and deprived them of time *to give to people,* and watch the results.

Allow time for the excellent formation programs now in existence to bear fruit, and the problem of the Sister shortage will be solved. With the solving of that problem, many others stemming directly or indirectly from it will disappear. It is incontrovertible that adequately prepared Sisters, strong in their religious spirit, poised in the company of cultured adults, understanding and compassionate with the underprivileged (for they are coming to know them personally and are no longer strangers to their problems) will attract thousands of American girls to share their life, their apostolate and their rewards. The complete formation of a Sister as a true religious, a wholesome woman and an excellent teacher requires time. It requires also a large financial outlay which Communities willingly make as an investment in the lives of their Sisters and the future of their religious Congregation. The triple investment of thought, time and money provides that which the Church so earnestly recommends: The *aggiornamento* of the Sister-teacher, and the attendant result she so prayerfully seeks—the holy and effective religious.

13

Aggiornamento of the Sister-Nurse

Nursing Sisters occupy an enviable position among the Sisters of the active Orders in the United States today. Professionally, they are in terms of percentage the best educationally qualified of any group. They have shown a dependable flexibility in meeting the demand of professional excellence. Far from offering resistance to change, they are found in the vanguard of such professional movements demanding—and achieving—incredible change. Nursing Sisters show no deterring devotion to the *status quo,* they have an open-mindedness in regard to tradition, an alert awareness of what today's world requires of the nursing profession, as well as anticipatory readiness to meet the needs of tomorrow. True, Sisters have not played the leading role of initiators in new educational patterns for nurses, but they have been faithful followers and able allies of those who did. Indeed, their readiness to follow important and unprecedented patterns of change marks them today as potentially among the best professionally educated religious women in the world. It is not so much their possession of the best possible education as their instinctive appreciation of what constitutes a truly liberalizing education, and their willingness to make sacrifices to increase their effectiveness as nurses through study, that makes their future so bright with promise.

Recognition of Nursing as a Profession

Sister-nurses played no small part in the long, uphill battle for full recognition of nursing as a profession. This battle still goes on, spearheaded by the profession's competently functioning associations. In these associations the Sisters participate, very frequently holding high office. In the atmosphere of these associations created by combined effort and common goal, they find something akin to that of Community life. They experience a congeniality in working with nursing leaders for the advancement of the nursing profession. All this should portend a very favorable outlook for the *aggiornamento* of the nursing Sister. However, a close study of the situation does not bear this out. Every person who succeeds has his Achilles heel.

The emphasis on the professional, not counterbalanced by equal concern for the other facets of a Sister-nurse's life—the religious, intellectual, cultural and social—presents a real obstacle to the *aggiornamento* the Church is calling for. The nursing profession itself now recognizes that the stress on the professional has led to narrow specialization and self-containment. It is moving powerfully and promptly to effect a change. Changes are needed, and Sister-nurses should be foremost in promoting them. But for them to do this purely for professional reasons would be indeed a sort of treason: "To do the right thing for the wrong reason."

A willingness to change can at times be only a cloak for conformity to current trends. A Sister-nurse needs to set her sights high; her goal should be all-encompassing. She must call upon the values of the religious life, its inner strengths, and adapt patterns of nursing education to a purpose consonant with these ideals.

These ideals have been bequeathed to the present generation of Sister-nurses by generations of Sisters who have preceded them. While neither the history of nursing nor the history of hospitals—both stemming from the same root, care of the sick—is within the province of this chapter, the *aggiornamento* of Sisters requires reference to both.

Emancipation of the Religious Nurse

Nursing as a work of mercy is identified with the beginning of Christianity. "I was sick and you visited Me" is its charter. The Church, mindful of its responsibilities for the care of the sick, approved many Orders of both men and women, which had nursing as their chief work. Because of social restrictions on the

activities of women religious, the Orders of men outnumbered
and overshadowed those of women. While there was much devoted
nursing care under the auspices of the Church, there was little
nursing education until the beginning of the 17th century.

That century marks, as it were, the ecclesiastical emancipation
of religious women; the establishment of uncloistered Communities
of women. That women bound by the essential vows of poverty,
chastity and obedience should be free to go wherever the needs
and sufferings of mankind called was more than a radical idea—it
was revolutionary. Nothing that religious women are being urged
to do today can compare with it. That is one heartening lesson
we can learn from the past. One might say that what Cardinal
Suenens in *The Nun in the World* now pleads for reverts to what
Sisters in the 17th century were doing. The nursing field was
foremost in taking advantage of the newly-accorded and Church-
blessed liberty of women religious. The Sisters cared for the sick
in their homes (Visiting Nurses); they conducted hospitals, both
Church and municipally owned (Administration); they served
on the battlefields (Army Nurses); they took note of and provided
for *all* the needs of their patients (Family-Centered Care); they
staffed hospitals for the mentally ill (Psychiatric Nursing); and
leprosaria and hospitals for the plague victims (Contagious-
Disease Nursing). Here we have all the modern specialties of
today.

These new and enlarged areas of service led to the beginning
of nursing education. New recruits to religious Orders were
instructed by the older ones. Instruction was of the apprenticeship
type, where one learned by doing—under observation—called
on-the-job learning today. Applicants to religious Orders were
carefully screened as to intelligence, health and morals. The more
experienced members considered it a sacred obligation to impart
to the younger Sisters the knowledge and skills they had acquired,
and spiritual motivation was constantly inculcated. This is why
Orders devoted to the care of the sick were able to produce the
finest type of nurse of their day.

To prove this, one instance may be cited. When Florence
Nightingale, the great reformer of nursing (excluding that done
by religious women), sailed on her epic voyage to Scutari and the

Crimean battlefield, of the thirty-eight members of her nursing staff, eighteen were religious. There were ten Roman Catholic Sisters of Mercy from Bermondsey and Norwood, and eight Anglican Sisters from an Order also called Sisters of Mercy, that had been founded at Devonport.[1] That Sisters met the exacting demands of "the Lady with the Lamp" attests eloquently to their intelligence, competency, generosity and devotedness.

High Quality of Nursing Sisters

These qualities the nursing Sisters brought from Europe to the United States, and imbued native Communities with their high ideals of service. From the very beginning, Catholic hospitals were popular with the public, persons of all faiths making use of them. Catholic hospitals were never considered as set apart from others, different from, or in conflict with other hospitals, and never used exclusively for Catholics. The Church-State issue was never raised—nor is it raised today. Catholic hospitals developed and progressed as the United States developed and progressed. Both voluntary hospitals, under whatever auspices, and tax-supported hospitals were accepted as the American way of life, and as part and parcel of the country's health facilities and program.

When the program required that hospitals expand their services to include the education of nurses as well as the care of the sick, Catholic hospitals were quick to establish schools of nursing. Briefly it may be said that they followed the evolution of nursing education from "trained" nurses to registered nurses; from three-year hospital diploma schools to college-affiliated schools; then to the basic-degree program in college or university leading to Bachelor of Science in Nursing; and on to the master's degree in nursing specialties.

It must be frankly admitted that this steady professional advancement was, to a certain degree, pressure progress. The double pressure (that is, State licensing and registration laws), and the further pressure of medical and nursing professional organizations,

[1] Lucy R. Seymer, *Florence Nightingale* (New York: The Macmillan Co., 1951), p. 43.

keep Catholic hospitals and their educational facilities abreast of the times. Certainly religious Superiors have other and higher motives for giving their Sisters the best possible professional education. They are motivated by reverence for nursing as a work of mercy, by justice to the patients, by their responsibility as representatives of the Church, and by the need to educate their subjects. But it is quite obvious that outside pressures, plus the heavy financial investment in hospitals, are strong factors in satisfying accrediting demands, which include the professional preparation of all those holding, as most Sisters do, supervisory or other key positions.

Trends in Professional Preparation

But professional preparation today is not what it was ten, or even five, years ago. The nursing profession fully recognizes that the trend must be reversed from the narrowing professional to the addition of liberal arts as a background or base on which to build. It is conceded that the goal of a Bachelor of Science in Nursing as the minimal professional requirement may take years to attain. The report of the Surgeon General Consultant Group in Nursing, *Towards Quality in Nursing, Needs and Goals,* shows clearly the disparity between supply and demand. It shows also that the chief source of registered nurses is the hospital-diploma schools, the majority of which have college-course affiliation.[2] Yet many Sisters today are meeting the maximum educational and professional requirements.

The projected increase to meet the nursing needs of 1969 from schools under Catholic auspices alone calls for 13,400 graduates from diploma schools and 1,655 from degree programs. In addition to the baccalaureate degree and the hospital-diploma schools there is the associate-degree program from which a candidate may choose. Regardless of the program chosen, all take the identical State Board examination for licenses as registered nurses.

For the nursing Sister there can be no choice. Her minimal

2 U.S. Department of Health, Education and Welfare, Public Health Service, *Toward Quality in Nursing* (Washington, D.C.: U.S. Government Printing Office, May, 1963), p. 12.

pre-service preparation must be the baccalaureate from the best available program in order that she be fully "formed" as well as educated to meet the requirements of nursing as an apostolate. The sick and others with whom she deals must find in her a woman of quick, intuitive empathy; a nurse skilled in both the art and science of her profession; a religious joyously living out her dedicated commitment in every action. In a triple sense, she is a handmaid—handmaid only, however, in the sense our Lady meant when she designated herself "handmaid of the Lord." She is handmaid to the priest, serving beside him in the daily cycle of life and death which is her world. She is the handmaid of the physician, who depends upon her powers of observation, her judgment, her ability to make decisions about the carrying out of his orders. She is the handmaid of the patient, who looks to her for spiritual aid, social companionship, psychological understanding, as well as nursing care. Rather, all of these ancillary services *are* nursing care at its professional best. It is love in action.

To produce this type of nurse, time is of the essence—time for the deepening of a Sister's religious life, the strengthening of Community ties, the maturing of her emotions, the flowering of her intellectual powers, the growth of cultural appreciation. This cannot be accomplished in less than five years (including the ascetical emphasis of the canonical year of novitiate) within the framework of a liberal arts program, strengthened, augmented and enriched to fit the Sister-nurse for the unlimited areas of service open to her. The goals of such a program are effectively summed up in the following passages from the Self-Study of an accredited basic-degree program in an institution which confines its enrollment to Sisters.

We believe that baccalaureate education for the practice of professional nursing must be built on a background of a broad liberal arts education and scientific principles. It must endeavor to promote critical thinking, and intellectual inquiry; self-understanding and self-direction, development of leadership qualities; purposeful working relationships with others; continuous individual growth as a Sister, a citizen, and a professional nurse practitioner.[3]

We believe that because Sisters freely and deliberately dedicate

3 Marillac College Department of Nursing, *Self-Study* (St. Louis: Marillac College Press, 1963), p. 10.

their lives to God by the vows of religion (poverty, chastity and obedience) and consecrate their service to the neighbor in the active apostolate of nursing they are committed to the pursuit of excellence in all its ramifications. We therefore believe that to lay a solid foundation in their religious life and to prepare them for effective service to society, Sisters need a special kind of education that will assist them to unify their whole life.[4]

Such a program is not only desirable but quite practical when one takes into account the three material advantages which, thanks to her religious Community, every Sister-student has: First, an all-expense-paid, all-inclusive, five-year pre-service education; second, job assurance; third, the certainty of going on for advanced study as her talents and taste dictate. When we contrast the Sister-student's favorable position in these matters with that of the lay student, it is evident that more can and should be expected of her.

American Way of Life

She has other advantages also, upon which to build a superior program. The Sister-student (in this chapter "Sister-student" has exclusive reference to one being prepared for the apostolate of nursing) has, previous to her admission to the Community, made the grave choice, the firm decision as to her role in life. She has, in a word, consecrated her entire life to God. This in itself differentiates her from the lay student, furnishes a strong motivation for her work and contributes to her maturity. Her religious Superiors, by accepting her, postulate their belief in her latent powers as a Christian and cultured woman of high ideals, stable concepts and seriousness of purpose. These highly desirable character traits will be solidified by study in all the major areas of learning which are the intellectual heritage of all Americans.

For the religious vocation operates no *a priori* change in a person. She remains a woman, a practitioner of a profession, and an American citizen. It is to serve on the American scene, in the American way of life, that she must be prepared. In general, the American way of life calls for a college education. For the Sister, the future representative of the Church in a particular field, a college education will not stop at the hours and courses required

[4] *Ibid.*, p. 9.

for a degree. It attaches small importance to the counting of credits. It means all that is implied in the philosophy "that baccalaureate education for the practice of professional nursing must be built on the background of a broad, liberal arts education and scientific principles."

When the implementation of this philosophy is challenged, not only by the time it takes, but by the ever-haunting spectre of "too few Sisters," the answer is rather a grim "There are fewer than you think." The Catholic hospital system is so vast, and it presents such an imposing picture, that one automatically—and erroneously—associates a tremendous number of Sisters with it.

Under Catholic auspices in 1962 there was a total of 863 general and special hospitals, representing 147,507 beds.[5] Religious Communities also operate a number of nursing homes and homes for the aged, which require the services of registered nurses. There are approximately 12,000 Sisters in hospital work, that number including those who have non-nursing duties, such as dietitians, pharmacists, technologists, accountants, etc. A close estimate would place the number of nursing Sisters at less than 9,000.[6] This very fewness is the most cogent reason for the Sisters' having the best possible preparation, so that they may make their impress on the nursing world in every type of excellence, including leadership. Numerically, they constitute a small percentage among the 550,000 lay nurses.[7] In order that Sister-nurses may play the role which God and man—particularly their fellow nurses—want them to play, theirs must be a preparation of the total person.

Importance of General Education

To achieve this preparation of the whole person, the curriculum, in addition to meeting the requirements of an accredited college with an accredited division of nursing, provides a preponderance of liberal arts subjects over the professional. This is to the great

[5] *Catholic Hospital Association 1964 Directory* (St. Louis: Catholic Hospital Association of the United States and Canada), p. 31.

[6] Data collected by a Survey of the Catholic Hospitals and Catholic Schools of Nursing, Fall, 1961. Available at Catholic Hospital Association, St. Louis, Missouri.

[7] *Toward Quality in Nursing*, p. 58.

profit of professional education, to which liberal studies give broader and deeper significance. To grasp the wisdom of this, one has only to recall that the profession of nursing is now calling strongly for "total patient care," "nursing the whole person," and even "family-centered care," "post-hospitalization home-nursing care"—all terms indicating the need for recognition of the many and varied elements, other than the pathological, which contribute to illness and need to be included in the nurse's interest.

With fifty per cent of all illnesses classified as psychosomatic, medical science admits that the most potent remedies come not in pill or capsule, box or bottle, but from the contact of a wholesome personality with one that is in some way damaged. This kind of supportive nursing is the result of the study of many disciplines, combined with professional knowledge and skills— all unified by a common element.

In the academic areas of a Sister-student's pre-service preparation this unifying, integrating element is found in philosophy and theology presented in a carefully planned sequence. Both contribute to the appreciation of one's self as a person, unique in the eyes of God, created for a definite purpose and having but one lifetime in which to fulfill that purpose. This appreciation of human dignity applied to all men will be the basis of a Sister's dealing with them. She will recognize it in her patients, whose worth, dignity and rights she will respect and will cause others to respect. She will refuse to admit the validity of any exceptions, even in cases where the patient may appear to have forfeited it, either deliberately by acts that have brought about his condition, or indeliberately as the victim of a materialistic philosophy. This is a situation which will be met in the world of the nurse many times.

By acquiring through study strong, rational, natural goals for desirable conduct, the Sister-student will more easily and strongly grasp supernatural precepts. Since the Council of Trent, the study of philosophy and theology have been mandatory for aspirants to the priestly function. There is no difference in *need* for these studies in preparing a religious woman for her apostolic duty; the difference is in *degree*. She needs it for her personal growth in holiness, and to lead others to want to become holy.

From other disciplines she will learn "life adjustment," but only from theology will she learn "life-adjustment-to-God's will," the *sine qua non* of holiness. The basic truth that man, having come from God, must return to God, and return by a particular path—a state of life—for which he has been created, strengthens a Sister against temptation: temptations in the form of a sensible attraction to another state of life; a questioning of the usefulness of the religious life itself; doubts, discouragement, discontent, and restlessness. To combat successfully these and other occasions for anxiety that she will encounter, a Sister must be armed with solid piety derived from a knowledge of theology in general, and in particular of the theology of the religious life. Her whole life as a good, practical religious fulfilling her apostolate in peace and purposeful security is based on her total pre-service formation as a Sister.

Need for the Cardinal Virtues

Religious life being a supernatural life, the need for theology to live that life, and to live it more abundantly, is obvious. This is further emphasized by the fact that in Catholic colleges theology is now a requirement for lay students. How much more need for it there is in the formation of a Sister, a functionary of the Church. By the successful integration of theology with all her studies, the integration of her life of prayer and apostolic action should be assured. The subject must be studied, not primarily for making the Sister an able exponent of the faith—though she will have many and unique opportunities for using her knowledge of doctrine and dogma in that way—but for its effect upon herself.

The infused virtues of faith, hope and charity should be understood and developed to so virile a degree that the moral virtues of prudence, temperance, justice and fortitude will characterize the Sister-nurse. These virtues are called continually into play in her social relationships. Sister-nurses dealing constantly with adults—and with adults under unusual stress—meet demands to exemplify these cardinal virtues daily.

1. *Prudence.* Prudence has been simply but cogently defined as "the sensible application of our theoretical knowledge (natural and

supernatural) to practical living."[8] This application a Sister-nurse is called upon constantly to make, both because of the confidence reposed in her and the responsibilities that devolve upon her. Both confidences and responsibilities often involve moral obligations to act or not to act, to speak or to be silent. She is faced with problems which can be solved only by a combination of professional competency and loyalty to moral principles.

Prudence enables a Sister-nurse to deal dispassionately, but with sensitivity, with her own problems and with those of others. It will prevent over-identification with patients, or more likely, with co-workers, while she exercises without limit the healing arts of understanding and sympathy. Prudence is a safeguard against the acceptance of too effusive manifestations of gratitude and of confidences which imply large future demands on her time. It might almost be said that prudence is *the* virtue most needed by a Sister-nurse.

2. *Justice.* Justice, temperance and fortitude may well be called the "show case" jewels of virtue, the presence or absence of which cannot be hidden from a Sister's associates. Other virtues, or the lack of them, might escape notice, but not these. A firmly embedded sense of justice will cause the Sister-nurse to "render to Caesar the things that are Caesar's, and to God the things that are God's." Her prayer life will not be neglected; purity of intention will guide her actions, and the presence of God fill her thoughts.

These inner practices her associates will not see, save reflexively. But they will notice if she fails in justice by preferences and partialities that ultimately result in disruption of that atmosphere of fraternal charity which she should engender. They will note if she condemns on scanty evidence, if she fails to give credit where credit is due, and if long-term faithful service is not rewarded financially as well as with praise. Without justice, there can be no real love of God or of the neighbor.

3. *Temperance.* Just as justice stems from and engenders charity, so does temperance stem from and engender hope; a hope

[8] J. D. Conway, *Facts of the Faith* (New York: Doubleday, 1959), p. 288.

which keeps a balance between all extremes; the extremes of doubt and confidence, gloom and gaiety, weakness and meekness, severity and laxity. Possessed of this virtue, a Sister-nurse will be temperate, not temperamental. She will *exercise* constructive control (most Sisters *exercise* supervisory positions) without inhibiting initiative. She will welcome but weigh suggestions for changes. Temperance enables her to be predictable, reasonable, cheerful and cooperative. Imbued with this virtue, the Sister-nurse will engender an atmosphere of hope, which will pass from her associates to the sick, imparting reassurance and confidence to both patients and colleagues.

4. *Fortitude.* Fortitude is founded on faith. How much in need of this virtue—a combination of confidence and constancy—is the Sister-nurse who must so frequently urge the practice of it on her patients. It is almost impossible to exaggerate the importance of this virtue for the Sister-nurse. One is apt to relegate it to the times and conditions under which pioneer hospitals worked—to twelve-hour (and at times twenty-four) duty, to the days of wood-gathering for heating and water-drawing from a well. But for these physical hardships there are now substituted more subtle demands to which Sisters must face up: The eight- or ten-hour day in a modern, professionally demanding, tightly organized, speed-paced hospital exacts more moral and physical stamina than did the hospital day of half a century ago.

Then too, whereas the hardships of a former day were calculated to emphasize dedication, it takes real effort to keep the clear image of God unblurred when working with every automatic and electronic convenience, and in surroundings where radio music and television programs, décolleté negligees and slack-clad visitors (where permitted), perfumes and flowers are as much a part of the picture as are oxygen tents, transfusion sets, and technologists' trays.

There is also the flattery—or the fury—of doctors to be reckoned with, professional rivalries to be held in check, and the constantly arising grievances—just and unjust—of patients and employees to be handled. Fortitude in no small measure is needed to carry a Sister unscathed and unscarred through such a day and enable her to be at the same time a serene tower of strength to her colleagues as well as to patients and relatives when they seek comfort and counsel.

The Hospital Milieu

The "others" amid whom a Sister spends her entire working day include a wide range of adults. These persons are doctors, nurses, technologists, members of guilds and auxiliaries, volunteers, skilled employees and those with only on-the-job training. They make up a Sister's steady contacts, in contrast to that which she has with individual patients, whose average stay in the hospital is less than a week. Such contacts offer an immensely fruitful field for the apostolate, and of this Sisters should be constantly aware. Again, this points up the fact that a Sister needs to be educated and developed as a person—a cultivated and cultured person in her own right, independently of her profession, although her profession will increasingly make more and more demands on these qualities in the Sister-nurse.

Avenues of Knowledge

This development predicates exposure, as we have said, to all the avenues of learning considered to be our intellectual heritage: the humanities—comprising a knowledge of world cultures, history, literature, music, art, and the philosophical ideas that have molded man down the ages. It means an introduction to the natural and social sciences and to the behavioral sciences, which give insight into the causes and effects of human conduct. The key concept is the idea of a sound religious formation, a well-rounded collegiate preparation culminating in a baccalaureate degree.

But why take five years for this when it can be accomplished in four? Why does the Sister need so many more liberal arts subjects than are required for a degree, and why in greater amount? Why, for example, such a subject as physical science? This is a practical question. There is a practical answer. Automation has been largely accepted in the hospital world. Not only is there "station-to-station" communication, but there are electronic devices which enable a nurse to monitor a whole "block" of patients from a single nursing station.

If a nurse is to be saved from an "assembly-line" mentality, she must be intellectually acquainted with the electronic equipment that she uses, thus fostering the attitude that although these things are for her use, they are not her usurpers. Again, such equipment as electrically controlled Hi-low beds, piped-in oxygen, drainage apparatus, and infusion appliances require a scientific knowledge of the principles of physical science, not just the "push-pull" instruction that suffices for a nurse's aide. This knowledge will enable the nurse, as occasion arises, to save a patient much discomfort, and possibly real harm.

The Humanities

A nurse's need for chemistry and biology is readily seen. (Though happily, no longer are such textbooks put on the market with the delimiting suffix "for nurses.") Her needs for literature (beyond the omnipresent "required"), art and music are not so readily accepted. Apart from the need every cultured woman has of these subjects, they play a considerable role in a Sister's professional world. Literature will give her that vicarious knowledge of life essential to one whose profession requires that she constantly give sympathy, understanding and support to others. Literature will not only broaden her knowledge of human nature; it will also exercise her emotions helpfully. The nurse will learn to respond to tragedy created by authors, before she deals with it daily as created by circumstances. Literature and the fine arts will enable her to reach her patients in a most helpful and—often, to them— surprising way.

This is to give the patient that "plus" service that not infrequently, like the last inch of a rescue rope, means all the difference between success and failure in his treatment. It is coming to be recognized increasingly that some patients can be helped more by the discussion of a book, current or classic, or of music and art appreciation, than by medicine or other forms of therapy. Nurses are coming to realize this more and more in their daily contact with the sick.

The cultural aspect of a Sister-nurse's education fills yet a deeper, personal need. Medical science and knowledge are ever reaching out to new truths. The orthodoxy of today becomes the heresy of tomorrow. As medical science changes, so does the professional education of a nurse change, for example, as to the administration of drugs, techniques and practices. A textbook of fifty years ago may now call forth laughter. It is certain that the textbooks of today—professional textbooks—will be equally obsolete and amusing less than fifty years hence. But the literature, art and music that were beautiful, harmonious and inspiring five hundred or more years ago—are equally so today. These, with moral truths, are the constants, the universals of man's life. They build up man's respect for his own nature; they engender a sense of security and pride. This security a nurse needs to save her from that faint touch of cynicism and skepticism to which she might be tempted by her professional experiences.

The Social and Behavioral Sciences

This profession is exercised in an environment that requires a knowledge of the other disciplines: Sociology and psychology, economics and government. For the world of the sick is a deviate world, vastly different from the world of health with its familial, social, economic and recreational activities. Indeed it might be said that every nurse serves on a battlefield, which starts with the patient's illness but spreads to many fronts.

Once stricken, the patient has not only a particular pathological condition to combat, but other insidious foes which are the allies of disease. He struggles against strong feelings of disorientation, for the hospital world is a foreign one to him. Pain often engenders impatience, irritability, anxiety; helplessness begets frustration; boredom leads to depression. In addition, the patient, man or woman, is frequently harassed and oppressed by the financial cost of illness, since rarely does health insurance of whatever kind cover all costs. He is further disturbed by the loss of earning power and the disruption of family life. All these accompanying factors must be included in a nurse's interest as she ministers to the original illness.

It is here that a knowledge of the behavioral sciences gives to the nurse's services an additional dimension. Both psychology and sociology furnish insights into the "why" of the normal and abnormal behavior of sick people. This enables the nurse to detect felt, but often inhibited, needs, anxieties and tension-building concerns for which she can suggest means of therapy. How often a patient's most desperate need is "just to talk" to someone whose attitude has elicited his confidence, and who is able to respond with wisdom and intelligence.

A Sister-nurse's increased knowledge of a person as a *human being* gives meaning to the concept of "total patient care." She recognizes that illness makes its impact on the social and emotional facets of her patient's personality; that it affects him morally and psychologically as well as physiologically and anatomically. Hence, her nursing must minister to his complete person. This concept is a stark truth to which the nurse must be prepared to give more than lip-service. She must be able to analyze her patient in terms of his varied needs, socio-economic, socio-familial, societal, his emotional needs, which are always changed, if not increased. Even his native intellectual needs are affected by his temporary loss of health, accompanied not infrequently by the shadow of death or fear of permanent disability. A Sister with a truly educated heart is quick to sense the hidden fears, the bewilderment, the mental anguish that so often accompany illness and physical suffering. It is to a Sister that even the proud and once self-sufficient patient will turn—once she has won his confidence— for sympathy and help to accept pain which, according to Bishop Fulton Sheen, has an inherent infinite value of its own, when "countersigned with the signature of the Saviour on the Cross." He says:

A feverish brow that never throbs in unison with a Head crowned with thorns, or an aching hand never borne in patience with a Hand on the Cross is sheer waste. The world is worse for that pain when it might have been so much the better. All the sick-beds in the world are on the right side of the Cross or on the left. . . .[9]

[9] Fulton J. Sheen, *The Rainbow of Sorrow* (New York: P. J. Kenedy, 1938), p. 30.

It is a Sister's privilege and prerogative by the right word at the right moment to make sure that the suffering of her patients is never wasted. This looking upon, accepting and treating the patient as a *whole* person points up the superior kind of education and formation a Sister-nurse must be given in order to develop in her the abilities necessary to fulfill her appropriate role as Sister-nurse.

The Nursing Apostolate

There are continuing returns from a Sister's education—or formation—to use the more comprehensive term—for it is a matter of forming the religious woman, as well as the Sister-nurse; a woman who, as a religious, will be in the profession for her entire life. The Sister represents a much more permanent investment than does the building. Catholic hospital construction is always in the forefront, often representing vision that is close to daring. This quality should be largely evidenced by the Sisters who exercise their apostolate in these buildings, according to the present pattern.

This pattern for the Sister-nurse is mainly supervisory in design. Besides the lay nurses working with her, both the degreed and the graduates of diploma schools, there is a host of auxiliary workers —practical nurses, aides, maids, ward clerks, messengers, etc.— whose services she must organize and coordinate. This is a task requiring no small amount of administrative ability and managerial skill. Organization and management of this teamwork is responsible in part for removing a Sister-nurse *from* the bedside of the patient—a situation the profession is striving to correct. Certainly Sisters should be foremost in this movement. It is what they want, as any nursing Sister will tell you. "But . . ."

This "But . . ." invariably points up a Sister's organizational, managerial and supervisory duties as insuperable obstacles to the bedside contacts she would like to have. So much of her time is required for the coordinating of the efficient performances of the nursing personnel for which she is responsible that she is "tied to a desk." Circumstances have obliged her to substitute administration for the ministry. No one will deny, still less disparage, the truth that a Sister by her kindness, understanding, patience and tolerance in dealing with her associates will impart these traits to others and thus have a large and beneficent effect on the quality of care given to the sick. But it is *not* getting her back to the bedside; it is *not* enabling her to bear witness to Christ through her personal holiness and professional competency directly to the patient—and to his family.

One familiar with Catholic hospitals knows that only too often, a patient's sole complaint is "I never saw a Sister while I was there." This, in itself, speaks volumes for what the presence of a Sister in a sickroom means. Knowing this, many Sisters try to "see" every patient daily, but it can be no more than a brief visit which does not really satisfy the patient. He wants someone who, through the exercise of her nursing skills, excites his confidence. Someone who has time to answer his questions concerning his illness with interest and intelligence; who can allay his fears—so often unfounded—by casually mentioning patients (without identifying them) who have conditions similar to his and who have successfully recovered. He wants a Sister-nurse who will increase his comfort by skillfully adjusting an appliance, massaging an aching area; one who will allay his anxiety by explaining in advance a medical procedure.

The Need for Understanding Care

Only one who has been a patient knows how far-reaching and remedial are the effects of such understanding care. It has been well said that "Life seen from the horizontal is vastly different from life seen from the perpendicular." If we take "horizontal" to represent one patient or all suffering mankind, then the Sister-nurse is the "perpendicular," her feet firmly based on earth and her heart right in this room. By reason of her dedicated service she makes bearable her patients' bodily pain, mental anguish and spiritual ills; her very presence suggests the strength emanating from Christ on His Cross.

Techniques of nursing change, miracle drugs come and go, but the Christlike virtues of patience, kindness, humility and meekness, combined in a Sister with superior professional efficiency, hold solace and healing for the sick now as they have always done. That the Sister-nurse having these qualities may not miss the choice opportunities she has of being the means of overflowing graces to others requires, perhaps, an entire re-thinking of the administrative and organizational structure of Catholic hospitals. To date they have followed the accepted pattern of educating Sisters for administrative and supervisory positions. The reasoning is that as Communities own the hospitals, the best interests of patients, hospitals and Communities require that Sisters be in key positions. But do they? Just what is meant by "best interests"? Which really are the true "key" positions?

Questions to Ponder

How are the best interests correlated—the best interests of the sick, of the nursing apostolate, of the Church?[10] Does not the very fact that Communities *do* own the hospitals give them greater freedom to experiment? How could they go about returning the Sister to the bedside of the sick, to whom she is really committed? How can they return her to the work for which she has been actually and professionally prepared, where she is wanted and needed? Where else will she experience the great satisfaction of personal ministry? These are questions well worth pondering.

Here again a change of attitude is needed, and what more propitious time for a change of attitude than now, when the Church is calling for it and is setting the example in so many ways? The change calls for vision, courage, and above all, sincerity. Have these questions ever been raised and looked at honestly: Do Sisters *always* have to be in positions of authority? Does not an affirmative answer negate the humility of Christ, who "came to minister"? Is not the redemptive role of a Sister diminished when the *virtue* of obedience is delimited to her response only to religious Superiors? Is not the practice of obedience which she must exercise towards doctors and others a response to the same, though delegated, authority? Would not a rejection of this view constitute a contradiction between what a religious professes to be

10 Interview with Sister Virginia Kingsbury, D.C., Nursing Education Consultant to the Daughters of Charity, St. Louis Province, Marillac College, July 3, 1964.

and what she is? These questions can only be raised. The right, the power and the duty of answering them belong to Major Superiors.

Fortunately, the Conference of Major Superiors offers an admirable forum for discussing such questions and formulating answers. This is exclusively within their province. There is evidence, from what has been accomplished, that the pioneer spirit is still strong among them, and that some startlingly courageous action may result —action much more in accord with the wisdom of God than with the wisdom of men.

New Horizons for Bearing Witness to Christ

It is fascinating, and at the same time sobering, to consider what might be done to widen the witnessing to Christ among Sisters dedicated to the care of the sick and suffering. What new horizons would be opened by facing these soul-searching questions: Is the best and most effective use being made of Sister-nurse power? In what areas can religious nurses make the greatest contribution? Could not Communities, through consultation and mutual stimulation, plan means for extending Sister-nurses' services beyond the walls of their respective hospitals?

Within a hundred miles or so of almost any of our large cities— cities with a population of 500,000 or over—there are areas where health facilities are sadly lacking. A rural population, widely scattered, poorly paid for whatever work is available, living on a marginal-subsistence level, is critically in need, both of medical care and of instruction in the rudimentary laws of health and hygiene. These situations represent opportunities for a Catholic hospital to render great service at a minimal expense—if doctors and Sisters are willing to work under what might be termed "missionary" conditions. They could establish—with the aid of the Catholic Physicians' Guild, if that is available—a rural clinic and health center where the inhabitants could receive weekly medical consultation and care and instructions on preventive measures to insure health. The round trip could easily be made from the hospital in one day. The plan is even more feasible if several Catholic hospitals pool their personnel, facilities, and resources.

The writer knows of one such clinic that has been successfully conducted for years. It is probable that there are others. The Sisters look forward to the long ride and a hard day's work under such challenging conditions with enthusiastic zeal. A network of such clinics dotting rural areas throughout our country would render vital service to those who need it most, while reflecting the image of the Church as the Good Shepherd.

Another example is the great need for Sisters prepared for psychiatric nursing. This is a large field indeed, since more than one-half[11] of all hospital beds are reserved for the care of the mentally ill. During the last thirty years the trend has been towards psychiatric units in general hospitals. How many Sisters are qualified to give such care, where a person-to-person relationship means so much? Not every nurse, not every Sister is fitted by temperament and personality for this type of nursing. Could not a large Community with vision and a desire to serve where the need is greatest prepare more Sisters for psychiatric nursing, and make the services of these Sisters available to other Communities? Multiple-Community faculties have been common—and highly successful—in high schools and colleges for years. Why would not the same plan work well in hospitals? Other examples of inter-Community cooperation could be suggested in cardio-vascular, maternal and child care, and rehabilitation nursing. Perhaps the first reaction will be "Impossible!" But with our witnessing daily the accomplishment of so many "impossible" things all around us, that word should be, not the first, but the last to be used towards a new proposition or line of action. It would be one of the finest examples of *aggiornamento* in Community collaboration in health service yet seen.

International Roles

There are international as well as national roles which the *aggiornamento* of Sister-nurses calls for; roles which will give them new experiences and enable them to grow in religious and social

---

[11] *Hospitals, Journal of the American Hospital Association, Guide Issue,* XXXVII, No. 15 (August, 1963), 482.

stature.[12] International exchange of Sister-nurses, both on an inter- and intra-Community basis, could be arranged for such length of time and in such fields as the Communities concerned would agree upon. (That the Sisters selected must first acquire a fluency in another language is a "plus" that will serve them well in many ways.) Both the Sister from the United States and the one coming in exchange would be excellent ambassadors of good will for both Church and State. Both would profit professionally by first-hand knowledge of different cultures and of nursing in countries other than their own.

It is exhilarating to think what an impact would be made on the Catholic nursing world—and beyond it—if an international exchange, involving a hundred or more Sisters annually, would be maintained. Here is a rich, ready-to-hand opportunity for Sisters to make their influence felt internationally. And the "too few Sisters" is no argument against it, since the exchange would be on a Sister-for-Sister basis.

The instances cited are but samplings of how the apostolic mission of the Sister-nurse could be expanded, were there a "divine discontent" with the *status quo* and an ever-increasing response to *Caritas Christi urget nos*. The huge complex of Catholic hospitals, so efficiently administered and held in such high professional repute, should not engender complacency. Rather, the Sisters responsible for them should feel keenly their obligation to the Church, to society, and to themselves, to pioneer in new areas of service and to broaden their sphere of influence. Never, as Cardinal Suenens says, should we ever cry "Enough," but continually seek more and more ways to bring Christ to the world.

The Spirit of Conquest for Christ

What else does bringing Christ to the world mean, save to be filled with the spirit of conquest? the same spirit that first brought Sisters to the shores of America, North and South; the spirit that enabled them to live in the most primitive conditions, to bear the most rigorous hardships, to brave the greatest dangers, that they

12 Cf. Sister Virginia Kingsbury, D.C., Member of the Surgeon General's Consultant Group on Nursing. *Report on the Status of Nursing Education in Ecuador*, 1963, pp. 21–22. (Mimeographed.)

might bring Christ to the new world. It is this spirit that is needed to break away from set patterns of service—patterns which, except in spirit, do not differ from those of non-Catholic hospitals. These patterns, it is true, have brought returns in professional satisfaction, personal growth and social prestige to the Church, but they must be updated. Time is rushing by. It is not too soon to be thinking in terms of 21st century demands for an ever more personalized service.

By way of preparation for a new, updated spirit, let us ask ourselves: How far have these patterns of service helped to confirm Sisters in their attitude of acute consciousness of overwork, of being under constant stress and strain? Would not these attitudes be drastically changed if, instead of facing her day's work with a harried, "There are so many persons for whose work I am responsible," she would say hopefully, "I have so many persons to assist me; so many whom my dedicated life will touch today and who will help me to live my dedicated life fully." A contrary view indicates a deplorable drifting with the tide of current secularism. It shows a lack of Christian awareness and religious integrity. How far from the pioneer spirit of conquest! Seeming success can lull us into a false sense of tranquility.

"Make no mistake about the age we live in," says St. Paul. "It is high time for us to wake out of our sleep." (Rom. 13:11, Knox) The tremendous force that lies in hospital Sisters must be aroused to its full power.

You should be true brides of the Lord: souls united indissolubly and intimately with him alone; souls without stain, detached from the world of the senses, from the world of money, from the world of vanities. And we willingly acknowledge that countless sisters do correspond fully to the ideal of their vocation or, at least, come very close to that ideal. If only there were never amongst them—we do not say betrayals, but not even the slightest indications of infidelity, the least evidences of indifference, coldness or lack of understanding! God alone knows what an increase of flourishing vitality and what a harvest of works the Church would behold. And it is the sick, who are entrusted to your care, who above all would become aware of it and would always truly see Jesus Christ in you.[13]

13 *The States of Perfection*, pp. 288–289.

It is for this excellent and unlimited service that the Church wishes the Sister-nurse to have a superior, unhurried, pre-service and continuing preparation. Since the life of a religious is but a prolongation of the life of Christ on earth, to live it fully the Sister-nurse must, like Christ her Exemplar, never succumb to weariness, but go about always doing good.

14

Aggiornamento
of the Sister in Social Welfare

Social work, reduced to its simplest definition, means helping others. It goes back, therefore, as a need and a fact, to the very origin of man. As a result of the primal fall, man's human nature was deprived of its original perfections. He became vulnerable to the effects of poverty—since he must earn his bread in the sweat of his brow—and to sorrow, infirmities, illness and death. Since his nature was not depraved, however, he retained a God-given instinct to help his fellow man in his sufferings, afflictions and trials; particularly those related to him by family or tribal ties.

The Old Testament sets forth clearly that man is his brother's keeper, and bound to observe the prescribed laws for the fulfilling of his duty. But the love of one's neighbor, with its consequent duty of rendering every form of assistance to him, came to its full flowering only in the Christian era. Christian social living calls for unlimited service to others. This has always been recognized as the responsibility of the individual Christian and of the Church.

Although social work in practice is as old as civilization, as a profession it has a very brief history, one which is still being written. The term social work came first to be used in the very early 20th century. It replaced the time-honored word "charity" dating from the beginning of the Christian era: works of charity, works of mercy. These works, and the persons devoted entirely to them (mainly religious men and women), were held in high esteem. It was generally accepted that, given the necessary qualities of intelligence, health, aptitude, understanding, sympathy, compassion and all that can be summed up in the one word, "love," anyone could minister to his needy fellow man.

Until a comparatively recent date, the State concerned itself only with the physical facilities of social agencies, such as safety measures, fire prevention and compliance with the requirements of health and hygiene. The competency of the workers did not come under its jurisdiction.

The Institutional Setting

Charitable works, whether private or tax-supported, were carried on chiefly within an institutional setting. The Church followed this pattern, and very early in its history in the United States established orphanages, homes for the aging, maternity hospitals for the unwed mother and her child, school-homes for delinquent youth, institutions for handicapped children, and settlement houses. These works were appealing to the Sisters and attractive to their numerous benefactors. They flourished. But neither the Sisters employed in them nor other employees in similar institutions, whether tax-supported or private, complied with any professional standards, for the simple reason that there were none. The performance of works of charity was not looked upon as a profession. It was considered the normal expression of a Christian's duty: a work of mercy, with love as its guiding principle.

Advent of the Welfare State

The development of the Welfare State, following the great depression of 1929, ushered in another era. It gave great impetus to social work as a profession. When the government accepted the premise that its responsibility extended to all needy persons, in every category, of every age and condition, financing loomed large. Tax dollars—first by the millions, and then by the billions—were needed to implement its new role. Over-all government agencies were quickly set up to receive the funds; but to dispense them wisely, equitably and intelligently was another matter. This required the services of persons with a very special kind of training. Such persons had to be possessed of a body of knowledge and skills needed for dealing with people—people with problems which they, without help, could neither cope with nor solve. The person aiding them had to know how to assess, weigh, and analyze the situation, and then come up with a solution, not merely by extending temporary aid, but by eliminating, where possible, the cause of the problem.

In addition to calling for desirable basic human qualities, this work demanded a knowledge of biology, psychology and psychiatry; of economics and civics, some acquaintance, too, with law, medicine, ethnology and the humanities was deemed helpful, and even necessary. Most universities offered such courses, but without the emphasis needed for one preparing to become a social worker; nor did they afford the needed practice or field experience. Quickly, however, and despite many handicaps, a profession was born. Universities set up schools of social work as early as 1916. The first Catholic school of social work was begun by Fordham University in 1929. One could almost say that this new profession came into existence full-blown.

To be a "social worker," properly so called, one must have earned the master's degree at a university recognized as having a good school of social work within its academic and professional disciplines. Surprisingly enough, there are few designated background requirements at the prerequisite level. A solid liberal arts program of general education is considered the best preparation for beginning graduate work.

The preparation differs quite radically from that required for the teaching and nursing professions, since both give official and professional recognition to the holders of bachelor degrees. Indeed, in some areas, a person may be designated as a "teacher" and eligible for membership in the National Educational Association on the possession of a "two-year certificate" while finishing undergraduate courses at a college or university. A person may become a "registered nurse" on the completion of a three- or even a two-year course at a recognized hospital-diploma school of nursing by passing "State Boards" (examinations). But to be a professional social worker, eligible for membership in the National Association of Social Workers, the M.A. degree is the minimum requirement. This beginning requirement of a master's degree has a very specific bearing on the small number of Sisters who are "professional social workers."

Curiously, the State, whose needs accented the new profession of social work, with few exceptions, has made no laws requiring registration and/or certification of social workers. It still relies entirely upon the National Association of Social Workers to set standards and to maintain them. One must face the fact, without implying that it is wholly regrettable, that had the State placed the licensing of social institutions on the same basis as it did schools and hospitals—that is, had it legislated for the professional qualities of the workers as well as the physical facilities of the work—a large number of Sisters would today have a master's degree in social work. As it is, the number is negligible, not more than five hundred. But factors other than the lack of State pressure, factors applying directly to Sisters, account for their small enrollment in schools of social work.

First of all, religious Superiors were somewhat averse to taking a modern view of works of charity. The traditional view was associated with institutional care. Orphans, the aging, unwanted infants, the needy and neglected of all kinds, connoted an institution and the presence and generous, loving care of the Sisters. It was difficult indeed to accept a concept other than institutional care, particularly since it had served the purpose so well for so long. This was true not only of Catholic but of all institutions. But the battle to strike a balance belongs to the history of social work as a profession.

Several other obstacles, which Superiors in their wisdom weighed well, militated against a large enrollment of Sisters in schools of social work. The first was the requirement of a master's degree for first-level competency. This precluded sending Sisters for their professional education very early in their religious life before Superiors had time and opportunity to study them well, to observe their inter-personal relations, their ability to stand up under pressure, and in general to determine if they had the personality and the qualities required for social work. Again, field work required that Sisters go alone into disadvantaged neighborhoods and to deal on a person-to-person basis with all sorts of people.

Yet another obstacle, one which made Sisters as well as their Superiors wary of embracing the tenets of professional social work, was its philosophy. As Msgr. Cooke so ably says: "The purpose of social work education is to help people to help themselves, by solving their difficulties and making an adjustment to life. You cannot help people to adjust to a philosophy of life if you have not a *true* philosophy yourself."[1] Succinctly, Christian philosophy looks upon the poor and sees Christ in their person. Secularistic philosophy looks upon the poor and sees a client. Thus, when the State replaced the Church as the largest dispenser of aid, secularistic philosophy replaced Catholic philosophy as the prime motive for the work. It came as a Trojan horse, for indeed it seemed good that the State should provide for those who could not provide for themselves. It even seemed Christian. Catholics were caught off-guard, and the works of mercy and charity, the very heart of the Church which manifests its faith acting by charity, might have been almost wholly lost to it, but for a providential development. Again one must revert to history to illuminate the present.

National Conference of Catholic Charities

Catholic charitable institutions and agencies were, up to fifty years ago, individual, isolated units, save for such communication as their respective Communities afforded. They were welded together by a slow and painful process, through the establishment, in 1910, of the National Conference of Catholic Charities. The significance of this for the Sisters can best be expressed by quoting the words of His Excellency, Patrick A. O'Boyle, Archbishop of Washington, D.C.:

The Catholic Charities movement in the United States had been blessed with a good sense of timing. The young and vigorous profession of social work was still in the process of its own formation when, in 1910, the National Conference of Catholic Charities was

1 Vincent W. Cooke, "The Infiltration of Secularism into the Catholic Social Field," *Sisters' Religious Community Life in the United States* (Glen Rock, New Jersey: The Paulist Press, 1952), p. 160.

established at the Catholic university in Washington, D.C. As a result of this initial effort, the Catholic Charities movement was prepared to coordinate and to perfect the activity of individual and institutional in the apostolate of charity in the Church, so that its distinct identity would never be lost in the wider development of the social welfare field.[2]

Beginning on the national level, Catholic Charities Bureaus spread to, and are now operating in, practically every large city in our country. This gave the Sisters an anchor to which they could hold in the fast-changing field; a guide they could trust, a counselor to whom they could turn with confidence. It gave them also a strong bond of unity and, through the conferences it sponsored, a means of consultation and collaboration. The hierarchy, in their whole-hearted approval of the Catholic Charities movement, were far-seeing. Priests of phenomenal ability and courage pioneered the cause. No words spoken today could be more daring than those spoken by Msgr. Kirby in 1910:

Let us hold to our philosophy, to our doctrine, to our supernatural motive and inspiration. Then let us seek progress in method and practical aim from critic, from conservative and from radical, from new and old.[3]

Bishops were quick to see the necessity of placing professionally qualified priests in charge of Catholic Charities Offices. As a result, priests were among the first to be graduated from schools of social work, Catholic and non-Catholic. Catholic Charities went further and offered scholarships to workers who would pledge a certain number of years of service to the agency after their graduation.[4] These offers were eagerly accepted by lay persons, rarely by Sisters. They had not yet felt the full impact of need for professional education, other than of the in-service type.

[2] "Foreword," *The National Conference of Catholic Charities: 1910–1960*, by Donald P. Gavin (Milwaukee: Bruce Press, 1962), p. v.

[3] William J. Kirby, "Problems in Charity," *National Conference of Catholic Charities Proceedings* (Washington, D.C.: National Conference of Catholic Charities, 1910), p. 410.

[4] Marguerite T. Boylan, *Social Welfare in the Catholic Church* (New York: Columbia University Press, 1941), pp. 201–204.

Flexibility in Welfare Work

But following the trend of the times, this in-service education was carried on sedulously. Beginning with the bachelor's degree, with which most of the Sisters were equipped, the Sisters supplemented this education by attendance at workshops, institutes and conventions. They attended college courses bearing on their work: psychology, community resources, guidance, dynamics of group work, etc. They continued to staff, exceedingly well, a vast network of Catholic agencies. The Sisters in social work manifested a marvelous and enviable flexibility in changing their programs and practices to meet the needs of the times. Many institutions, inheritors of century-old names, operate today in the most modern manner.

The profession was not slow to create its own vocabulary. The words "orphanages" and "asylum" disappeared. "Institutional" became a bad word with a "bad image." Children's institutions built for group care were subdivided into modern "apartments" where ten to twelve boys or girls have their own family living and recreation room, dining room and kitchenette. One Sister with several helpers is responsible for such a group, and is referred to as "group mother" or "group Sister." The children attend parish schools, take part in all extra-curricular school activities, stay overnight in their chums' homes, and, in turn, invite their friends for overnight visits with them.

Children under six are rarely found in a child-serving institution today, as foster-home placements are deemed best for them. Actually, social workers would prefer that no child under twelve should be in a congregate home. For the adolescent, the troubled and troublesome teen-ager, foster homes are often inadequate, and, truth to tell, few prospective foster parents can be found who want to assume responsibility for adolescents. The care and interest and love of the Sisters, in a modified and modernized institutional setting, appears to be the best answer. The girls can enroll in the various diocesan, parochial or private schools. Within the institution they have, not only what the Sisters have to offer, but the possibility of drawing on the skills of professional lay social workers, therapeutic recreations, non-directive guidance, psychological, and (when indicated), psychiatric aid. All this is a vastly different concept from what the word "orphanage" once signified. Today's dependent children are rarely orphans, but rather the products of disrupted homes, "wards" of the court, or of the local Catholic Charities Bureau.

Philosophy Concerning "Illegitimate Parents"

The same spirit of progress and change is evidenced by Sisters in social work everywhere. No longer is an infant born of an unwed mother raised in an "infant asylum" until three or four years of age. In most cases, the birth of such a child takes place in a Catholic general hospital, and the infant is placed from the hospital in either an adoptive or a foster home. In every case the wish of the mother is paramount and always previously ascertained. This leaves the Sisters and the personnel of their institutions free to focus on the mother, to aid her recovery from the psychic trauma to which she has been subjected, to foster her Christian and social rehabilitation, to help her plan wisely and prudently for the future. Incidentally, it was a Sister (one who held a M.S.W. degree) who first called attention to the need of case work with the unwed father.

The plight of the unwed mother had always been, more or less, well understood. That she had need of wise and prudent counseling; that a special psychology was imperative for her rehabilitation to wholesome womanhood, that her deepest need was restored self-respect and self-confidence unmarred by a feeling of rejection —these were needs intuitively seen by doctors, nurses and social workers dealing with the unwed mother, whatever her age, background or experience.

It is comparatively recently that anyone thought of the unwed father except as the villain of the piece. But one Sister—some two or three decades ago—contemplated with understanding compassion the idea that somehow, somewhere, a tortured masculine mind might well be engulfed in guilt feelings at the thought, "Somewhere in this world is a son of mine—a son I shall never know." The Sister followed her intuition with action. She found the need for counsel, restored self-respect, and wholesome self-renewal almost as urgent—and sometimes more so—for the unwed father as for the unwed girl, who carries the heavier onus of guilt, but whose plight is more readily recognized.

Settlements and Day-Care of Children

Settlement houses, too, owing to the Sisters' alertness and vision, have been changing over the decades from centers of recreation, custodial day-care of children, and depots of material supplies, to an entirely new role in the community. This role is changing from day to day. Case work was done with the parent or parents wishing to place a young child in day-care, to determine if such care was best for the child and the family. The necessity for both mother and father to work has always been a leading problem, especially if it means unsupervised children, who will possibly turn into truants. What are the home conditions? Does not the child need preparation for this change in his life? Such checking becomes an ongoing process through staff-parents conferences held at regular intervals. Day-care for the child has progressed from custodial care to a meaningful Christian experience, with strong educational, social, and psychological overtones.

Inner-City Problems

Broadening their territory, the Sisters found that systematic visiting of homes brought to light many needs that, with their aid, could be remedied; for example, aid could be secured for a helpless aged person, eligible for old-age pension but not getting it; excessive rents could be redressed through a protest by an informed, interested person; truancy problems with which the parents were unable to cope could be solved. Sisters with their lay staff of Settlement houses initiated various forms of community organization for the betterment of the neighborhod.

A modern phenomenon is seen today in that more and more the Sisters in social agencies are drawn away from their institutions and brought into closer contact with the pulsing life of misery, squalor and degradation in the community around them. They are necessarily brought into more and more contact with civic officials, and welfare workers, and with the inner-city problems of large urban centers. To work with maximum efficiency, the Sisters should have the necessary knowledge of sociological techniques, the insights into ethnic mores, customs and outlook that regulate or modify the conduct of disadvantaged families and promote inter-group factions and street gang warfare.

Public housing in the form of high-rise apartments, in our inner cities, was the material, numerical, mathematical answer as to how a given number of families—running into the thousands—could be adequately housed in a certain amount of space. The psychological and social factors were largely left out of the planning, and every city is plagued with the results of that lamentable omission. That very often the crime rate is highest where such housing predominates is not due to the type of families that live in them, but to the abnormal manner of living into which these families have been forced. If "stone walls do not a prison make," it is equally true that row upon row of impersonal concrete buildings whose residents rarely so much as meet each other do not make for friendliness; these people are not really even neighbors. Their situation does make for hostility, resentment, and many other forms of anti-social behavior.

This concentration of disadvantaged persons in certain areas offers to the Sister-welfare-worker the same opportunity for service offered to nursing Sisters by large hospitals with a concentration of sick persons with every type of malady. This, Sisters in some of the large cities have been quick to sense. Satisfied with small successes, their aim is to bring to the people not so much material relief—the State takes care of that, after a fashion—but to make themselves acceptable and accepted by their genuine Christ-oriented interest in every family and every individual. Their work is as heroic and their vision as great and far-seeing as that of their pioneer predecessors.

The Sisters of this generation may but lay the groundwork for reaching the masses at their door, but a great beginning has been made by their recognition of the challenging opportunity. These contacts they have made, their seeing and hearing the multiple moral, religious, family and financial problems of the poor have made Sisters realize their unpreparedness to render maximum service. They have learned that heart-and-head compassion combined with natural talent and a supernatural desire to help is not really sufficient. Just as these qualities would not make Sisters good nurses, good teachers, good accountants or good house-mothers, neither do they fit them to be of maximum and lasting help to persons profoundly distressed and disturbed by these environmental problems. Graduate study in a school of social work or in the area of counseling is required, not only that a Sister herself may do more constructive work, but that she may exercise effective Christian leadership where it is so sorely needed. By leading others to see Christ in the poor she is rendering the greatest service to the poor in their panic flight from facelessness.

That action is needed *now* in this matter is disclosed by a recent (1962) survey[5] which shows that the six Catholic schools of social work have graduated only a total of 106 Sisters during the five-year period, 1957–1962. Previous to 1957 they had graduated 169, making a total of 279 graduates since Catholic universities set up schools of social work. It is certain, of course, that some Sisters received degrees from other than Catholic universities. An estimate of 500 Sisters with a master's degree in social work is a generous one. The actual number is, conceivably, far short of this.

Understandable Doubts

There is still some reluctance among the laity and not an inconsiderable number of the clergy to "see" a Sister-welfare-worker in her new role. They eye questioningly Sisters doing social work on a permanent and extensive scale outside of an institution. Some Major Superiors, too, have doubts about the propriety and the desirability of Sisters combating social ills where they arise—in the home and in the neighborhood. They fear that working in unconventual settings, in areas labeled "undesirable," may affect adversely a Sister's religious spirit. These doubts and fears should be resolved, because Sisters, for their peace of mind, must have the whole-hearted support of their Superiors on all levels. Lacking

5 Sister Bertrande Meyers, D.C., *An Investigation into the Social Work Study Policies of Sisters*, 1962, p. 1. (Mimeographed.) Prepared for the Special Committee of the National Directors of Catholic Charities.

this, they cannot go joyfully about their work. This joyousness is never more needed than when a Sister's assignment brings her in daily contact with those who, for one reason or another, can no longer bear life's burdens unsupported.

Sisters who work with the disadvantaged, most frequently in congested urban areas, are deeply convinced by their experiences of the necessity of going out to those in need rather than waiting for such people to come to them. They have experienced how much more readily confidence is established when, sitting on a wobbly chair in a nondescript kitchen, they talk to a woman about her delinquent daughter, than were the same woman "on the other side of the desk" in a well-appointed office. To hear the drunken snores of a husband in his home and witness the family fearfully await his awakening is quite, quite different from hearing *of* him, and reducing the information to a neat "Father drinks" in a case history. It is one thing to try to make ragged, neglected children in their own homes presentable for school, and a different thing to receive such children into an institution with every facility for the removing of rags, grime and vermin. Yet how can the Sisters live the gospel if, when they are assigned to serve the poor and the deprived, community customs and regulations delimit the place, time and extent of their services?

Sisters and Inner-City Needs

The idea is often advanced by good lay people: "I think Sisters who have made vows should be protected from all that squalor. Why clutter their minds with it? Is it *right* for Sisters to see the seamy side of life? Wouldn't they be better off in their convent Chapel praying for the poor and needy?"

Prayer is good and necessary. Without it one can do nothing. But Christ did not hesitate to say, "I have not come to call the just, but sinners, to repentance." (Luke 5:32, Conf.) Hence His interest in the woman at the well, the woman taken in adultery, the Publicans and sinners, Mary Magdalen. The grace that comes from the vow of chastity will be the Sister's protection in the foulest places. The love of neighbor for the love of God cannot be bounded by "safe neighborhoods." Good people, needy people, are to be found in these inner-city areas, and the disadvantaged need Sisters to secure aid and social justice for them; to bring God into their lives.

Naturally (and supernaturally) prudence should be exercised, in the same way that a public health nurse would exercise prudence if she were working in an area besieged with an epidemic of communicable disease. One would send there experiencd nurses, certainly. They would be well prepared to handle such an assignment. That is why it is of tremendous importance that a Sister be thoroughly formed in the religious and intellectual life before undertaking social service. She needs maturity, social and psychological; she needs the stability and self-control that the discipline of hard study gives. But to be adequately prepared for welfare work, she needs the know-how to be gained from the supervised field experience that is an integral part of the course work that leads to a master's degree in social work. Most importantly, Sisters chosen for this field should have a natural, as well as supernatural, aptitude for the work.

There should be no reversal of values either by Superiors or Sisters in assessing the spiritual worth of social welfare. It is not only what a Sister *does* for others that makes her a better religious, it is what the doing of it does *for her*. Christ has said plainly that in the final balance every person born into this world will stand or fall by one single entry: What each did, or failed to do, for Him in the person of the poor. St. Vincent de Paul has said he who has loved the poor during life will behold the approach of death without fear.

The Beatitudes—Creed and Code of Sister-Social-Worker

Christ gave His beatitudes (Matt. 5:3–11) to all people as a set of rules to guide them. Probably most Sisters can say: "All these have I kept from my youth" (Matt. 19:20), but no one needs these maxims more than the Sister in welfare work. They should be for her not only a professional creed and code to live by, but a source of confidence that they are Christ's own words of reassurance as to her conduct in the service of the poor.

They are a series of hard sayings in a way, albeit they come from Christ's own lips. They fall harshly on the unaccustomed ear. "Blessed are the poor in spirit. . . . Blessed are they that mourn. . . . Blessed are they that hunger after justice . . ." social justice, racial justice, economic justice. These are happy? are blessed?

A Sister-welfare-worker, living the beatitudes as her personal commitment calls for, interprets the beatitudes to those whom she serves by her *being* even more than by her doing. Thus a reciprocal service is established, as there is a mutual sharing of Sister and client in the beatitudes themselves—purity of heart, meekness, thirst for justice and all the others. There is, too, a mutual progress towards the rewards promised: the kingdom of heaven, the possession of inalienable lands, the comfort of Christ.

"Blessed are the poor . . . the meek. . . ." A Sister-social-worker has that "understanding concerning the needy and the poor" (Ps. 40:1) which governs her entire approach to them. She does not identify the poor with the poverty she seeks to alleviate—she identifies them with Christ. This gives to her services not only a warm, personal element, but the attitude of one who is receiving rather than giving.

This identification of the person in need with the need itself is the greatest affront to human dignity. This depersonalization by welfare agencies is scarcely avoidable, perhaps, when "Relief" has become a multi-billion-dollar, complex program of aid. The needy person or family slips like a slot into a machine, fitting neatly into a category: "Unemployed," "Unemployable," "Broken family," "Sub-marginal income," "Mentally handicapped," according to his need of assistance. He is given an impersonal appointment to be in a certain building, in a certain office, on a certain day and hour. The card on which these instructions are written, and which is the *sine qua non* of his being interviewed, is equated with himself. Contrariwise, a Sister who has become poor for Christ's sake equates every poor person with herself. She has a oneness with the disadvantaged and a deep concern for them, whether they be materially or morally poor, culturally or educationally deprived, or devoid of incentive and ambition.

Does the Sister-welfare-worker wish to "possess the land" of the trust and confidence of those whom she serves? She must indeed exercise meekness; meekness when her best efforts are thwarted through lack of cooperation; meekness when her advice, given through long hours of counseling, is disregarded; meekness when the chronic truancy of children is encouraged by the parents. But even as she meets these tests, she is humbled by the greater evidence of meekness shown by her clients: A woman who reports uncomplainingly that she waited five hours at a hospital clinic; a man who takes back his errant wife "for the sake of the children"; a teen-age boy or girl who returns day after day from fruitless job-hunting with the explanation, "They don't hire Negroes." So does the work of a Sister-welfare-worker, which might, to the uninitiated, appear to be always strenuous, often drab and sometimes fruitless, become in her eyes truly blessed.

"*. . . shall be comforted . . . shall be filled. . . .*" All men are in need of comforting because suffering is the universal lot of mankind. In listing the absolutes of man's life, Solomon says: "There is a time to weep . . . and a time to mourn." (Eccles. 3:4) But not everyone, even the well-intentioned, is capable of comforting—as witness the term, "Job's comforters." However, a Sister who knows well the paramount place of suffering in salvation history, who personally and vicariously has experienced the purifying power of private pain, holds the secret to the art of comforting.

Comforting must go deeper than the surface; it must have the penetrating power of love. It must needs be the kind of love which gives food to a poor family without leaving the breadwinner starved for self-respect. It must be the kind of love that can pay a person's rent without substituting for it a sense of debt of another sort. True comforting stems from understanding, sympathy and compassion—it begins with love and ends with love.

The hunger and thirst after natural justice with which the world is today seething has its source in man's God-given instincts for those conditions—political, financial and social—in which he is free to become his best self. From the same source come the hunger and thirst of the disadvantaged for the justice of decent housing, adequate education, equitable wages, equal job opportunities and social acceptance. Sisters who openly by word, writing or deed join with the deprived in their efforts to obtain elemental justice will "have their fill" of Christ's approval. In what a new light is the Church seen when Sisters join in marches of protest, head a minority grievance group to the mayor's office, or prevent, by their presence, the eviction of a family on a bitterly cold day! If, in doing these things, they draw upon themselves the displeasure and disapprobation of conscientious objectors; if, in fact, they "suffer persecution for justice' sake," in the way of hostile public opinion, opposition of really good people, loss of some benefactors, they have Christ's word for it that they are blessed. Indeed not a little of their own "beatitude" may well derive from their contribution to the Church's renewal—making the Church truly, in all times and places, the Church of the poor.

"Blessed are the merciful . . . the clean of heart. . . ." Deprivation and want only too frequently engender bitterness, and the needy are not always merciful, one to another, as witness the parable of the two debtors. One of a Sister-welfare-worker's great services is to make of the common needs which bring persons together a bond and not a barrier. Nothing so builds up a person's morale and heightens his self-concept as to extend aid to others. When a man is moved to the "mercy" of gratuitously giving to a fellow employee a ride to work in his jalopy, or does "for free" a bit of repair work on the sagging windows of a neighbor's house, he is receiving more than he gives. When a woman offers to "baby sit" to free another woman to go shopping; when a skilled seamstress donates her sewing skills so that her neighbor's children may have new dresses for school, we have examples of that mercy which is indeed ". . . twice blest, it blesseth him that gives and him that takes."[6] A Sister-welfare-worker readily generates this give-and-take atmosphere because her own life is one of gratuitous giving. How often are her words of commendation for a generous act stopped with: "Sister, you work for us for nothing. Why shouldn't we do our part?" There is simply no end to the good a Sister does by the example of love she gives to the poor she serves. The whole atmosphere of a tenement house can be changed from hostility to friendliness by a Sister's continued

6 William Shakespeare, *The Merchant of Venice,* Act IV: Scene I.

visits; and this influence, begun in one shabby building, extends to an entire neighborhood.

"*. . . shall see God . . . be called the children of God. . . .*" "Blessed are the pure in heart, for they shall see God" is perhaps the strongest article in the Sister-welfare-worker's creed. It seems to anticipate the eternal reward reserved for heaven—the Beatific Vision. But how can one see God in this world in a slum area; where the Man-God said explicitly *He* would be found? "Amen, I say to you, as long as you did it to one of these my least brethren, you did it to me." (Matt. 25:40) These words have all the simplicity, all the directness, all the challenge a Sister needs to know that in serving the needy she is serving Christ Himself. A Sister working among the least of His has the special grace of seeing Christ in all. She sees His image in the derelict, the criminal, the corrupt, the cruel, as well as in the disadvantaged whose patience and dignity elicit her respect and admiration.

Holy Habit and Viewpoint Make the Difference

Armored with her religious Habit and all that it symbolizes, a Sister walks safely and serenely in places where a laywoman, or even an officer of the law, might hesitate to go unaccompanied. It is not the services she renders which have won for her a rough veneration—others render like services and on a larger material scale—but it is the sense of something "different" about her. Here, in the holy Habit, is the outward sign, the symbol, that marks her as "different"—the servant, the *friend* of the poor.

No Substitute for the Charity of Christ

Any fear that the Welfare State will leave no place for the charity of Christ should be laid to rest. Christianity has something to give beyond all material aid. This is exemplified in the confident action of Peter and John as told in the Acts of the Apostles. When a certain cripple sitting at the gate of the temple asked for an alms, Peter's ready answer was: "Silver and gold I have none; but what I have, I give thee: In the name of Jesus Christ of Nazareth,

arise and walk." (Acts 3:6) The apostles' very lack of a small coin
—that is, their poverty—with which to satisfy the beggar's request,
and their own conscience, made them draw on their inner resources and thus give to the suppliant, not an alms, but the cure
of his incapacity. That there was a spiritual healing also is indicated by the closing lines of the scene: ". . . And he went in with
them into the temple, walking, and leaping, and praising God."
(Acts 3:8)

While realizing only too well that welfare benefits sometimes fall
short of providing sufficiently for the needs of the recipients, Sisters
may well feel satisfied that, in many instances, they need no longer
concentrate on providing food, clothing and shelter, but rather
direct their efforts to building up their clients' self-confidence,
arousing latent ambitions, strengthening family ties, affording protection against moral dangers, fostering neighborhood cooperation, and developing a sense of responsibility. This form of social
work requires a persistence and stamina, a faith and fortitude, far
greater than were needed in the older institutional setting. It calls
also for a thorough knowledge of those basic factors underlying
effective human behavior, the principles of group dynamics, and
an unwavering conviction of the importance of every individual.
In a word, it calls for faith as well as love.

The Sister-Social-Worker's Hour of Destiny

This is the Sister-social-worker's hour of destiny. No greater
proof is needed than that found in the words of Pope Paul VI, who,
while yet Archbishop of Milan, addressed, in 1961, the Women
Religious of his archdiocese. He first paid high tribute to the
Sisters, stating that the Church had greater need of them than
ever before. He then traced the evolution of religious life for
women from the cloister to the active life, making use of the
penetrating words: "St. Vincent de Paul is the most important
precursor of the apostolic monasteries which took form as 'action'
and as 'charity.' " The term "apostolic monasteries" dissolves
completely the supposed dichotomy of work and prayer. The
Archbishop of Milan continued:

You have served in education, in the service of the sick, in schools. At this time the Church says, "And now I ask yet more, my dearest daughters. Become capable of doing and of giving even more. . . ." I will scatter you among the Christian people, who have such need of seeing the consecrated virgin in the midst of their profane society. I will put you into the very midst of society and of youth. . . . This is the modern vocation of the Sister—to become a collaborator in pastoral action. . . .

Do not refuse this vocation! . . . The mission I will point out will give you infinite preoccupation and worries because the apostolate, the service of souls, is sacrifice, not comfort. . . . It will place you in direct contact with this modern humanity so polluted and so in need of being purified and saved. . . . You will see from close up, what sin is. . . .[7]

Here the eminent speaker, knowing that love and a right intention would not alone suffice, added a needed word on *aggiornamento:*

Preparation, competency, is needed in every field today. . . . We must learn from the children of darkness (I mean from the lesson of the modern world) the awareness of perfection that it has. It calls for technical excellence, it calls for professional excellence, it calls for perfection in scientific aids, etc. Prepare yourself and see to this, even though it will disturb and upset your daily program and will change some of your customs. The Church of God calls you.[8]

While this broadening of the apostolic-professional is urged upon all Sisters, it has a special appeal, a magnetic attraction, for Sisters engaged in social work. To answer the call of the Church and the needs of society, Sisters must be professionally equipped.

Three Attributes of Sister-Social-Workers

The delay in this preparation has, providentially, been turned by the Sisters to good account. Sister-social-workers (without benefit of the master's degree) have learned, and learned well, three lessons with which Sisters in other areas of service are now

7 *Address to the Women Religious of Milan*, pp. 4–5.
8 *Ibid.*

struggling: first, to accept changed programs as the needs of the times require; to be open to concepts of their work which run counter to tradition, and to adapt their horaria to the needs of the apostolate. Second—and in this they have an immeasurable advantage—they have learned to work well with lay persons, not only with them as colleagues but also under lay people who are in the role of superiors because of their position as supervisor or administrator in an agency where the Sisters work. Third, they have not been poured into a professional mold; they have not acquired attitudes and viewpoints which they would find hampering in the new avenue now flung open to them, and into which the Church urges them to move. Sister-teachers and nurses, knowing their work to be by its nature apostolic, will have to battle with themselves to broaden that concept, to add a fourth dimension to their profession. Sister-social-workers have already conquered this difficulty.

Superiors should have no further misgivings concerning the appropriateness of providing further professional education for Sisters in social work who have already earned their first degree. Nor should the fewness of vocations deter them. This has not been a deterrent in other professional fields; and social work should not be the outstanding exception. Two concurrent courses of action could be taken to increase the slow trickle of Sisters professionally qualified in the social field to a steady, increasing stream. The first is to select, from Sisters now in social work, those who are best qualified by solidarity in their religious vocation; Sisters who are intelligent in a truly Christian way, and who have already demonstrated emotional stability, health, and the ability to work with others. A liberal-education foundation at the baccalaureate level is the *prerequisite* for enrolling for full-time study in a Catholic school of Social Service.

Superiors will have many such Sisters in the desirable age-range —loosely speaking, from twenty-five to forty years—who have demonstrated their ability to deal constructively and compassionately with human problems, and who are fully capable of profiting by higher education. The fact that a Sister is doing the work assigned her well should not carry the penalty of depriving her of educational opportunities to do it better. "Do it again," to quote Pope Paul VI, "with even more professional excellence."

The second action Superiors can take is to give a special preparation in their undergraduate work to those Sisters who express a wish for social work and who, apparently, have the qualifications needed. Observation may indeed reveal potential ability, but it remains only potential until preparation, education, and formation have been synthesized and made ready for use. Within a truly *liberal* education with good sequences in philosophy, theology, psychology and the social sciences (where the first two are the instrumental basis and integrating principle for the behavioral and professional sciences that are to follow) an excellent background will render the two years' graduate study interesting, challenging and not too difficult. Only such a foundation can make fruitful the professional subject matter and field work that are the core of the master's program.

The undergraduate work should so weld *being* with *doing* that the Sister-student emerges, not merely a person who knows what ought to be done, but one who does what needs doing capably and with prudence, knowledge, and fortitude.

"Seasoning" Needed Before "Serving"

Where possible, a Sister thus prepared in an undergraduate program should have a few years of "seasoning" as a Sister in a social agency before going on to graduate school. The former is an excellent and enriched foundation for future professional studies. During the several years that the Sister would serve as "a social work aid" in a Catholic agency, she would be under the direction of a Sister who had her master's in social work, so that guidance would prevent her making mistakes in dealing with those persons whom the agency was trying to help. As an apprentice she would have errors pointed out and she would be shown better, more constructive, methods of dealing with persons and their problems. The Sister would see, at first hand, the role lay social workers play, and this should lead to well-founded respect and friendship, as she continues to work in cooperation with them or under their supervision.

Inter-agency relationships would also unfold, and she would learn the role of the Catholic Charities Office in maintaining common policies and practices among Catholic as well as non-sectarian agencies; the help it extends in preparing and presenting budgets to the United Fund or similar voluntary fund-raising and dispensing organizations. She would become aware of the watchful eye it keeps upon proposed legislation which could be in ill-accord with Catholic philosophy or contrary to Christian principles. She would become familiar with State and City Welfare policies and practices, learning both their extent and their limitations. In the meantime, the Sister would be getting the "feel" of social work in the duty assigned her and would be growing in a desire for greater competency evolving from a deep consciousness of her need of it. Thus would she be strongly motivated to graduate study.

Long-Range Planning for the Making of a Sister-Social-Worker

Another well-chosen pre-placement for a Sister destined ultimately for social work is a school, particularly a school in the inner-city, where the pupils or students come mostly from low-income families or from racial or national minority groups. In the classroom the Sister will learn one of the basic principles of case work: not to be disturbed or misled by undesirable conduct, even the most gross, but always to seek the "why" of such behavior, while accepting the person guilty of it—accepting and loving him. Seeking the "why" will frequently lead her into conditions with which, later, as a social worker, she must know how to deal understandingly and effectively.

The "why" of a youth's behavior may be rooted in the home in marital discord, physical neglect, sibling rivalry, parental cruelty or immoral conduct. If she is permitted to visit the homes of the children, as school-Sisters are urged to do now, she will soon note the far-reaching effects of racial tensions and strife, clashing cultures, and national resentments. Seeing these situations, and being able to offer only minimal aid or marginal solutions, she will be eager for that professional education and guided field work which will enable her to be of deep and lasting service to society as a social worker and without which she will forever feel uncertain and insecure.

In adopting this preparatory plan for graduate study in social work, religious Superiors will be doing, deliberately and prudently, what social agencies in every part of the country are forced to do through necessity. There are approximately 29,000 persons with the master's degree in social work, and there are 129,000 positions open. Administrators of agencies fill the gap as best they can, preference being given to persons holding a bachelor's degree with a major in sociology and a minor in psychology, or vice versa. Very often these persons do part-time study for their master's degree while working. However, by no means can all agencies afford to be so selective, and hundreds of positions in social agencies are held by persons with no special professional preparation and an education that falls short of college graduation.

Comparatively speaking, Catholic social agencies are better off in the matter of prepared personnel—except on the executive and administrative level—than are tax-supported agencies. This is due in large measure to the initial qualities of the Sisters, their stability and supernatural motivation, their love of people and sympathy for their problems, along with their ability to inspire others with similar sentiments. However, Sisters cannot be satisfied, still less complacent, with the quality of their work. The Church deplores mediocrity in the service of God and demands excellence as His due.

Major Superiors Key Leaders in Promoting Excellence

The attainment of this excellence is in the hands of Major Superiors. These Superiors have responded promptly and vigorously to the call of the Church for the *aggiornamento* of Sister-teachers and nurses. They have maintained at all costs, financial and otherwise, a vast system of schools and hospitals because they hold as a sacred commission the education of youth and the care of the sick. Now the focus should be broadened to include the preparation of Sisters who minister to mankind in the person of dependent children, the aged, the handicapped, the improvident, the delinquent, the socially incapable and the morally incompetent as professional social workers.

The Church, religious Communities, and the Catholic laity have evidenced their determined defense of the Church's right to educate. There must be equal vigilance where the works of mercy and charity are concerned. Secularistic forces are constantly pressing, sometimes covertly but in most instances overtly, to preempt entirely the field of social work. These forces continue to urge making the State the legal guardian of all dependent or neglected children, assuming the responsibility for their care and education. In taking over budgetary management of a needy family, the State seeks to control many other aspects of family life, by its power to give or withhold funds.

How can the poor of all categories, while accepting State aid which is their due, be protected against the secularistic philosophy which dictates and accompanies it? Obviously, by the same means by which the Church has retained her schools and made Catholic hospitals the equal of any and superior to most—by adding high-level professional preparation to the Sisters' intelligence, spirituality, devotedness and dedication. Superiors have long and prudently pondered the fitness of professional social work for Sisters. Now the same prudence would seem to demand that they ponder the fitness of their individual Sisters for professional social work, and send them, in the same numerical proportion that Sisters in other works are sent, for the master's degree in social work. In a word, the same prudence that once dictated cautious hesitation now dictates prudent, prompt, large-scale action.

Sisters Indispensable to the Needs of Society

It can safely be said that while the Church has need of more religious in all fields, its need for qualified Sister-social-workers is paramount. The need now is for Sisters to go out to the people, not to wait for the people to come to them. There is a great need for Sisters to become a meaningful part of the life of the masses. They need to have the "feel" of the poverty of the poor; they need to know that a job lost can be a major catastrophe to a family; they need to sense keenly the moral dangers and the psychological trauma arising from thousands of persons being housed under one roof in high-rise government building projects.

Sisters should be increasingly aware of the dangers to youth in the accelerated rate of high-school drop-outs and subsequent un-skilled, under-paid employment, or no employment at all. This constitutes a chief problem in our society today. But to what pur-pose do the Sisters sense and feel and know the problem if they are not prepared to offer solutions? Competency in handling human problems must be added to compassion in understanding them. The Sisters need to be fully acquainted with sources of help; they should, because of their professional preparation, be able to command the respect of state officials and the regard of their fellow social workers among the laity. One such Sister touches the lives of thousands. Such Sisters should be multiplied.

Think what it would mean to the works of charity, if each exclusively teaching and nursing Community were to educate and maintain just two well-prepared Sister-social-workers! These Sis-ters could either function as school social workers within their own school system, or they could be "loaned" (for a salary) to work in social agencies of other Communities (living in their own convent, "commuting" to work). This is but another example of possible inter-Community cooperation and collaboration. The Church and society await these Sisters. The war against poverty needs them.

15

In His Image and Likeness

Twentieth century man has been accused both in literature and life of being preoccupied with his own identity: Who am I? What am I *for?* The farther he draws away from God, the less certainty he has. A superficial manifestation of this deeper inner questioning and search is seen in the current popularity of the word "image" and how it is applied to almost any given situation. A man's bank balance is referred to as his "fiscal image"; his home in suburbia, the way his family dresses and perhaps the church they attend will inevitably contribute to or subtract from his "social image." Man wonders about his professional or business "image"; what image he projects at work, at home, among friends.

Man's True Image

Man has always known intuitively or by instruction that he was created in the image and likeness of a Higher Being; he has read or heard, or has been taught by his readings in the Old Testament, that God has said: "Let us make man to our image and likeness." (Gen. 1:26) But, after the first man's revolt and fall, his darkened intellect and weakened will could scarcely grasp the glory that, by creation, was his. Yahweh, for all of His watchfulness over His chosen people, was an Image inspiring awe and fear. He was a Voice, speaking from a burning bush, or a Power thundering His commandments from Mount Sinai, moving the people to cry in terror to Moses: "Let not the Lord speak to us lest we die." (Exod. 20:19)

The Purpose of Life

God, divinely paternal, in due course of time, fulfilled His promise to man to send a Redeemer. In the drama of the Incarnation He reversed, as it were, the creative act. Where once He had said: "Let us make man to our image and likeness," He now willed to make His Son, always co-equal with Himself, to the image and likeness of man. "Being made in the likeness of men and in habit found as a man." (Phil. 2:7)

In Christ, man found the God of love, Christ Jesus, an Image he could truly worship in the Flesh and a Likeness he could see, appreciate, and by the grace of God, imitate. Here man saw that both the "image" and "likeness" are free gifts of God bestowed by His grace. The image stamped him indelibly as belonging to His Maker. Man could mar this image, deface it, and even debase it; yet he could never destroy it. But St. Augustine tells us that "God, who created you without your cooperation, will not save you without it." Likeness, therefore, though present in the soul by God's grace, was something man was required, in a sense, to earn, something to be wrested by effort, to be worked for in the depths of his spirit and the sweat of his brow. As Exemplar, the Ideal to be followed, man was given the Model on the Mount— the Mount of the Beatitudes. By following the pronouncements given there, and the pattern of His daily life as lived in the gospels, man can not only bring into bold relief the "image" of His Maker; by correspondence with grace, he can radiate the "likeness" of Christ. Implicit in this way that God *made* man, is the purpose for which He made Him: to show forth God's goodness and greatness; to learn to know Him; to love and serve Him; and to teach others to know, love and serve Him in this world, in order to be happy with Him forever in the next.

For those who accept this simple but clear-cut purpose, life is no riddle. It is the testing ground that leads to man's final destiny —happiness in eternity. God's call to perfection, to follow Him according to the "Model shown you on the Mount," applies to all men indiscriminately. "If thou wilt be perfect, come follow Me." Men, from all times, have followed Christ, not only individually but collectively. His apostles were the first to leave all things to follow Him. Patterned on their example, the religious life came to be organized for both men and women, under the protection of the Church. Down the ages it has projected the "image" of Christ, poor, chaste, obedient.

Religious Life in Modern Perspective

Each age has received the "image" of the religious life according to its mode of receiving, its viewpoint, and in terms of its needs; for the religious life has always been relevant to the times in which it was lived. It has been reserved to the modern world to see a new image of the religious life, an image that differs in appearances and in accidentals from the former ideal, though the strict essentials remain unchanged. There is a more general understanding today that the religious life seeks no escape from reality; the convent is no haven of refuge from the world, grown more hectic with its complex trials and tribulations. It is coming to be seen for what it is, and truly always was, a courageous following of Christ, an imitation of Him, as He walked among men; it is a sharing of His concern for all people. It is a sharing, too, of the misunderstanding and contradictions that were Christ's, the trials and temptations that He underwent. It is a brave facing up daily to a life of sacrifice.

The Sister, favored with a religious-apostolic vocation, the call to be another Christ to all men, does not flee from the world. Like Christ, her Model, who first retired to the hidden life of Nazareth, and then to the desert, to pray and prepare Himself for His apostolate among men, a Sister does absent herself for a time to be fashioned and fitted to return to the world to play therein a redemptive role. Having answered Christ's call to a more perfect way, having pondered the purpose of life, she knows that henceforth she is to bring to all men a surer image of God's goodness, and she is to bear about her a more radiant and relevant likeness to Christ. Henceforth, *this* is the "image" with which she will be preoccupied.

A Sister's Concern with Her Image

A Sister's concern is always with God. To see herself as He sees her, to show forth His goodness to all men, is the purpose for which she has been created. She knows that God will see in her an image of His divine Son whose prototype was Abraham, answering the call of God, "Go forth out of thy country and from among thy kindred, and out of thy father's house, and come unto the land which I shall show thee." (Gen. 12:1) A Sister, twenty, thirty or forty years in religion may long since have ceased reverting to the struggles she experienced in following the call of vocation, her first sacrifice eagerly, earnestly and willingly made, but nonetheless heartbreaking, considered from the human viewpoint. But God sees in her now, as He saw then, the impress of His divine Son deriving from her acceptance of His invitation to love Him more than father and mother, sister and brother, lands and possessions. God sees her as one whose pole-star is His will, even as it was that of His divine Son, "I seek not My own will, but the will of Him that sent Me." (John 5:30)

In this confidence, a Sister lives her life in the sight of God, in a state transcending the most acceptable holocaust of the Old Law. For she knows with a certainty that brings serenity and peace of soul, that her "image" is bound up with her example of sacrifice, found rather in the sacrament of the New Law, in the Eucharist, where Christ remains perpetually at the disposal of mankind, daily giving them His Body to eat and His Blood to drink. A Sister, devoted to serving God through her fellow man, can joyously see herself consumed in the services of others; and like her divine Model, she can say at the end of life *"Consummatum est."*

The Sister's Image in the Church

A Sister has a special relationship with the Church which sees and helps to fashion a further complementary facet of her image. It sees in her, not only an individual member of the Mystical Body, as are all the people of God, but also a member of a particular religious Congregation, brought into existence, not only through the God-given inspiration of its founder, but by the juridical process which the Church exercises as an organization. This it is that gives a Sister a special relationship to the Church as well as to the other members of her Order. Herein the Sister realizes that she projects a twofold image: first, as a member of the Church, to which she is bound, even as she is bound to Christ, by the vows of poverty, chastity and obedience; and second, as a member of her Community. As a whole, healthy member, functioning perfectly gives renewed strength and vitality to the body, so the fervor and fidelity of a religious assures to her Community a state of spiritual health, which, in turn, affects the whole Mystical Body.

In the daily life of every Sister, this concept of the Mystical Body is a real and moving force that animates and motivates her spiritual as well as her apostolic activity. She realizes that here she reflects, not only the image of Christ crucified, inasmuch as she has, for His sake renounced, and, in a sense, died to those things which she may have held normally and legitimately most dear, but by her joyousness in her state of immolation, she reflects the brightness and the glory of the risen Christ. This, she realizes, is a source of strength, of courage and of hope to other members of the Mystical Body.

Religious—Elite Corps of the Church

In the Church there is another image which the Sister seeks by daily devotedness to bring out in clear and militant relief. She sees herself as a member of an elite corps which numbers almost one million strong—a corps, single-purposed, well disciplined, totally dedicated. Thanks to the Church's directives, the members of this corps are now well-equipped with modern intellectual and spiritual "weapons" and are growing daily more familiar with the terrain on which their battles must be waged. Like other forces within the Church, the host of Sisters is being brought up to maximum efficiency in order to meet the social, economic and psychological forces that are threatening to disrupt and de-Christianize the contemporary world. Religious Orders project the image of an always dependable corps, ready to serve at home and abroad, wherever there be need to bear witness to Christ.

It is a glorious thing to belong to this corps, to have answered the summons as Sisters have, voluntarily. For although Christ's call was clear, it was also conditioned by: "If you will." No one is ever drafted into a religious Community. Before entering, a Sister knows, in a general way, the triple renunciation she must make, the price inherent in a call to "take up your cross" and an invitation to "follow Me." But motivated by love of Christ, the "recruits" place themselves in the hands of the Superiors of the Community they select, ready and willing to be formed and fashioned as the Church requires. Thus do they enter the ranks of those who are not only Church-oriented, but wholly Church-directed.

The Sister as a Member of Her Religious Community

The Sister is naturally, as well as supernaturally, concerned with the image she presents to the members of her own religious Congregation. This is her family, its members are her comrades-in-arms; with them she will serve God, the Church, and contemporary society. It is within the confines of her life as a member of this particular Order, with its unique spirit, that she will be distinguished from members of other Communities by the emphasis which the founder or foundress placed on some feature of Christ's life, or some special virtue which He exemplified in an unusual degree.

This particular spirit, this spiritual emphasis, however, is but the five or ten per cent of religious life which differentiates the Sister of one Congregation from that of another. Basically, fundamentally, the religious life is the same for all. The end is always the love of God and the neighbor; the manner of expressing this love, and its manifestation of zeal for its special apostolate, may hold some minor differences or variety; but only minor. Yet a Sister is particularly aware of her special identity as a Benedictine, a Dominican, a Sister of Charity. In her mind, the Benedictine "image" is not the same as that of the Franciscan; the Dominican "image" is not the same as that of a Sister of Charity.

But all religious life in every Community is ideally structured to make possible the fulfillment of Christ's prayer: "That they may be one, as we also are." (John 17:11) It will be helpful and

heartening to most religious to recall that this plea for oneness
—of oneness with the Father—was made in behalf of men who
had shown many faults, serious weaknesses, and glaring defects
of character. The apostles, even after having answered the call
of Christ and having lived closely with Him for nearly three
years, were still contentious and ambitious; they were weak and
fearful, sometimes motivated by human respect and often stirred
with a desire for power. Yet, it was to such men that Christ
entrusted His Church, giving as the badge of discipleship with
Him, the observance of a new commandment: "By this shall all
men know that you are My disciples, if you have love one for
another." (John 13:35)

Religious life, then, is but the extension and intensifying of
the Christian life—discipleship with Christ through fraternal
charity. Each Sister knows that this love should predominate in
the image she reflects to her Community. She is equally aware
that, just as an applicant enters a Community *seeking* perfection,
fully conscious of her defects and failings, she gradually learns
that the search for sanctity is a lifetime endeavor even as it is for
each of her companions.

Christ's Measure of Holiness

Fraternal charity, or the lack of it among those with whom we
live, is something that can be more easily detected than can love
of God or love of the neighbor. Fidelity to spiritual exercises, the
scrupulous observance of every external rule, large or small,
adherence to every tradition and custom—all these can be tested
in the close association of Community life by the criteria of
fraternal charity. This was Christ's own measure. The scribes and
Pharisees, strict observers of the law, censorious of those who
failed, and quick to condemn them, were the only classes of
persons to whom Christ spoke with unmitigated severity. Wither-
ingly He called them "whited sepulchers" and accused them of
binding heavy and intolerable burdens on the backs of others,
which they would not touch with their own fingers. Yet He made
it clear, both by word and example, that the keeping of the law
was always to be subordinated to the higher law of charity. As a

case in point, He healed on the Sabbath day; He defended His apostles when, to satisfy their hunger, they plucked grain on the Sabbath; and, when contrary to the ceremonies prescribed by law, they ate with unwashed hands, He excused them.

As fraternal charity is the touchstone revealing the genuine love of God, so zeal in the apostolate is subject to the same test. Patience with the lay people a Sister serves must be matched with patience in dealing with Sister companions. Sisters who ardently, for the love of God, wish to project an image of generosity, devotedness, kindness and compassion towards the poor they serve in the apostolate, realize that such an image is false if it does not project the same love and compassion for those with whom they live within the convent.

Sisters who radiate fraternal charity among their companions, within the religious family at home, can make of the poorest house or mission a place of peace, joy and continued satisfaction. The kindness, the solicitude of a Sister Superior is often taken for granted, equated with her duty as an official. More appreciated is the kind act, the sympathetic word from a Sister companion when something has evidently gone wrong, and even more appreciated is the hearty word of praise when all has gone well.

Praise is all too little cultivated among Sisters in their relationships with one another. Yet, is not the image of Christ notably lacking when well-earned praise is withheld? Curiously enough, the laity are often lavish with their praise of Sisters for merited action; often, their appreciation knows no bounds. But Sisters, alleging fear of fostering pride, too often allow a conspicuous opportunity for proffering words of recognition to pass with no attempt to express their appreciation. Yet, nothing is so satisfying to a Sister, nothing so arouses so deep a sense of humility, so keen a sense of belonging, as does some spontaneous expression of loyal commendation from one or more of her companions.

Significant indeed are the answers received by a retreat master who sent questionnaires to a large number of religious asking them what subjects they preferred to hear discussed during their annual eight-day retreat. The subject of fraternal charity led by a wide margin—seventy per cent as against the second-highest subject, which was rated by only fifty-one per cent. (It may be remarked, in passing, that the choice of fraternal charity did not seem to emanate from any marked presence of unhappiness among the religious answering the questionnaire, since out of twenty-four possible topics, death came last with only two per cent of the Sisters interested in the Grim Reaper.)

Fraternal Charity and Potential Vocations

Not to be overlooked—indeed to be given a prominently thoughtful place—is the effect fraternal charity, or the lack of it, has on potential vocations. While willing to admit with indulgent understanding that "Sisters are only human" when there are lapses in meekness, patience, or cordiality towards a lay person, the same lay person finds no such indulgent excuse if there has been a lapse of patience towards another Sister. A high-school girl will smilingly accept a quick retort from a Sister, but recoil when the retort is directed by a Sister to a Sister. When even a brief encounter of this kind takes place, there is surprise, dismay, and sometimes real shock on the part of those who witness even a passing discord.

Quite possibly the following incident is not of frequent occurrence. Let us hope that it never really happened. But that it could be "thought up" should "set a guard about our lips" and increase interest in the image a Sister might momentarily project, with momentous results. A priest, deeply interested and zealous in promoting vocations, tells of his dialogue with a mature young Catholic woman, twenty-five years of age, who remarked that while reading the gospel she sometimes felt as though the words, "Come, follow Me" were addressed directly to her:

"How fine! So you want to be a Sister!"

"Oh, never, never, never!"

"May I ask why? Can you tell me what you know about Sisters?"

"They don't live according to the Gospels. They don't love one another. They don't pray—they recite prayers. They are not poor, they are sparing. Their chastity makes spinsters of them; and obedience, infants."[1]

[1] A. Plé, O.P., *Religious Life in the Modern World*, Selections from the Notre Dame Institutes of Spirituality (Notre Dame, Ind.: University of Notre Dame Press, 1961), p. 16.

Father Plé rightly called this image of Sisters a caricature, and certainly it is exaggerated. But analyzed for what grains of truth it might contain, it could point to a lack of love, lack of love of God, lack of love for Sisters and lack of love for their fellow man.

With all the helps a Sister receives today from courses in psychology, group dynamics and human relations—and even without them—she knows that to reflect the image of God she has to know how to love, unselfishly and even selflessly. The vows of religion are intended to free her from those obstacles that would hinder a reflection of the likeness of Christ from shining through.

Through the actions of Christ we glimpse the perfect "Community life" He lived with His apostles and disciples. As man He felt a human need to be with His companions. With them He talked freely; He relaxed with them; to them He explained His parables and sayings; He encouraged them and He admonished them. He was interested in them; never was He repelled by their faults. He sustained them; He defended them. He was the perfect Superior, understanding, approachable, patient. This is the atmosphere, this is the environment that fraternal charity produces in the religious life. This is the climate made possible in each convent by those deeply interested in tracing in themselves the image and likeness of Christ.

Today, the Best Day for Religious Life

It is this atmosphere of fraternal charity, reproduced, fostered and developed, under the directives of the Church, supported by modern theological teachings, which makes the present day the best of all times in which to be a religious. Sisters, grounded in their vocation, can be daring in their apostolate, embracing all the needs of a modern world, because they know their lives are built on the firm foundation of discipleship with Christ. They can become engrossed in complicated business affairs and not lose, nor even lessen, the peace of Christ which is theirs; they can be warm, helpful and loving to others, because of the warmth, help and love ever engendered and ever renewed in their Community lives. Sisters live, not in Utopia, where all things are perfect—how utterly that would unfit them for dealing with reality—but in a state where all, knowing full well their imperfections and faults, are striving to bring out in themselves, more and more clearly, the image and likeness of Christ.

Today's Sister is being steadily and solidly prepared for today's apostolate, and the preparation goes far deeper than a change in externals, such as habits, rules and customs. Those changes are important and there will be more of them. But, more important are the changes quietly and gradually taking place as all Sisters learn more of how the natural can aid the supernatural. Discoveries are not confined to the field of natural science alone. The social sciences, the behavioral sciences, the newer reaches of human and interpersonal relationships are unexpectedly contributing to a better understanding of human conduct, making the gospel more real and vital in everyday living. The liturgy of the Mass, the daily participation in the Eucharistic Meal, emphasis on Paschal joy—all of these are aids to a deep renewal in the essentials of the religious life, bringing to the surface a more Christlike way of living.

Thus, gone for the most part is the inflexible, authoritarian form of government; gone is the suppressing of natural talents under guise of fostering humility. Gone is the ignoring of special aptitudes in order "to die to self" and the human desire for self-realization. Gone is the attitude, on the part of religious Superiors, that for a Sister to ask an explanation is to question authority and impugn her grace of office. Alive and ever-growing is an attitude of understanding that now makes it comparatively easy for a Sister to combine obedience with initiative, success with generous recognition of the contributions of others, outstanding accomplishment with genuine humility, and finally, public fame with private self-evaluation.

It is safe to say that today's Sister knows more of the world today than the world knows of today's Sister. When the achievements of a Sister in the fields of art, science, literature, sociology or theology, make headlines, the majority of Sisters see nothing extraordinary in it. They know that such results come from the unusual opportunities given to Sisters by their Communities to develop their potentials on every level. Herein we see the image of Christ dealing with His disciples. Having prepared them by His grace and instruction, and having given them the mission to "Heal the sick, raise the dead, cleanse the lepers, cast out devils" (Matt. 10:8), He later listened with interest as they recounted their successes to Him. After these discussions He would gently draw them aside to pray with Him in solitude. Here their powers would be renewed, even as the Sisters are renewed by stronger application to prayer and closer companionship with Christ. Never did Christ dampen His apostles' sense of achievement, even though they knew all power to perform derived from Him. But He was careful always to draw their attention to the Source whence they drew the power to achieve.

Brethren Aided by Brethren

"A brother, aided by a brother, is like a strong city." The present age with its exhausting anxieties, its overwhelming fears, its shifting sense of values, and its crumbling standards calls critically for a showing forth of Christ's image, sureness of purpose, and sense of mission. Communities that are not sensitive to the impact of the world crisis will be powerless to assist in solving its problems.

Bishop Pursley, after enumerating graphically the terrors of technology, the ever-present threat of nuclear warfare, the almost constant strain of national and international tensions, and the frustrating search of modern man for self-identity and fulfillment, adds:

It would be futile to deny the impact of these realities upon the integrity of religious life, even in the safe seclusion and comparative isolation of convent and monastery. As never before, we dare not ask "for whom the bell tolls." We are all in the same boat, and even though it be the barque of Peter, it rides the same waves that are whipped up by the storms of the world. Fear and anxiety are natural responses to an awareness of danger.[2]

This awareness of danger adds to, rather than detracts from, the privilege of being a religious in today's world. Stability, of which

2 Leo A. Pursley, "Keynote Address," *Religious Life in the Church Today,* p. 20.

some Communities make a vow, cannot be tested in the midst of calm, freedom from strain, and the absence of great difficulties. A soldier's bravery and loyalty to his country and its ideals of freedom are tested and tried more on the battlefield than in the barracks.

That there is a certain danger inherent in the following of Christ is shown by His stern rebuke to Peter, who had protested Christ's foretelling of His passion: "Go behind Me, Satan: . . . thou savourest not the things that are of God, . . ." (Matt. 16:23) Neither misunderstandings nor contradictions, calumny nor scorn, persecution nor ultimate death however ignominious, could swerve Christ from His appointed purpose. "For this was I born, and for this came I into the world; that I should give testimony to the truth." (John 18:37)

The Challenge of Ideas Versus Ideals

A Sister today has perhaps—as never before—the privilege and the need to give testimony to the truth of her divine call, her religious vocation. Someone has said that every Sister founds her Community anew because the duty of preservation devolves upon every generation. This is a challenge today's Sister will meet *today*. She will meet this challenge by distinguishing between the *ideals* of the religious life and certain *ideas* that have come to be associated with it. Ideas connected with the religious life are changing today so that its ideals may be vitally renewed. A clear distinction of their relativity is needed.

Certainty and stability from within must combat doubt and questioning from without. If the Church is seeking to change her image from that of a static institution to one of dynamic vitality and keen relevance to the world of today so that modern man may turn to her for guidance in his perplexing problems, it is not surprising that the Church would wish religious Communities to improve and update their image in today's world, the more competently to serve society as it needs to be served. Popes have reiterated the need the Church has of her religious Orders:

How could the Church have fulfilled her mission of education and charity during recent years, especially in the immediate past, without the aid given, with so much zeal, by hundreds of thousands of Sisters? How otherwise could the Church fulfill her mission today?[3]

There is every evidence that, far from losing their relevance in today's world, Sisters are becoming more and more essential to the apostolate in the modern world. In the same allocution Pius XII adds,

Chastity and virginity (which imply also the inner renunciation of all sensual affection) do not estrange souls from this world. They rather awaken and develop energies needed for wider and higher offices beyond the limits of individual families. *Today there are many teaching and nursing Sisters who, in the best sense of the word, are nearer to life than the average person living in the world.*[4]

Nearer to life. This is the image every Sister wants to convey: that the vows of religion have liberated her from any obstacles that could keep her from serving the modern world as it needs to be served *today*. When Pius XII speaks in admiration of Sisters being "nearer to life" than the average layman living in the world, he by no means advocates that a Sister become "worldly" or less a religious than were Sisters of an earlier generation. What he is approving is that Sisters know the century in which they live; that they understand the problems of modern man and his scale of values, the pressures exerted in a secular environment, the need to view life in terms of God while still maintaining close and constant contact with 20th century reality. Implied in the statement that a Sister is "nearer to life" is the belief that she will be alert to the rapid changes made in today's way of thinking as well as in today's way of doing.

For one example—and there should be several to illustrate this point—Pope Paul VI speaks of Vatican II as a new spring, "an awakening of the mighty spiritual and moral energies which at present lie dormant" but which the Conciliar Fathers feel should be roused into action. An implied reference to religious life as one of the mighty forces in the Church may here be seen. The present

[3] Pius XII in an Allocution to Teaching Sisters, September 13, 1951, *Education: Papal Teachings*, p. 403.
[4] *Ibid.*, p. 407. The italics are mine.

Pope adds: "The Council is evidence of a determination to bring about a rejuvenation both of the interior forces of the Church and of the regulations by which her canonical structure and liturgical forms are governed."[5]

Community Responsibility to the Church

To follow the Church in its program of change and renewal, and so bring out the image of Christ more clearly, is not only a Community responsibility but the individual responsibility of each Sister. In following the call to the religious life a Sister places herself wholly at the disposal of the Church. In theory all Sisters accept this idea. But in actual practice it can well be that for all of her religious life a Sister has seen herself strictly as a member of her religious Community, and only vaguely has she seen herself within the larger frame of reference, the Church.

This over-identification with one's religious Congregation and under-identification with the Church was a commonly accepted attitude among Sisters before the Church began its steady and insistent effort to end insularity among Communities. This attitude did not escape notice on the part of the Holy See. An official of the Sacred Congregation of Religious, in addressing Major Superiors, Mistresses, and other groups of Sisters, while conducting Institutes in the United States commented on the ecclesial services rendered by Sisters as follows:

The religious life is a service of the Church. To embrace it is to put one's self wholly at the disposal of the Church; not of some particular group or organization, but of the Church as such. . . . Here it is necessary to explain something that is not always correctly understood and which some religious find disturbing and do not want to accept. Characteristically and specifically the religious life exists for the well-being and holiness of the Church as a whole, rather than for the individual sanctification of those who embrace it, though it is only through the sanctification of the religious themselves that the characteristic end can be attained.[6]

5 Pope Paul VI, "The Task," *Council Speeches of Vatican II*, ed. Hans Küng, Yves Congar, O.P., and Daniel O'Hanlon, S.J. (Glen Rock, New Jersey: Paulist Press, 1964), p. 80.
6 Elio Gambari, S.M., *Religious-Apostolic Formation for Sisters*, pp. 4–5. Cf. also Notes of Institute for Junior Sisters conducted by Father Gambari at Marillac College, August, 1961.

Certainly it seems odd that Father Gambari should find some Sisters unwilling to accept the fact that it is the Church that makes possible a Community life for individuals; that all constitutions, rules and customs must have the approval of the Church before a religious Congregation may offer membership. Yet, this thinking in terms of one's Community before thinking of the Church as a whole may well be one of the root causes of unease in a considerable number of Sisters.

An *aggiornamento* in thinking, in bringing one's evaluations in line with the renewal and reappraisals now taking place in the Church through Vatican Council II, will save Sisters many disquieting hours of worried concern that the religious life as a way of service to God has outlived its usefulness. Only when the Church ceases to be, will the religious life cease to be, for, essentially, it is a part of the Church which has Christ's promise to be with her always.

Contemporary Concept of Obedience

Another example of needed updated thinking is seen in the changing concept of obedience, which for some older Sisters is sometimes hard to accept. Like the essence of the religious life, which can never really change, so the essence of given virtues does not change, nor do the principles that govern their practice. It is the application of these principles that can be updated without changing the nature of the virtue.

Obedience dominated the life of Christ from Bethlehem to Calvary. The greater part of Christ's life is condensed in five words: "He was subject to them." (Luke 2:51) Calvary closed that life with its poignant: ". . . becoming obedient unto death, even to the death of the cross." (Phil. 2:8)

If there is one virtue dear to the heart of every American Sister —quite possibly because there is nothing she values more than independence—it is obedience. Having sincerely renounced that independence in favor of her religious vocation, she wants, quite laudably, to succeed in the practice of complete obedience. Every fervent, earnest, stable Sister wishes to project a clear image of obedience, the obedience of Christ. It is quite a matter of honor with her, and even among the new breed there is no one who wishes to stand out as a rebel, nor is there any among the group eager to applaud aggressive independence. Yet there is, perhaps, no area of the religious life in which the "new thinking" is more evident.

With the opportunities now afforded Sisters of deepening it through theological studies, their appreciation of the ascetical life is more alive. Maturity and growth are made possible by their liberal studies in all areas of the humanities and social sciences. New insights are gained from serious reading provided almost lavishly today by Communities who want their members well-informed in all fields, and who, for this purpose, arrange weekly discussion experiences. With all these aids the understanding of the various virtues is not geared to routine practice but rather to an intellectual as well as practical assent. The contributions of psychology to everyday living have shown that too often the conformist grade-school child becomes the anarchist citizen; the "good" child grows into the troubled adult; passive acceptance builds up aggressive hostility. On the other hand, and in the long run, on a natural as well as supernatural plane, nothing pays off so well as the golden rule, which reaches its zenith in human relations when individual dignity is always respected—and recognized as always present in every human person.

Changes in Human Relationships

With advancement in this knowledge has come a perceptible change in human relationships. Authoritarianism belongs to the past. Some Sisters, who received their initial training before the new impetus the Church has given to religious life, are honestly and deeply troubled by the change—and on no point more so than in the area of obedience. Their idea, and even their ideal, of this virtue was acquired in an atmosphere of authoritarianism which freed them from all personal responsibility for their actions, save in those things morally wrong in themselves. At times it took a struggle to accept this type of rule, but in Community life it resulted in an abiding peace of soul.

When some older Sisters who have not kept up with readings on the Church's *aggiornamento,* hear now—something faint and

far off, scarcely credible, but still, threatening—that young Sisters
are being asked to express their preferences as to an assignment,
their reaction is: "Obedience is losing ground. It must not happen
to me!" In their relations with Superiors their Open Sesame to
absolute security is "Whatever you say, Reverend Mother." When
Reverend Mother seems unimpressed with this detachment, and
says kindly, but firmly, "Sister, I would really like you to express
a preference," the older Sister may be deeply troubled, disturbed
lest there be now a breaking down—as she sees it—of that bulwark
of the religious life, obedience.

Choices within a Framework of Alternatives

Many older Sisters feel threatened today; they fear their
spiritual security is in jeopardy, when they are offered choices
within a framework of alternatives. "Would you prefer teaching
older students—or younger ones?" a local Superior may ask.
'Sister, would you like to go on for library science as a change from
teaching?" asks a Major Superior. "Sister, you have been in charge
of geriatrics for seven years. Do you ever think in terms of change?
Is there another hall you would prefer?" The older Sister-nurse
is probably pleased that Reverend Mother would consult her; long
faithful years have merited this trust. But the young Sisters too,
untroubled about making decisions, are often consulted as to
their preferences. The Junior Sisters are encouraged to express a
preference for nursing, or teaching, or social work. Indeed, the
young Sister *expects* to be consulted. Where is their submission
of judgment; where is the opportunity for suppressing one's will?

Submission of judgment, an essential of the religious state, is
not so simple as the words indicate; it is never to be equated with
abdication of intelligence or the negation of responsibility. This
responsibility is given wholesome opportunites for development
when Sisters are asked to take an active rather than passive part
in large areas of decision-making regarding certain of their
activities.

The same virtue of obedience that was formerly (and formally)
fulfilled by "Whatever you say, Reverend Mother" now requires a
higher—and perhaps holier—response on the Sister's part, and

one which many find disturbing because they, as well as their
Superior, share the responsibility for decisions. These may entail
professional assignments, time, place, and subject of higher studies;
the desirability of a home visit in particular circumstances; matters
concerning medical care, attendance at conventions and other
such occasions where a Sister's personal interests, abilities and
inclinations are concerned.

When asked, as frequently occurs, to state an opinion or preference, the obligations of obedience require that a Sister place at
the disposal of her Superiors her intellectual observations, the
resources of her experience, the frank exposition of her capabili-
ties, as well as those tendencies, not always apparent, which
would be either an asset or a liability to the choice in question.
Responsibility is a burden which a Sister can be led to elude under
guise of practicing virtue. Father Gleason tells us:

Obedience is our way of growth. It is not shrinking of our true selves,
but a development, for we become more fully human by becoming
identified in will with the Humanity of Christ. We set our wills to
the tasks of Christ for the love of Christ, that they may be perfected
by sharing in the power, love, initiative and activity of the will of
Christ our Lord.[7]

To accept and practice this "newer" and higher form of obedience
is by no means to embrace an opportunity for greater independence and disregard for the wishes of Superiors. It is, rather, to
share in their responsibility that the will of God be done more
perfectly.

Conformity May Breed Psychological Dependence

Father Maher says that there are too many religious who seem
incapable of making firm acts of the will; they live, he says, in the
religious life by a mere process of conformity.[8] Such religious
will never achieve excellently or brilliantly for Christ. This, at
base, exhibits two traits: an unwillingness to accept the part the

7 Robert W. Gleason, S.J., *To Live Is Christ* (New York: Sheed and Ward,
1961), p. 141.
8 Maher, *Lest We Build on Sand*, p. 205.

intellect must play in the consecration of the will; and basically a psychological dependence on Superiors to make all decisions. Obedience never releases the Sister from the use of her judgment and will; above all, it can never require the subject to abrogate the use of her intelligence. Writes Father Dubay:

If only through what we may term a nebulous feeling of supernatural discomfort, no thoughtful religious long escapes the knotty problems in his reasoned reactions to his Superior's directives. Sooner or later he wonders how the perfection of obedience could possibly and honorably require that he judge to be wise and prudent what he may on occasion strongly feel to be unwise and imprudent.[9]

It is generally on the local level of authority that problems regarding the changing concept of obedience occur. Major Superiors have kept closer to the thinking of the Church on religious life as explained in their various Institutes of Spirituality, their Congresses, and their contacts with theologians approved by the Sacred Congregation of Religious. Local Superiors whose loyalty and obedience are beyond question have not had these opportunities for growth in outlook and acceptance of the contributions made by advances in knowledge of how the human personality can be developed by using the natural as well as supernatural aids they make possible. Major Superiors are also in closer contact with the formation programs through which the young Sister is helped to develop her critical powers by analyzing principles—once accepted without scrutiny—for possible flaws and to apply these principles as criteria for human conduct.

Decision-Making a Learning Situation

A local Superior is often much more bewildered when a young member of the Community questions the wisdom and prudence of a certain course of action than is her Major Superior, who welcomes the expression of a differing viewpoint if it is expressed with due regard for the amenities required by good social deportment and the respect all should have, one for the other, regardless

9 Thomas Dubay, S.M., "Personal Integrity and Intellectual Obedience," *Review for Religious*, XX (September, 1953), 493.

of the position held in the Community. The Major Superior is much less concerned with a submissive manner on the part of the young Sister than she is with seizing every opportunity to use it as a learning situation through which the young members of the Order may be brought to a better understanding of the obligations which the religious life lays upon them. For this reason Major Superiors are willing to take time to answer the "why's" propounded by young Sisters, to answer their questions with sometimes detailed explanations. This is always done with a view towards helping the Sister develop maturity in the practice of obedience, or indeed of any other virtue required to live a full religious life.

This represents not so much a departure from the concept of "blind" obedience as a forward step in making obedience a collaborative act, a sharing of the responsibility entailed. It implies the acceptance of an easily verifiable fact: no one's judgment, whether he be superior or subject, is ever infallible; it implies further that human judgment, being human, will most certainly be fallible in some instances.

When a Sister is given a direction to which her judgment cannot give assent, how far can she waive all personal responsibility for the outcome of following those directions? While obedience is founded on a supernatural, and not a natural basis, she is justified in considering thoughtfully and prayerfully why her Superior's judgment might be correct: The wider experience if such be the case, the knowledge of the whole situation which includes other persons, and their reactions, involved in the directive, the over-all response which the Superior is in a better position to appraise— all these should receive the objective attention of the Sister who has been given the directive.

If, after honest study of the situation, the Sister still cannot accept the directive, she would violate her own integrity by hesitating to make the representation and explanations called for by her conscience, even should the results be unpleasant. Once having made these representations with as much objectivity as she can bring to the problem, she should rest satisfied as to the outcome. This very human situation is foreseen in the rules of most Communities and should not occasion undue anxiety.

As an example, a Sister in a school may be assigned to a sixth grade for which she conscientiously feels inadequate. Her judgment, freed from all ulterior motives, tells her that she could, quite possibly, handle with some competence a fourth grade. She makes this representation to her Superior, who nevertheless does not change the assignment. The Sister is not called upon here to do violence to her judgment and bring it in line with that of her Superior. Her peace of soul lies in accepting the assignment, with its possible consequent failure, as something that God is asking of her *now*.

Obedience and Personal Integrity

A more troubling problem lies in a situation where a local Superior might require, more by example than by precept, a course of action that would ask for a less perfect realization of fraternal charity. Here the Sister desires to show complete loyalty to her Superior, but at the same time recognizes fraternal charity as a virtue absolutely integral to the religious life and her call to it. The requirement indirectly asked by obedience may be slight, but the Sister recognizes that compliance, even in a small degree, whittles away at her own personal integrity as a disciple of Christ. Here is a real dilemma.

Or another situation may call for a reappraisal of the apostolate as conceived by the local Superior and the Sister engaged therein. It may be a matter of emphasis, or a difference of opinion as to priority and importance. Where a Sister is truly disturbed, her rule supplies the answer. She is to have recourse to her Major Superior for a clarification of what may be considered the "wise and prudent" judgment. This, Father Dubay, in the words quoted, describes as a knotty problem, one which can never permanently escape a truly thoughtful religious. Sooner or later she is faced with a situation where obedience may offer a conflict with the demands exacted by one's personal integrity.

For obedience is an active not a passive virtue. Just as stability is tested, not in calm and serenity, but amid the storms of opposition, contradiction, and misunderstandings—so a virile obedience, founded on supernatural motives, will not fail when a Sister finds

that her judgment is not in strict accord with that of her local
Superior. When she has made the representations and suggestions
deemed necessary by her judgment, she should accept the decision
whether she agrees with it or not. The point is that she is never
called upon to violate the dictates of her own integrity of purpose.
Unthinking conformity, or conformity dictated by fear, is never a
virtue. A spirit of faith sometimes requires that a Sister accept,
as the will of God for the present moment, a directive to which
she cannot give intellectual assent. Conscience may oblige her
to represent her difficulty to the local Superior, and, in a serious
case, to her Major Superiors. Such an occasion gives a Major
Superior an opportunity to share with a local Superior the re-
thinking that Vatican II has inspired on all levels of Community
living.

Problems Concerning Local Superiors

By placing responsibility on the Sisters for the practice of
obedience; by giving them an opportunity to express their doubts
and perplexities, Superiors are but encouraging a Sister to use her
God-given faculties to grow in maturity as well as in grace. The
Major Superior will always support the local Superior, who, in
turn, will be grateful for the help she is receiving in exercising
authority in an intelligent and maternal manner. No local Superior
deliberately makes obedience difficult for a subject; yet it cannot
be disregarded that they are often puzzled by the attitude Major
Superiors now take towards obedience—an attitude unthought-of
and unheard-of in decades past. One is reminded here of the wise
adage: A humble soul can manage any situation. A young Sister
may learn a more lasting lesson of obedience from the example
of a local Superior's acceptance of "new ways" than she could
learn from a dozen sermons or several treatises on the subject.

The so-called "new" concept of obedience is not exactly new; its
emphasis is really on old wine in new bottles. There is, in the
thinking of today, a greater accent on more personal responsibility,
and less reliance on what makes for psychological dependence on
someone else; an older type of acquiescence that demanded less
reflection and returned more peace of soul. In a strong founda-

tional program of formation, young Sisters should learn their own weaknesses, the tendency of all youth to believe that it has all the answers. Where there is permission for participation in decision-making, there is the factual assumption of responsibility for the consequences of each decision. To whomsoever more is given, of him much more will be required.

Local Superiors should recognize this effort on the part of Major Superiors to form a strong sense of personal responsibility in young Sisters when they allow them to exercise choices within a framework of given alternatives. This permissiveness should lead to a broader understanding on the part of the younger Sisters and a more intelligent acceptance of the obligations of the vows. Poverty becomes to them something much more than a matter of fidelity in asking permission; chastity becomes the liberating force to give one's self whole-heartedly and without reserve to the apostolate assigned by her Community. They come to see that obedience raises each Sister, however humble in origin, to the highest dignity possible for a human being to achieve, since it gives importance to the smallest act she performs, stamping it as done in conformity with God's holy will, a condition essential to holiness.

Leadership for the Future—Responsibility of Major and Local Superiors

On the other hand, Major Superiors recognize that the local Superiors of today need more than ordinary help and guidance in understanding young Sisters. They have seen for some time now that this is a critical problem area and they are well aware that there are no easy solutions. They appreciate that their own national association offers an opportunity for fruitful consultation and a free exchange of ideas within small, well-planned discussion groups. But a similar conference or convention for local Superiors would not only prove unwieldy as to numbers but would present difficulties in creating the very special learning situation needed to achieve the specific results desired.

Some Communities have found that sessions held at the Mother-houses for all local Superiors—regardless of the varying apostolates involved—offer the best opportunity for Major Superiors to impart ideas gathered at national and international congresses. In these sessions they can share much of what they have learned from their guided study of the Church's directives concerning the preparation of the Junior Sisters for their religious life. Added help can be given to counsel the young Sisters on the application of principles learned in the Juniorate concerning the apostolates of teaching, nursing and social work. Major Superiors are understandably concerned that local Superiors bring the young Sisters to see that personal holiness, no matter how engrossing and demanding the apostolate is, remains the primary need, and always concerns itself with great love of God and an active, eager fraternal charity. This fraternal charity of the young Sister must be evident in all her dealings with her Sister companions, as well as the children she teaches and the parents she serves. Then her apostolate will be truly love-of-God-and-the-neighbor in action.

The Reverend Mothers are well aware that local Superiors are *ex officio* the spiritual leaders of their group and that the young Sisters sent to them expect to find in them that image. They are disappointed and feel deprived and often frustrated when they do not get the spiritual as well as professional help they need for their continuing formation as mature religious. Major Superiors have been quite outspoken in their belief that if educating the local Superior on how to deal with young Sisters today is neglected, serious results will follow. In this solemn duty they realize that there can be no abrogation of responsibility. It is both edifying and encouraging to see the lengths to which some Communities go to insure this in-service preparation for their better understanding of the role played by local Superiors and other professional administrators.

In-Service Education of Local Superiors

In speaking of the proposed sessions at the Motherhouse, the suggestion was made that carefully selected speakers, well-versed in the theological principles that undergird the newer thinking on the religious life, should be brought in. Updated concepts of obedience, of the development of social and spiritual maturity, a consideration of the stultifying effects of formalism and passive conformity, the Church's view on the application of the law of subsidiarity—these and many other topics were listed as possible subjects to include in a syllabus for a course for local Superiors. Such a course, it was thought, would do much to aid and encourage local Superiors in achieving a correct understanding of the exercise of obedience and authority.

It was further suggested that local Superiors should be encouraged to do wide reading in all areas that will help them to become spiritual and professional leaders of the late 20th and the 21st centuries. Proposals were made—but not completed—to appoint a committee to compile a list of such readings. The dual obligation of rounding out and crowning with experienced leadership the remaining decades of the present century, and the solid preparation of intelligent leaders who will make a better world possible for the 21st century, was discussed as a responsibility of today's Major Superiors. Creative leaders have always had a sense of history. They realize how essential the present is for creating a past on which the future can build to insure enduring stability—a stability that carries within itself the wholesome seed of ongoing progress. Many practical Major Superiors suggested that they themselves should neither offer nor accept, from those concerned, the easy excuse of "not having sufficient time." What duty is more important? What other task would be more worthy of a Superior's time and effort? This represents some of the forthright and intelligent thinking of our Major Superiors today.

Another suggestion made was the appointment—and good use —of one or two assistants who might give the local Superior added time and incentive for these more vital Community needs. It was further added that an important re-examination of how often and how *well* she delegates authority might prove enlightening. A consensus was that one usually finds time for the things one really wants to do. To critics of Major Superiors who think they are too slow in acting, it may well come as a surprise that so much "pondering the question" is going on behind closed doors. That there is no impulsive rush is a good omen that the Church-directed *aggiornamento* is in good hands and will come in God's good time. One further example will serve to highlight the interest and awareness of Major Superiors.

Speaking of the need to give necessary experience to local Superiors, one Mother General wrote to the author:

We spend a good deal of money educating the newly received Sisters—why not spend an equal amount in educating the local Superiors how to guide wisely and develop intelligently the "new breed" we are sending into the apostolate? Money spent on having two or even three one-week sessions a year at the Motherhouse would solve this problem in a comparatively short time. We all know it is our most acute domestic problem.

And perhaps we should all give more careful thought to the duties of the assistant Superior. Perhaps her authority and assignments can be broadened to give the local Superior more time to be with the younger Sisters, which is, after all, her primary assignment.

If it becomes necessary, there could be appointed a lay assistant administrator. For my part, Sister, I hope many of these points in your book will serve as subjects for group discussion at our national meetings. We all have the same problems. In such discussions we may find solutions that will save us positive grief.[10]

In one way or another any predicted "positive grief" is tied in with giving young members of religious Communities all the helps they need to become holy and effective Sisters. To the extent that they are helped to give, and taught *how* to give, totally of themselves in the active and almost fearfully challenging apostolates ahead, to that extent may Major Superiors be at ease about the future of their Communities.

The Sister's Image in Society

A Sister's concern with God is inseparable from her concern with her fellow man. In society she is eager to project an image of being all things to all men because she is, by her vocation both as a Christian and as a religious, her brother's keeper. This brotherhood of man is dear to her, for she has made every sacrifice to earn the respect, reverence, appreciation and love society has so generously accorded her. The love she returns so

10 Quoted with permission of the writer, who asks to remain unnamed.

abundantly enables her to radiate a sureness, a strength, a sense of purpose for which the world, so uncertain of itself and its goals, hungers. Her determined feet, her willing hands, her loving heart give sureness to the world, for none of its problems are foreign to her. With Christ as her Model she has accepted the invitation of the world to walk with it, to talk with it, to suffer with it.

Journals of opinion tell us today that Sisters have responded to the mandate for change more quickly, more readily, than almost any other class of people. Why? Because the Church asks it. Their sense of mission brings them into contact with all groups: the powerful and the powerless, the affluent and the indigent, the law-makers and the law-breakers. And the world, now that it has taken time out to notice, finds the modern, the updated Sister—interesting. Disconcertingly so.

The laity is discovering that she has an opinion on matters unconnected with report cards, uniforms and the proceeds from a bake sale. The friendly parishioner who dropped in at the convent before a coming municipal election found the Sisters conversant with the issues and learned that, among themselves, they held opposing views. And many a politician who sent his limousine to take the good Sisters to and from the polls rather ruefully suspected that the gesture had been wholly ineffectual. The "Sister says" with which Catholic households have echoed for generations now frequently refers to Sister's analysis of a controversial book, the effects of foreign policy on domestic economy, her ideas on racial tensions and job inequities.

But above all, a Sister's image in society today may be summed up in the one word—service, for service is love in action. It is this motivation of total love and total giving that differentiates her from thousands of others engaged in the same occupations. She is a person with a purpose from which nothing can deflect her— the purpose of showing forth the image and likeness of Christ.

A Golden Age for Sisters

This will go down in history as the golden age for women religious. It is indeed their finest hour. Never has God, the Church and society asked so much of them and never have they been so well prepared and so eager to give it. The Church in the United

States now presents the fairest picture of Catholicism ever known in the entire world. It is universally acknowledged that women religious are in no small part responsible for this picture. The forerunners of the present generation of Sisters faced obstacles of forest and wilderness, poverty and loneliness, prejudice and hostility. They succeeded because of that "Faith that worketh by charity." (Gal. 5:6) They had faith in God, faith in themselves, faith in their cause.

Today's Sister, working under changed conditions and more complex difficulties, needs in an unlimited degree this threefold faith: Faith that God has made her what she is, placed her where she is, and formed her for the times in which she lives. Just as knowledge of God is incomplete without a knowledge of self and of God's will, so faith in God is incomplete without faith in self and in one's mission. St. Paul has summed it up for all time: "Not I, but the grace of God with me." (1 Cor. 15:10) Serene in the certainty of their vocation, Sisters, in this age of fear, will show the world an image of faith in Christ. To a society that has a gnawing dread of nuclear destruction, they will show the hope of Christ. To all men, made to the image and likeness of God, they will show the love of Christ.

The nearly one million religious women in the world today— one-fifth of whom are in the United States—are the representatives, one might even say the direct descendants, of those holy women who followed and ministered to Christ during His earthly pilgrimage. They have experienced His look of love, they have obeyed His mysterious call, "Come, follow Me"; they have left all things to serve Him. In accepting the call they accepted Christ as a Way to be followed, a Truth to be witnessed, a Life to be lived. With Mary, His Mother, they have said, "Behold the handmaid of the Lord," and with her they share in a faint, echoing way, the promise: "Behold all generations shall call you blessed." They are a continuation of a long, unbroken procession that began nearly two thousand years ago with the active apostolate of Christ. They, the Sisters of today, will faithfully follow Him into the 21st century—and beyond.

CONTENTS ACCORDING TO TOPIC

INDEX